Praise for
The Mystery of Olga Chekhova

"This was an extraordinary life, which Mr. Beevor handles with disciplined speculation."
—*The New York Sun*

"An extraordinary drama of exile and espionage, celebrity and concealment. . . . As in the *Stalingrad* and *Berlin* books, though in a less deeply tragic key, Beevor's new work brings home to younger readers what he calls 'the fate of the individual within the mass' during Europe's age of tyranny, genocide and total war."
—Boyd Tonkin, *The Independent*

"Beevor has clearly enjoyed picking through the legends and his fascination with Chekhova's story shines through."
—Anne Applebaum, *Daily Telegraph*

"Beevor's work is, above all, the fascinating story of an extraordinary family living through extraordinary times. On those grounds alone it's a great read. Families, as so many novelists have discovered, provide a wonderful window into the past . . . Beevor tells the story with seemingly effortless grace and it reads like the very best novels. He is a gifted writer and this is an enthralling tale."
—Gerard DeGroot, *Scotland on Sunday*

"Antony Beevor's engaging and revealing memoir . . . tells the parallel stories of sister Olga and bother Lev with clarity and panache . . . as engaging a read as *Stalingrad* and *Berlin*."
—David Edgar, *The Guardian* (London)

"This compelling work . . . fascinates the reader by making Chekhova and her despicable brother Lev Knipper prisms through which one examines the degraded life of the citizens of Nazi Germany and Soviet Russia and explores the shadowy, morally ambiguous world of the Russian émigré. . . . As in his other books, Antony Beevor is remarkably astute at digging out testimonies from living descendants and closed archives."
—Donald Rayfield, author of *Anton Chekhov*,
in the *Literary Review*

"Beevor uses the story to evoke a world—the vague ideological borderlands of Nazism and Communism. . . . Exhibits Beevor's big-book knack: he can write excitingly yet with restraint, and never resorts to grand guignol to grip you."
—Felipe Fernandez Armesto, *The Times* (London)

"Fascinating. An intricate, gracefully told and often moving social history of a talented family in times of revolution, civil war, dictatorship and world conflict."
—Rachel Polonsky, *New Statesman*

"A true story that is dramatic, evocative and well worth unearthing"   —*The Observer* (London)

"Literate, lucent, and well researched; a fascinating glimpse into how artists respond as the world explodes around them."
—*Kirkus Reviews*

"Given its colorful subject matter and Beevor's well-placed narrative, *The Mystery of Olga Chekhova* never fails to absorb."
—*The Times Literary Supplement*

PENGUIN BOOKS

THE MYSTERY OF OLGA CHEKHOVA

Antony Beevor was educated at Winchester and Sandhurst. A regular officer in the 11th Hussars, he served in Germany and England. He has published several novels, and his works of nonfiction include *The Spanish Civil War*; *Crete: The Battle and the Resistance*, which won the 1993 Runciman Award; *Stalingrad*; and *The Fall of Berlin 1945*. With his wife, Artemis Cooper, he wrote *Paris After the Liberation: 1944–1949*, now issued in a new edition. *Stalingrad* was awarded the Samuel Johnson Prize for Non-Fiction, the Wolfson History Prize, and the Hawthornden Prize in 1999. *The Fall of Berlin 1945* was a number-one bestseller in Britain and has been translated into twenty-four languages. Most of his titles are published by Penguin.

Beevor is a Fellow of the Royal Society of Literature and a Chevalier de l'Ordre des Arts et des Lettres in France. In 2003 he received the first Longman History Today Trustees' Award. He was the 2002–2003 Lees Knowles lecturer at Cambridge and is a visiting professor at Birkbeck College, University of London. He is now chairman of the Society of Authors.

www.antonybeevor.com

The Mystery of Olga Chekhova

ANTONY BEEVOR

PENGUIN BOOKS

PENGUIN BOOKS

Published by the Penguin Group

Penguin Group (USA) Inc., 375 Hudson Street, New York, New York 10014, U.S.A.
Penguin Group (Canada), 90 Eglinton Avenue East, Suite 700, Toronto,
Ontario, Canada M4P 2Y3 (a division of Pearson Penguin Canada Inc.)
Penguin Books Ltd, 80 Strand, London WC2R 0RL, England
Penguin Ireland, 25 St Stephen's Green, Dublin 2, Ireland (a division of Penguin Books Ltd)
Penguin Group (Australia), 250 Camberwell Road, Camberwell,
Victoria 3124, Australia (a division of Pearson Australia Group Pty Ltd)
Penguin Books India Pvt Ltd, 11 Community Centre, Panchsheel Park,
New Delhi - 110 017, India
Penguin Group (NZ), cnr Airborne and Rosedale Roads, Albany, Auckland 1310, New
Zealand (a division of Pearson New Zealand Ltd)
Penguin Books (South Africa) (Pty) Ltd, 24 Sturdee Avenue,
Rosebank, Johannesburg 2196, South Africa

Penguin Books Ltd, Registered Offices:
80 Strand, London WC2R 0RL, England

First published in the United States of America by Viking Penguin,
a member of Penguin Group (USA) Inc. 2004
Published in Penguin Books 2005

1 3 5 7 9 10 8 6 4 2

Photographic credits appear on page xi.

THE LIBRARY OF CONGRESS HAS CATALOGED THE HARDCOVER EDITION AS FOLLOWS:
The Mystery of Olga Chekhova: was Hitler's favorite
actress a Russian spy? / Antony Beevor.
p. cm.
Includes filmography. Includes bibliographical references and index.
ISBN 0-670-03340-5 (hc.)
ISBN 0 14 30.3596 7 (pbk.)
1. Tschechowa, Olga, b. 1896.   2. Actors—Soviet Union—Biography.
3. Spies—Soviet Union—Biography.
PN2728.T8M95 2004   792.028'092—dc22
[B]   2004043076

Printed in the United States of America
Set in 12/14.75 pt. Monotype Bembo

For Artemis

CONTENTS

Contents

LIST OF ILLUSTRATIONS

Photographic Acknowledgements

AD-MCY Arkhiv doma-museya Chekhova Yalta (Archive of the Chekhov house-museum at Yalta): 8, 12, 14
AKG Archive: 29
The David King Photographic Archive: 1, 2, 3, 4, 5, 11, 15, 16, 38
Andrei Knipper private collection: 13, 25, 26, 27, 37, 39, 42, 43
Aleksandr Melikov private collection: 36
PAK/T Privatarchiv Knipper/Tschechowa, Berlin: 6, 7, 17, 18, 19, 20, 21, 22, 23, 24, 28, 30, 34, 35, 40
Harvey Pitcher, *Chekhov's Leading Lady*: 9
Russian State Film Archive: 41
Mariya Shverubovich private collection: 10
Olga Tschechowa, *Meine Uhren gehen anders*: 32, 44
Ullstein: 31, 33

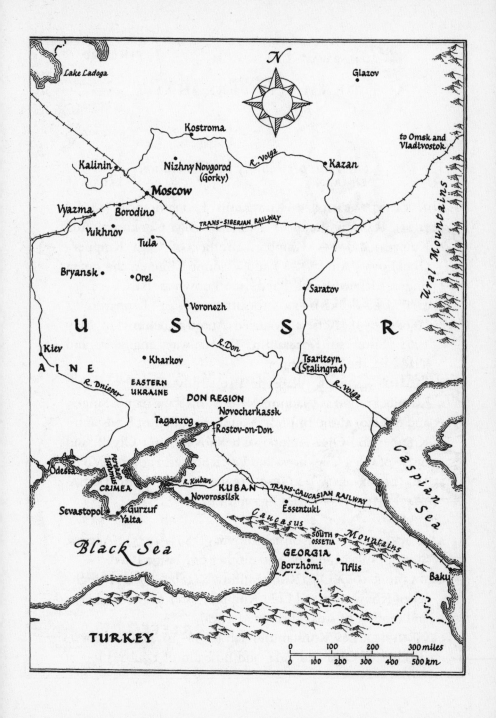

DRAMATIS PERSONAE

The Knipper Family by Generation

KONSTANTIN KNIPPER Konstantin Leonardovich (1866–
1924). Railway engineer. Father of Olga Chekhova, Ada
Knipper and Lev Knipper. Brother of Olga Knipper-
Chekhova ('Aunt Olya') and Vladmir Knipper, the opera
singer. Married 'Lulu' Ried, later known as 'Baba'.

'AUNT OLYA' KNIPPER-CHEKHOVA Olga Leonardovna
(1868–1959). Actress. Married Anton Chekhov in May
1901. Sister to Konstantin, the railway engineer, and
Vladimir, the opera singer.

VLADIMIR KNIPPER Vladimir Leonardovich (1877–1942).
Usually known as Vladimir Nardov, his stage name. Singer,
and director at the Bolshoi. Younger brother of Konstantin
Knipper and Olga Knipper-Chekhova ('Aunt Olya'), and
uncle of Olga Chekhova and Lev Knipper. Father of Vova.

LULU (LATER BABA) RIED-KNIPPER Yelena Luise (1874–
1943). Mother of Ada, Olga and Lev.

ADA KNIPPER Ada Konstantinovna (1895–1985). Actress.
Sister of Olga and Lev, and mother of Marina Ried.

OLGA CHEKHOVA Olga Konstantinovna (1897–1980). Daughter of Konstantin and Lulu Knipper, sister of Ada and Lev,
and mother of Ada (christened Olga).

LEV KNIPPER Lev Konstantinovich (1898–1974). Composer.
Brother of Olga and Ada, and husband of Lyuba, then of

Mariya Garikovna Melikova and finally of Tatyana Alekseevna Gaidamovich. Father of Andrei Knipper.

VOVA KNIPPER Vladimir Vladimirovich (1924–95). Son of Vladimir, the opera singer, and first cousin of Lev Knipper and Olga Chekhova.

ADA CHEKHOVA RUST Ada Mikhailovna (1916–66). Daughter of Olga Chekhova and Misha Chekhov. Married Wilhelm Rust. Mother of Vera. Killed in a plane crash.

MARINA RIED Marina Borisovna Rschevskaya (1917–89). Daughter of Ada Knipper and Boris P. Rschevsky (1872–1922), and niece of Olga Chekhova.

ANDREI KNIPPER (1931–   ). Geologist. Son of Lev Knipper and Lyuba (Lyubov Sergeevna Zalesskaya).

The Chekhov Family by Generation

ALEKSANDR CHEKHOV Aleksandr Pavlovich (1855–1913). Writer. Brother of Anton and Masha, and father of Misha. Husband of Natalya Golden.

ANTON CHEKHOV Anton Pavlovich (1860–1904). Writer, doctor and playwright. Married Olga Knipper in May 1901. Brother of Aleksandr, and uncle of Misha, Volodya and Sergei.

'AUNT MASHA' CHEKHOVA Mariya Pavlovna (1863–1957). Keeper of the Chekhov museum in Yalta. Sister of Aleksandr, Anton and the other Chekhov brothers. Aunt of Misha, Volodya and Sergei.

MISHA CHEKHOV Mikhail Aleksandrovich (1891–1955). Actor. Son of Aleksandr Chekhov and Natalya Golden, nephew of Anton Chekhov, husband of Olga Chekhova and father of Ada (Olga Mikhailovna) Chekhova.

VOLODYA CHEKHOV Vladimir Ivanovich (1894–1917). Student and lawyer. First cousin of Misha and Sergei. Committed suicide 1917.

SERGEI CHEKHOV Sergei Mikhailovich (1901–73). Family historian. First cousin of Misha and Volodya.

1. The Cherry Orchard of Victory

During the night of 8 May 1945, lights stayed on all over Moscow. People waited impatiently for news of the final German surrender. Only the most privileged members of the Soviet élite, such as the writer Ilya Ehrenburg, possessed a radio set which they dared to tune to foreign stations. In Stalin's Russia, victory did not bring freedom from the secret police.

The announcement of the German surrender taken by Marshal Zhukov in Berlin was eventually made by Levitan, the Radio Moscow newsreader, at ten past one on the morning of Wednesday 9 May. 'Attention, this is Moscow. Germany has capitulated . . . This day, in honour of the victorious Great Patriotic War, is to be a national holiday, a festival of victory.' The Internationale was played, followed by the national anthems of the United States, Great Britain and France.

The inhabitants of communal apartments did not wait for the music to finish. They surged out on to the landings in all stages of dress to congratulate each other. Those with telephones rang their relations and closest friends to share this historic moment with them. 'It's over! It's over!' they kept repeating. Many broke down in tears of relief and sorrow. With some 25 million dead as a result of the war, there was barely a family in the whole Soviet Union which had not known suffering. By four in the morning, Ehrenburg noted, 'Gorky Street was thronged: people stood about outside their buildings, or poured along the street towards Red Square.'

It was, as Ehrenburg wrote, 'an extraordinary day of joy

and sadness'. He saw an old woman, crying and smiling, showing a photograph of her son in uniform to passers-by and telling them that he had been killed the previous autumn. It was a festival of remembrance as much as a celebration. When bottles of vodka were passed round, the first toast was to those who had not lived to see this day, although loyal party members should have first paid tribute to Comrade Stalin, the 'great architect and genius of the victory'.

Officers in uniform, above all those with medals, were cheered and sometimes bounced in the air as victors. Even Ehrenburg, the most famous propagandist of the Red Army, was recognized in the street and suffered the same honour, to his great embarrassment. Foreigners too were 'kissed, hugged and generally fêted'. Around Red Square, 'foreign cars were stopped and their occupants dragged out, embraced and even tossed in the air'. Outside the American embassy, the crowds shouted their admiration for President Roosevelt, who had died just over a month before, to their genuine sorrow.

Khmelev, the director of the Moscow Art Theatre, addressed a spontaneous meeting of the company in the foyer. 'What immense joy is ours today!' he said. 'We've been waiting for this so long, but now that it's come, I can't find words to express what we feel. When the radio played victory marches, I saw a woman through the brightly lit window of a house, dancing and singing to herself.'

During the course of that day between 2 and 3 million people packed the centre of the capital, from the embankments of the Moskva river up to the Belorussky station. Most of them came armed with bottles of vodka or Georgian champagne, which had been hoarded religiously for this very day. Workers and their families from the suburbs had come into the centre wearing their best clothes. Muscovites who had stayed in the capital during the war were better dressed than those from elsewhere because, during the panic of October 1941, evacuees from the city had sold all the clothes they could not take with them to the thrift shops. Moscow, although it had been bombed that winter, had been truly fortunate. Comparatively few buildings had been damaged. Elsewhere, to the south and west, towns and villages lay in ruins for hundreds upon hundreds of miles. Some 25 million people were homeless. Survivors lived in dugouts – literally holes in the ground covered by trunks, branches and turf.

That evening, Stalin's victory speech was broadcast and a salute of 1,000 guns was fired, the shock waves rattling the windows. Hundreds of aircraft flew overhead, releasing red, gold and purple flares. Searchlights from Moscow's anti-aircraft batteries illuminated a huge red banner held up by invisible balloons. Stalin was cheered spontaneously. Many, like his protégé Ehrenburg, did not reflect until later upon the fate of all those whose lives had been wasted or who had been executed on false charges to cover up the blunders of their leader. Yet even as strangers embraced each other in the streets on that deeply emotional day, a true feeling of victory and joy somehow still seemed just beyond their reach. The only certain sensation was an exhausted, slightly numb relief.

After these celebrations, members of the Moscow Art Theatre felt that they too should mark the end of the war. The Kremlin was planning a huge military parade on Red Square to commemorate the achievements of the Great Patriotic War. They, meanwhile, decided on a special performance. They simply wanted to give thanks that Russian culture had survived the terrible onslaught of the Nazis.

With Anton Chekhov's flying seagull emblazoned on the curtains, the choice of author was not in doubt. The plays

which he had written for the Moscow Art Theatre, giving it
such international prestige, used to be known before the
revolution as its 'battleships'. And the work decided upon for
this occasion was Chekhov's last, *The Cherry Orchard*.

Chekhov's widow, Olga Knipper-Chekhova, a founder
member of the company, would take the part of the unworldly
landowner Ranyevskaya. She had played it during the very
first performance in January 1904, watched by their friends
Feodor Chaliapin, Maxim Gorky and Rachmaninov. It had
painful memories. Anton, her husband, had been seriously ill.
In fact he was so 'deathly pale' that there had been gasps
of horror when he appeared on stage to receive a tribute.
Konstantin Stanislavsky, the presiding genius of the Moscow
Art Theatre, remarked that this triumphant occasion 'smelled
of a funeral'. Six months later the playwright was dead.

In those days, Olga Knipper-Chekhova, with her small,
animated eyes and firm jaw, had possessed the clean good
looks of a determined, intelligent governess. But now, aged
seventy-six and quite stout despite the short rations of the war,
she was a living monument of the Russian theatre. She had
been appointed a People's Artist of the Soviet Union as early
as 1928. Yet under Stalin, this was no protection. She had
spent much of the war fearing arrest at any moment by the
NKVD secret police.

In the spy-mania of the time, her anxieties were perfectly
understandable. Both her father and mother were of German
origin. Her brother had assisted Admiral Kolchak, the White
commander in Siberia during the civil war. Her favourite
nephew, the composer Lev Knipper, had been a White Guard
officer fighting the Bolsheviks in the south of Russia. But
most dangerous of all by far, her niece, Olga Chekhova, had
been the leading movie star in Berlin, honoured since 1936
with the title of 'State Actress' of the Third Reich and allegedly

adored by Hitler. There had even been photographs of her at Hitler's side at Nazi receptions. And her niece's former husband, Mikhail Chekhov, was in Hollywood. They were a family of émigrés at a time of Stalinist xenophobia.

The elderly actress was almost the last survivor of that extraordinary group led by Stanislavsky which had started to revolutionize dramatic art in 1898. Stanislavsky, whom she described as 'a huge chapter' in her life and who had fired them all with his artistic ideals, had died in 1938. Tall and elegant, with white hair and black eyebrows, he could have been an immensely distinguished professor or diplomat when not disguised in one of the many parts in which he immersed himself. The intensity with which he engaged in a role left him exhausted after a performance. Actors entering his dressing room discovered that he relaxed by taking off all his clothes and smoking a cigar. 'Just as he could wear any kind of costume,' observed one of the cast, 'he could wear his own naked flesh genuinely, with the utmost Hellenic simplicity.'

Shortly before his last illness in 1938, Stanislavsky had wanted the brilliant actor and director Vsevolod Meyerhold, a companion of the early days, to succeed him at the Moscow Art Theatre. But Meyerhold had attracted the hatred of the Soviet authorities, and Stanislavsky could do little to help from beyond the grave. Meyerhold, who had been a supporter of the Bolsheviks at the time of the revolution, had fallen foul of the Stalinist regime because his plays did not conform to the new doctrine of Socialist Realism. He attacked the sterile state of Soviet theatre in a suicidally brave speech at the All-Union Congress of Stage Directors. He was arrested in June 1939. Two weeks later, his Jewish wife, the well-known actress Zinaida Raikh, was murdered in their apartment. Her body was mutilated and her eyes were gouged out. Meyerhold may well have been one of those personally tortured by Lavrenty

Beria himself before being killed. Stalin signed his death warrant. Few now dared to mention his name, or that a former mistress of Beria had been given the Meyerhold apartment.

Even the play chosen to celebrate the Soviet victory over Germany seemed to have its own ghosts. In 1917, the Moscow Art Theatre had performed *The Cherry Orchard* on the night of the Bolshevik *coup d'état*. And in May 1919, Olga Knipper-Chekhova had been in Kharkov with a touring party to escape starvation in Moscow, when they heard during the second act of the play that the city had suddenly fallen to the White Army of General Denikin. But the heady advance of the White armies was short-lived. Denikin's forces fell back in chaos towards the Black Sea coast. Along with a stampede of civilian refugees fearing Bolshevik vengeance, they were decimated by typhus and starvation. Olga Knipper-Chekhova and her companions in the travelling group escaped south across the Caucasus to Georgia. There, *The Cherry Orchard* had been their last performance in the capital, Tiflis, just before crossing the Black Sea into an indecisive exile.

From September 1920 until their return to Moscow in the spring of 1922, Olga Knipper-Chekhova had been an émigrée: a category of deep suspicion to the Soviet authorities. But this brief period, although dangerous in itself, was nothing in comparison to the flamboyant career of her niece and namesake in Germany.

In the autumn of 1943, the Moscow Art Theatre had requested a special honour for their greatest actress to mark her seventy-fifth birthday, but this had been received with an ominous silence from the Soviet authorities. Throughout the war she had never been invited to speak on the radio or to give solo performances as before. Other members of the family encountered similar sinister rebuffs. In the Soviet Union such signs could not be ignored. And now people were finding that the great victory had not eased the paranoia of the Stalinist regime. The recent wave of denunciations and pre-dawn raids by the NKVD made Muscovites afraid that another round of purges had begun.

At least the building was reassuringly familiar. This theatre had literally been a second home to her for over half a lifetime. Apart from a great Art Nouveau bas-relief above the entrance, the outside was not so very different from most Moscow three-storeyed façades. Inside, the circle of ceiling lamps and door handles of the auditorium were also of Art Nouveau design. The fronts of the seats were upholstered in plush, but otherwise the walls and floors were bare of decoration. Stanislavsky had disapproved of anything which distracted attention from the performance. On the grey-green curtains, the only emblem was Chekhov's single stylized seagull in flight. This symbol of a new reality in the theatre had remained in place throughout the revolution and the famine-stricken civil war. It had even survived the Stalinist Terror and the company being forced to stage Socialist Realist plays of pure propaganda.

Olga Knipper-Chekhova had little to fear professionally in such a well-known role as the one she was to play for this special performance of *The Cherry Orchard*. In the autumn of 1943 she had played the part for the thousandth time for the troops and received fan letters from the front afterwards.

Anton Chekhov had not written the part of Ranyevskaya with his wife in mind – he had in fact intended it for a much older actress – but this worked later to her advantage. It allowed her, even in her seventies, to continue playing the character and receive tumultuous applause, although the acclaim was perhaps more for a revered institution. She was known for her expressive hand movements – in the role of Ranyevskaya, they were fluttering and elegantly clumsy to express her emotional confusion – yet Olga Knipper-Chekhova herself overdid things when nervous. Nemirovich-Danchenko once sent her a message which she had never forgotten: 'One pair of hands is enough. Leave the other dozen pairs in the dressing room.'

That evening, as the curtains closed on Stanislavsky's final sound effect off-stage – the hollow thud of an axe chopping down cherry trees in the lost orchard – the 500-strong audience gave a standing ovation on this highly emotional occasion. Olga Knipper-Chekhova took her bow a few moments later. Her lowered eyes focused on the front rows. A beautiful, well-dressed woman in her forties gave her a discreet wave. Olga Knipper-Chekhova reeled back in shock and collapsed behind the curtain in confusion and terror. The glamorous woman who had waved to her, right there in the triumphant Soviet capital, was her niece, Olga Chekhova, the great star of the Nazi cinema.

2. Knippers and Chekhovs

Olga Knipper-Chekhova, People's Artist of the USSR and *grande dame* of the Moscow stage, had no Slav blood in her body. Her husband, Anton Chekhov, had never ceased to be bemused by the utterly un-Russian family into which he had married in 1901. To the consumptive playwright, the Germanic Knippers looked so healthy; and they seemed so tidy and organized and bourgeois in comparison to his own chaotic family.

The Knippers originally came from Saarbrücken, where the name was common. They were said to have been builders, which may explain the choice of family motto, *Per ardua ad astra*. Olga's father, Leonard Knipper, had made enough money during those nineteenth-century boom years in the volatile Russian economy to allow his family to adopt the upper-middle-class style of the period. There was a grand piano in the drawing room and well-upholstered furniture. They had five servants, and the children were sent to private schools. Konstantin studied to become an engineer, while Olga, usually known as Olya, took lessons in languages, music and singing. She longed to be an actress, but her father and mother considered a career on the stage unthinkable for a well-brought-up girl.

When Leonard Knipper died in 1894, a shock awaited his family. He had concealed his bankruptcy, but his death revealed their desperate situation. His widow, Anna, had to move to a small apartment with Olya, by then twenty-five, and Vladimir, who was just starting as a law student. Konstantin had already embarked on his career as a railway engineer. In their dramatically reduced circumstances, the small apartment had to be shared with two eccentric uncles.

To make ends meet, Anna Salza-Knipper gave singing lessons. Her musical talents were clearly considerable. She eventually became a professor at the Moscow Conservatoire. Olya, meanwhile, gave music lessons to earn money to help her through drama school, opposition to a stage career having collapsed after her father's death. Vladimir, the youngest in this handsome and talented family, later proved to have an even better voice than his mother and sister. After a brief career as a lawyer, he became a famous opera singer.

Olya Knipper, in spite of the memory of her father's bankruptcy, showed little regard for the accumulation of money or personal possessions. The theatre was all that mattered to her. She impressed the theatre director Vladimir Nemirovich-Danchenko at the Moscow Philharmonic School, and was one of the young actors chosen in his crusade to revolutionize the theatre with Konstantin Stanislavsky. They wanted to throw out the pompous and melodramatic, and focus instead on everyday life, using new acting techniques which re-created that reality. Stanislavsky's theory, which became known as the 'System' – the idea that actors should immerse themselves totally in their part – later became famous in Hollywood as the 'Method'.

Nemirovich-Danchenko and Stanislavsky, helped greatly by Stanislavsky's family money and the subsidies of rich supporters, set up the Moscow Art Theatre in 1898. Olya became the mistress of Nemirovich-Danchenko, a great friend of Anton Chekhov and the champion of his play *The Seagull*. It was presumably quite an energetic relationship, since Nemirovich-Danchenko's pet name for Olya was 'my vaulting-horse'. But this did not stop her and Chekhov from falling in love after their first meeting that September, during rehearsals for *The Seagull*. Chekhov had sometimes railed against actresses – he once called them 'cows who fancy they are goddesses' and 'Machiavellis in skirts' – but this was partly due to his inability to keep away from them, and they from him.

The love affair between Anton Chekhov and Olya Knipper was mostly a curious long-distance process. Except for summer visits, she stayed in Moscow with the theatre. The consumptive writer, meanwhile, was forced to remain for much of the year in the far warmer climate of Yalta in the Crimea. He called this exile 'my hot Siberia'. The gap was bridged by letters to and fro. They sparred, sometimes quite mercilessly. She joked about Anton's adoring former mistresses, whom she nicknamed the *Antonovkas* – the name of a variety of luscious apple. He teased her about her relationship with her former lover, the theatre's elegant director. 'Have you been carried away by his moiré silk lapels?' he wrote. Occasionally, his jester's mask slipped, revealing his jealousy. But he had little to fear. Nemirovich-Danchenko, a pragmatist more than a cynic, knew that Olya's relationship with the playwright was of great importance to the Moscow Art Theatre. He and Stanislavsky privately viewed the relationship as the theatrical equivalent of an important dynastic marriage.

In the summer of 1900, as Chekhov settled down to write *The Three Sisters*, he resolved to marry Olya Knipper, his 'little Lutheran'. But even when he had finished the play and they arranged their marriage the following year in Moscow, he still did not quite have the nerve to warn his mother and his utterly devoted sister, Mariya, always known as Masha. Olga's mother, Anna Salza, was also unhappy about the marriage. After the brief service, Olya Knipper-Chekhova, as she now became, and Anton slipped away to see his friend and fellow playwright

Maxim Gorky. An amazed Gorky slapped her on the back in congratulation. After this impromptu visit, the bride and groom departed for the railway station. Bewildered guests at the wedding reception were left to wait in vain, but this does not seem to have been that abnormal in the spontaneous chaos of the Chekhovian circle. Only after the wedding was over did Chekhov send his mother a telegram to announce it.

The Chekhov and the Knipper families could not have been more different, as the playwright had so often joked. Yet there were odd similarities. Anton's father, Pavel Chekhov, who had been born the son of a serf, became a hard-nosed shopkeeper in Taganrog on the Sea of Azov, but he also went bankrupt like Leonard Knipper.

The bankruptcy of a parent often proves a powerful influence on the children affected. Some become determined to make so much money that they will feel beyond such dangers, but others long to emancipate themselves from a poverty of experience and knowledge, even more than from financial hardship. The Chekhov children took the latter route. The eldest, Aleksandr, wanted to be a writer. Nikolai became an artist and caricaturist. Anton trained as a doctor while writing his early comic pieces and short stories. Ivan was a primary school teacher, Mariya a painter and Mikhail, the youngest, a translator and general dogsbody on a literary magazine.

Anton was the only one who made any money, so the others frequently turned to him for help and burdened him with their private catastrophes interrupting his work. Many friends and former mistresses who had fallen on hard times did likewise. In the prodigal and disordered world of the late-nineteenth-century Russian intelligentsia, few bothered to save money against unforeseen disaster. That was regarded as bourgeois and disgracefully un-Russian.

Chekhov's choice of subject for the play *The Three Sisters* was not entirely surprising. He had always been fascinated by such trios. One family in particular, the Golden sisters, had become closely linked with Anton and two of his brothers in St Petersburg's bohemia of the early 1880s, a smoky demimonde of debts, drinking and fornication. It was no wonder that the young Dr Chekhov, like most of his medical contemporaries, had to spend a large part of his professional life coping with venereal infections.

The Chekhovs and Goldens lived and worked in the same round of literary weeklies, the boys as contributors, the girls as secretaries. The eldest of these three Jewish sisters, Anna Golden, a divorcée, became the common-law wife of Anton's brother Nikolai, or Kolya. The youngest, darkest and thinnest of the three, Natalya Golden, fell in love with Anton, and their affair lasted two years. She was his 'little skeleton', even though her appetite for food was apparently as voracious as her sexual desire.

They drifted apart, but then, in October 1888, Anton received an astonishing letter from his brother Aleksandr. 'Natalya is living in my apartment, running the household, fussing over the children and keeping me up to scratch. And if she crosses sometimes into concubinage, that's none of your business.' Perhaps the greatest surprise came at the end of the letter. 'If our parents, whose old age I intend to console by exemplary behaviour, don't view this "intimacy" as incest, fornication and onanism, then I have nothing against marriage in church.' Natalya also wrote to Anton professing her own astonishment at how things had turned out. She too was now keen on the idea of middle-class respectability; in fact the 'onanism' mentioned by Aleksandr was almost certainly due to her fear of becoming pregnant before they were married. The condoms he bought at thirty-five kopecks apiece did not seem to work. He bragged to Anton that they burst because they were not large enough.

Nobody could accuse Natalya of being maritally ambitious. Aleksandr was a writer whose lack of financial and critical success was cruelly highlighted by the growing renown of his younger sibling. He was reduced to journalism for the right-wing Suvorin press in St Petersburg. Aleksandr was a big, powerful man with a 'thunderous voice' who loathed modern inventions such as the telephone or typewriter, preferring a goose-quill pen. He was also decidedly eccentric. He tried to train his chickens to use one door of the henhouse for entry and the other for exit, but they failed to understand such logic and neither threats nor inducements would alter their random behaviour. Utterly unpredictable in his own life, squalid in his surroundings and obscene in his language, both on the page and in public, he had often sought escape in the bottle and in the beds of indulgent women.

Anton, who visited the couple in St Petersburg just over two months later, was appalled by his eldest brother's crude behaviour in front of children and servants and his mistreatment of Natalya. On 2 January 1889, he wrote a letter of devastating criticism. It had a marked effect. From then on, Natalya ruled the marital roost. Yet her position of virtual ostracism within the wider Chekhov family improved only when she gave birth to a son, Mikhail, on 16 August 1891. This was the first legitimate grandchild for Pavel and Evgenia Chekhov and they were overjoyed. Aleksandr was soon trying to convince Anton of the blessings of marriage – or 'God-fearing coitus', as he preferred to put it – but it was not long before he started to suffer from impotence, probably as a result of his semi-chronic alcoholism.

The marriage continued to undergo severe strains, mainly according to whether Aleksandr was on or off the bottle.

Sometimes he just disappeared. A telegram would arrive saying: 'Am in the Crimea' or 'Am in the Caucasus'. Sometimes Natalya threw him out of the house when he lapsed again into alcohol and impotence. It was perhaps typical of this morally anarchic circle that the demanding Natalya, Anton's former mistress, should write to him, complaining of his brother's inability to satisfy her. She asked what he, as a doctor, could do to help. The answer was clearly discouraging.

Natalya nevertheless remained devoted to Anton, especially if he came to see them on visits to St Petersburg and praised his young nephew Mikhail's emerging talents. 'Misha is an amazingly intelligent boy,' he wrote in February 1895. 'There's a nervous energy shining in his eyes. I think he's going to grow into a talented man.' Aleksandr was also boastful of his son's precocious prowess. He later claimed that, as well as speaking French and German, Misha at the age of twelve was already chasing girls. Natalya, however, had been so determined to protect her precious Misha from bad influences that she had made Aleksandr send Kolya, the unruly fourteen-year-old elder son from his previous liaison, away to the merchant navy. She became increasingly eccentric. Misha could do no wrong in her eyes, but her overpowering possessiveness evidently unbalanced him. He later told friends that she had seduced him. This was almost certainly untrue, but the brilliant youth who was to marry Uncle Anton's niece by marriage was slightly unbalanced. He seems to have inherited his father's self-destructive streak.

During these turn-of-the-century years, Anton Chekhov's brother-in-law Konstantin Knipper, had become a successful engineer in the great days of Russian railroad expansion. With his immaculate beard and the official frock-coated uniform of the imperial railways, Konstantin Knipper had the air of a better-looking version of the Tsar himself. He directed the construction of the Trans-Caucasian line, living with his young family near Tiflis. His wife, Yelena, usually known as Lulu, was also German, and also musical. Their daughter Olga, Mikhail Chekhov's future wife, later claimed that Tchaikovsky had been her mother's first love, a particularly improbable invention. She also claimed, in her exasperatingly disingenuous memoirs, that her mother was close friends with Tolstoy, Rachmaninov and the Tsarina.

A slight confusion even surrounds Olga's birth on 26 April 1897. Official Soviet documents, including later reports of the NKVD and SMERSh, record her place of birth as Pushkin (the former Tsarskoe Selo, near St Petersburg), yet she was undoubtedly born at Aleksandropol in the southern Caucasus. The family did not move to St Petersburg until several years later.

Olga Chekhova's first recollection of childhood in Georgia focused on a summer afternoon. She and her elder sister, Ada, tiptoed about the house outside Tiflis, because their parents were nervous and irritable. Their little brother, Lev, lay in a darkened room, with his feet fastened to the end of the bed. Traction was exerted on his back through weights attached to his feet and a leather loop under his chin. Anton Chekhov, then the lover but not quite yet the husband of their Aunt Olya, as they called her, had come to see the invalid child. He diagnosed tuberculosis of the bone. Their mother, Lulu, having tried many medical practitioners who all agreed with this diagnosis, had turned in desperation to Chekhov, the only doctor close to the family. In later years, Lev's sister Olga could not resist embroidering the event in her memoirs, with the unlikely detail that Anton Chekhov had brought the two-year-old a gramophone as a present because he was already aware of this future composer's musical gifts. Lev's love for music did not become evident until much later.

The house – Olga later described it as 'a hunting lodge' – was made with wood from the mountain forest. It had a library, a billiard room and a sitting room with a piano on which Olga and Lev's parents played four-handed duets. A nanny supervised them from breakfast until bedtime prayers, but they still seem to have had adventures. Olga claimed that, as a baby, she had been dragged from the garden by a jackal which emerged from the surrounding wilderness, and that, at the age of five, she was molested by the gardener. Neither experience appears to have daunted her.

Lev, after being sent to Moscow for treatment, recovered gradually and slowly began to walk again. But his childhood illness made him a solitary, rather introverted character. He did not join his two sisters when they played in laundry baskets, pretending that these were ships in which they sailed from room to room, each one designated a different country. The girls read *Robinson Crusoe* and *Don Quixote*, and adored dressing up. Yet even though they were not unduly noisy or ill-disciplined, Konstantin Leonardovich Knipper often exploded into rages, especially if his authority was questioned. Olga claimed that she once threw herself out of a ground-floor window in protest at one of her father's outbursts. Whether or not the father's rages were a contributory factor, Lev appears to have grown into a boy who controlled and concealed his emotions. Nobody knew what he was thinking.

Konstantin Knipper, although he loomed large when at home, was frequently taken away by his work on the railways. In 1904, with the onset of the Russo-Japanese War, he was summoned to rebuild a large section of the Trans-Siberian railway to help transport troops to the Far East. Whenever possible, Lulu Knipper accompanied her husband. On one of these occasions, she left the four-year-old Lev in the custody of his Aunt Olya. She adored Lev and wrote to Anton, now her husband, afterwards: 'I hellishly wanted a son like that for you and me.' From then on she saw herself virtually as Lev's surrogate mother.

It was around this time that the family left Georgia for Moscow, a temporary resting place, before they moved on to St Petersburg once Konstantin Knipper became an official in the Ministry of Transport. The fact that he was of German origin and a Lutheran did not impede his career. Konstantin Knipper made clear at home that he wanted his only son, Lev, to follow in his footsteps as an engineer. Lev showed little reaction, as usual.

He started to recover from his childhood illness. Aunt Olya gave him boxing gloves and a football, which provoked energetic protests from the boy's mother, convinced that he should take no risks. But it was not long before Lev became attracted to dangerous physical activity, almost certainly to compensate for the humiliations of an over-coddled childhood. He was also to become extremely competitive. His only foray into engineering as a child was to build a rudimentary plane 'which looked like a see-saw'. It crashed, injuring his spine. The two sisters, Ada and Olga, looked after him for a whole summer holiday, and Aunt Olya also came to care for him.

Behind his controlled mask, Lev was clearly intelligent, so his overt refusal to indicate any special interest exasperated his father. Lev had in fact discovered his vocation, but did not reveal it to anyone, including himself, for many years. When he was about six, his parents took him to a concert in St Petersburg, presumably hoping like most adults that he would not embarrass or irritate them by shuffling around out of boredom. But the music – it was Tchaikovsky's 6th Symphony – struck him with such exquisite power that he was quite overcome. He later described it as his 'first music shock'. It was so intense that, to his mother's alarm, he burst into tears. An evidently displeased Konstantin Knipper had to lead his young son out of the concert hall and take him home.

The two Knipper girls received piano lessons as a matter of course, but even in this musical family Lev did not. His mother used to organize musical soirées at home, so Lev hid in the drawing room to listen. He loved the Gypsy folksongs called *romans* performed by a friend of his mother: they seem to have had a lasting influence on some of his subsequent work. And whenever Aunt Olya was visiting St Petersburg with the Moscow Art Theatre during its spring season, she used to play adaptations of Beethoven symphonies with her brother Konstantin or sing *bergerettes* to her own accompaniment. Clearly Lev had so sealed himself off in boyhood that he never expressed his musical yearnings and nobody in the family guessed them until he became an adolescent.

Lev's secondary schooling took place at the First Classical School Gymnasium. He was fortunate to have an excellent music teacher, and at last his inclination blossomed. In the school orchestra he wanted to learn all the instruments – wind, percussion and string. He even started to become a normal boy of his time, reading Jules Verne, Fenimore Cooper and *The Three Musketeers*. Most strikingly, he showed himself determined to conquer all the feelings of physical inferiority he had experienced as a child. He spent time running and engaging in the Russian version of 'French wrestling'. Aunt Olya, thrilled to see this physical improvement, and proud of the presents she had given him to such family outrage, now brought back a full footballer's outfit from one of her foreign trips.

At home as well as at school, Lev followed one passion after another. He was given a chemistry set and experimented constantly until an explosion led to its instant confiscation.

His parents finally found a piano teacher for him, but the teacher in question was clearly of the old-fashioned school, making him play scales the whole time. After the freedom and innovation of the orchestra, this irritated Lev profoundly and his 'unruly character' revolted against this 'scale torture'. The lessons were stopped.

Lev's sister Olga showed none of his academic promise at all. In 1913, at the Stroganov Art School in St Petersburg, her final marks for religious education, Russian, maths, algebra, geometry, history and physics could hardly have been lower. Her French and German were adequate and she distinguished herself only in art. The reaction of many within the family was that 'such a beauty didn't need to go to school anyway'.

Young Olga longed to go on the stage, but her father, Konstantin, absolutely forbade any idea of the theatre as a career. He could not say so, out of loyalty to his sister, the great symbol of the Moscow Art Theatre, but actresses, like ballerinas, were seen in imperial Russia as not much better than high-class prostitutes. Yet Lulu, her mother, seems to have secretly sympathized. According to young Olga, her aunt, when acting for a season in St Petersburg, brought the great Italian actress Eleanora Duse to the house. Duse, she later claimed, patted her head and said: 'You will definitely become an actress one day, my little one.' Nobody, however, would have predicted that, like Aunt Olya, Olga too would marry into the Chekhov family, although in her case the marriage would prove disastrous.

3. Mikhail Chekhov

The acting talents of Olga's future husband, Misha Chekhov, were evident from an early age. In 1907, when he was just sixteen, his besotted mother, Natalya, moved him to the school of the Maly Theatre in St Petersburg. He studied there for three years and graduated with distinction. In October 1911, aged only nineteen, he was given the lead role in the Maly's production of Aleksei Tolstoy's *Tsar Feodor*. It was the play which had launched the Moscow Art Theatre just before *The Seagull* and brought fame, as well as Chekhov's attention, to Aunt Olya in the role of the Tsarina Irina.

Misha was an instant success. He had an extraordinary gift for mimicry, both facial and vocal, while his mesmerizing eyes and haunted face allowed him to play old men convincingly even before he was twenty. A first cousin, Sergei Chekhov, described Misha in the spring of 1912: 'He was short, thin and moved restlessly. He dressed carelessly in a shabby velvet jacket and, horror of horrors, he did not just lack a starched collar, he wore no collar at all. But he had a captivating tenderness about him. He was warm and had a sweet smile which made one forget that he was not handsome. He would pull up his trousers in a characteristic gesture of exaggerated elegance, and rolled his eyes in an amusing way.' The two of them went for walks together, fooled around and danced the tango, which was then the rage in St Petersburg. Misha gave his cousin a photograph of himself frowning and signed it with the words: 'This is how I look after the tango.'

During the spring of 1912, the Moscow Art Theatre came

to St Petersburg for its annual season. Anton Chekhov's sister, Masha, the devoted guardian of the playwright's flame, arranged for him to meet her sister-in-law Olga Knipper-Chekhova, still the star of the Moscow Art Theatre, and she in turn promised to arrange an audition with Stanislavsky. Misha spent a sleepless night beforehand, so keen was he to join the company. The next morning he found that the collar of his only suitable shirt was so tight that it produced a ringing in the ears, and his trousers had to be hauled up so high 'as if I had to step over puddles'.

'Thank you, Aunt Masha,' he wrote afterwards. 'I can imagine what a silly and funny impression I made upon them. I am terribly shy. I can't speak, and when I meet a person for the first time, I can't even say two words.' But Stanislavsky recognized his talent immediately and invited him to join the Moscow Art Theatre. The fact that he was a nephew of the theatre's patron saint was certainly not a hindrance. In August of that year, Misha left St Petersburg for Moscow.

At first he lived under Aunt Masha's wing in her apartment on Dolgorukovskaya ulitsa. She was a vegetarian at the time and was teased by the rest of the family. Misha called his aunt 'the Countess', and kissed her hand most elaborately. When he returned to St Petersburg the following year with the Moscow Art Theatre on its spring tour, he found that his father did not have much time left to live. Natalya had thrown Aleksandr out in 1908, because of his relapse into alcoholism. Since then, Misha's father had been living in a small dacha with one servant, his dogs and his chickens, and he was now dying from cancer of the larynx. Misha spent his spare time by his father's deathbed. Despite the pain, Aleksandr continued to make jokes until the end came in May 1913. Misha was deeply touched. The experience, as he admitted later, influenced his portrayal of death on the stage.

When Misha returned to Moscow after his father's death, Natalya moved there with her two dachshunds to join him. They began to enjoy a style beyond his modest salary at the theatre. Perhaps they were living off the proceeds from the sale of the house near St Petersburg. In any case Misha, with his success on the stage, had acquired a taste for theatrical extravagence. 'I visited Mishka several times,' Volodya Chekhov, another first cousin, wrote to his mother, who was staying during that last summer of peace in the playwright's house at Yalta. 'He is living in a four-roomed apartment with electric light near the Patriarshie ponds. He has bought a new piano and now he no longer borrows twenty kopecks from the porters, but is constantly handing out tips all round. He pays eighty-five roubles for his apartment. Natalya Aleksandrovna sits there in a black robe, squints and smokes, while Misha, in red shoes, grey unbuttoned trousers and no jacket, lies on the sofa and "spits at the ceiling" [an old Russian phrase which means doing nothing].'

Volodya, younger by nearly three years, hero-worshipped Misha. He also felt himself to be in his shadow and something of a poor relation. Volodya had secretly longed to be an actor too, but lacked sufficient confidence in his own talents. He also faced parental disapproval. His father, the fourth of the five Chekhov brothers, had not even graduated from secondary school. Ivan Chekhov, who appears in family photographs as elegantly bearded and bearing a faint resemblance to the young Stalin, had taught in a primary school. There he had met Volodya's mother, a beautiful young fellow teacher with fair hair. But his career had not been a happy one.

Their side of the family saw comparatively little of the more artistic members, perhaps partly because Ivan Chekhov had convinced himself that actors were 'second-rate people'. Volodya had not met Misha before because his parents would have nothing to do with Natalya, Misha's mother and Anton's former mistress. Volodya, now studying law at Moscow University, finally set eyes on him at one of Aunt Masha's family dinners. Volodya adored the way Misha could not stop performing, often with brilliant improvisations and imitations. The two of them would invent and act out whole scenes together. And for Volodya, such associations with the theatre must have had a heady whiff of the forbidden.

The cousins used to play charades after Aunt Masha's dinners, using all the shawls, rugs, old hats, sheets and even the big carpet from the floor in the sitting room. Sergei remembered 'Volodya wrapped in this carpet, wriggling on the floor, pretending to be a whale'. Misha, draped in a sheet and holding a staff, played Jonah and plunged into the carpet's mouth. Another night, however, when perhaps playing the part of Noah too literally, he fell asleep having drunk too much.

On some evenings, to Aunt Masha's considerable distress, Misha would arrive already inebriated. She dreaded him inheriting his father's alcoholism and offered him twenty-five roubles a month if he gave up drink. He promised to do so and took the money. Aunt Masha was very relieved, but then one evening he turned up swaying and slurring his words again. Volodya, who was with him, said gloomily that he had found Misha in this state outside in the street. Aunt Masha burst into tears, reproaching him. Misha, who had been putting on an act for fun, was horrified by the intensity of her reaction. He fell on his knees. 'My darling Mashechka, calm down,' he called to her in a sober voice. 'I was pretending. Please forgive me.' Aunt Masha was consoled and later used to tell the story, boasting how great an actor her nephew was. Yet the reprieve from alcoholism was only temporary.

The cousins' charmed life continued after the announcement of war in August 1914. They had ignored the middle-class crowds rejoicing in the streets. Even the terrible news when the First and Second Russian Armies were destroyed in East Prussia seemed to make little difference to their existence. Volodya was in his second year at university and, during that autumn season of 1914, Misha played in Turgenev's *A Woman from the Provinces*. He also enjoyed great success in an experimental version by the Moscow Art Theatre studio of *The Cricket on the Hearth* by Charles Dickens.

Stanislavsky's 'System', Misha found, produced great demands on the actor, but he felt that he was learning far more than he ever had in St Petersburg at the Maly Theatre. It was not up to the actor simply to follow the director's instructions. He had to create the role in a literal sense, by imagining the character he was playing and inhabiting his life. Stanislavsky did not want an actor to imitate the externals. The actor's own emotional memories were to be used to help his re-creation, making it personal and real to him, and thus to the audience. Stanislavsky loathed the stock gestures of the theatrical profession which had made acting so mannered.

'Agitation is expressed by pacing up and down the stage very quickly,' he wrote, 'by the hands being seen to tremble when a letter is being opened or by letting the jug knock against the glass and then the glass against the teeth when the water is being poured and drunk.' He regarded this as a lazy shorthand, a caricature of human behaviour, a copy of a copy of a copy, which had evolved into a standard pattern of theatrical clichés. The point for Stanislavsky was to convey inner feelings through every other means.

Misha often had breakfast with Stanislavsky, who would suddenly tell him to eat in a manner which expressed a particular mood: for example, as if he had just suffered the death of a child.

★

In the winter, the cousins went skiing in the Sparrow Hills outside Moscow. The ill-constructed trenches of the eastern front, in which several million men from the Tsarist army stood in icy mud up to their knees, must have seemed a whole world away. Misha and his mother dreaded his conscription into the army, yet the Moscow Art Theatre carried on as before.

The younger generation of Knippers as well as Chekhovs also started to move to Moscow from St Petersburg, now renamed Petrograd by the Tsar in a gesture of wartime Russian nationalism. Olga was sent to Moscow by her parents in 1914 to study art. She moved into Aunt Olya's apartment on the first floor of 23 Prechistensky bulvar, a typical late-nineteenth-century Moscow stuccoed building with Italianate windows on the top two floors. It still stands on the broad Boulevard Ring, with a promenade bordered by large maples and grass running between the two carriageways. The view from Aunt Olya's windows was of trees and the magnificent town houses of magnates on the far side of the boulevard.

The following year, Lev too came to Moscow to attend a new school. Aunt Olya made sure that she saw her favourite nephew frequently and she encouraged him in every way. The school, which was progressive for the times, put on a performance of Aleksandr Blok's play *The Rose and the Cross*, for which Lev was allowed to select and adapt the music. Lev had mixed feelings about the move to Moscow. He had fallen in love with the beauty of St Petersburg a year or so before leaving it, yet the city in its wartime guise of Petrograd was starting to change. There was a new, ugly mood. The Knipper parents had discussed the political unrest quite openly at table. They were extremely concerned at the strikes and the ossified reaction of the Tsar and his entourage to an increasingly dangerous situation.

4. Misha and Olga

Along with Aleksandr Chekhov's alcoholism, Misha had also inherited a compulsion to seduce, although mercifully in a rather more romantic fashion than his father. 'From my earliest youth,' he wrote later, 'I found myself in a constant state of falling in love.'

Misha must have first met Olga Knipper when he was still at the Maly Theatre in St Petersburg. Just before the First World War, two or three of the Chekhov cousins went out to the Knipper house at Tsarskoe Selo to play tennis, swim and dance. Misha presumably did not pay much attention to her then, for she was almost six years younger than him. But when Olga came to Moscow in 1914 to study art she was seventeen and enchantingly beautiful. She had not yet emerged from an innocent naïvety and a tendency to day-dream, even though she had already demonstrated on occasion a streak of determination.

Her own account of these early years is heavily roman-ticized. She claimed that as a child she used to play with the little Grand Duchesses at Tsarskoe Selo and that she had encountered Rasputin in alarming circumstances. She even recounted that she had been accepted at the Moscow Academy of Art at the age of twelve and later studied under Bakst and Rodin. But this compulsive mythologizing may well have been provoked by the patronizing attitude of a family which refused to take her seriously because of her beauty.

Misha and Volodya met her at the apartment of Aunt Olya Knipper–Chekhova and at Aunt Masha's Sunday night supper parties. In one after-dinner charade, Misha, wearing a white coat, played an unskilled medical assistant in a clinic. He rushed back and forth to a patient, played by young Olga, carrying medical implements and water, which he spilled in his clumsiness, all the time being shouted at by the doctor. Misha and Volodya became increasingly competitive in their acting and their joking. They had both fallen for their fair cousin-in-law.

Perhaps inevitably in such a story of tangled love, none of the accounts agree. According to Sergei Chekhov, Volodya followed Misha to St Petersburg for the Moscow Art Theatre's 1914 spring season. Misha came across Volodya carrying a tennis racket and dressed in check trousers, white shoes and a boater. Volodya was apparently intent on proposing to Olga during a moonlit walk, but then Misha, his best friend and hero, insisted that, since he was three years older, he had priority. Volodya answered that there was no priority in love. Misha retorted that he already had some standing in society, while Volodya was still a student and his future was uncertain. Volodya replied that he would make Olga promise to wait for him until he graduated from the university.

'Your father is not going to let you marry her!' Misha almost shouted.

At this Volodya just grinned.

'So what are we going to do?' Misha asked more calmly.

'Let's toss a coin,' Volodya replied. 'The one who gets tails will leave Olya for ever and keep no place for bitterness in his heart.'

He tossed the coin and it came down tails. The cousins embraced without a word.

Volodya recounted all this to Aunt Masha in 1917, when he was staying with her down in the Crimea. Misha never really gave his side, except in the most offhand way. The only other version of events is that written by Olga herself. She was utterly besotted with Misha, her cousin by marriage, who appeared to be as brilliant an actor as his uncle had been a playwright. Olga, then studying at the Moscow Academy of Art, went to as many of his performances in the Studio of the Art Theatre as she could. She helped paint the scenery for *The Cricket on the Hearth*, in which he had the lead part. But carried away with the story, she claimed in her memoirs that the key moment in their romance took place after she played Ophelia to his Hamlet in the Moscow Art Theatre for a charity performance. Her version includes everyone, including Stanislavsky and Aunt Olya, congratulating her on her performance after the curtain. An emotional Misha then pulls her into the wings and kisses her passionately. Although the circumstances are unlikely, she was so innocent of the facts of life that she may well have thought, as she claims, that she would have a child if such a man kissed her.

'But now you must marry me,' she told him.

'What could be better?' he laughed.

Misha and Olga, whatever the exact details surrounding their decision to get married, undoubtedly acted on the spur of the moment without telling anyone. They knew that if they did ask for permission, it would be refused on the grounds of Olga's age and Misha's circumstances, and she would be taken home to Tsarskoe Selo immediately.

So early one morning in September 1914, soon after the outbreak of war, Olga packed a small suitcase with her passport, wash-bag and a new nightdress and slipped out of Aunt Olya's apartment on Prechistensky bulvar without being seen. It must have taken considerable courage, even when carried away by romantic fever. She took a *drozhky* to join Misha and together they drove to a small Orthodox church at the other end of Moscow. Misha, saying that they did not have much time, handed their passports to the priest, a very old man with a wrinkled face. The priest clearly did not want to be hurried and kept shaking his head in disapproval. The bride and groom each grasped a flickering candle, and two bystanders, engaged by Misha, held the crowns over their heads. The fact that Olga was a Lutheran does not appear to have been a problem. By Orthodox standards it certainly seems to have been a simple, short ceremony. Even so, Olga claimed later that Misha was constantly looking at his pocket watch, afraid of being late for that afternoon's performance.

For Olga, the enormity of what they had just done sank in only after they had returned to Misha's apartment. They sat down to drink some tea from the samovar in his bedroom. The bed was so small that she wondered where she was supposed to sleep. Although the apartment had appeared large to Sergei Chekhov, it must have seemed very small to Olga, brought up in the houses at Tiflis and Tsarskoe Selo. And they had to share it with Misha's old wet nurse as well as her mother-in-law. The atmosphere must have been unbearably oppressive. Next door, Natalya lay prostrate in her darkened bedroom. She had collapsed in shock and grief at discovering that her beloved son had married without telling her. That afternoon, even the egocentric Misha must have realized that he could not go to work at the theatre on the day of his wedding, leaving together these two irreconcilable women in his life.

Aunt Olya found out a few hours later. One of the actors at the Moscow Art Theatre came up and congratulated her. She asked why.

'Oh, but your nephew has got married,' he said to her.

'Which nephew?' she asked.

'Mikhail Aleksandrovich.'

'Who's he married?'

'Your niece, Olga Konstantinovna.'

Distraught, she went straight home to Prechistensky bulvar. Olga wasn't there, so she rushed round to Misha's apartment. Olga herself opened the door. Aunt Olya fainted on the landing and Misha had to carry her into the apartment. Volodya, the defeated rival who turned up soon afterwards, described the situation in a letter to his mother: 'You can't imagine what a scene it was. [Aunt Olya] wanted to give Mishka a beating, then she changed her mind. She started to faint, she sobbed. In another room [Olga] was in hysterics. In the third one Natalya Aleksandrovna was lying unconscious. The scandal was grandiose and is still going on. I can't imagine how it is going to end. Aunt Olya sent a telegram to St Petersburg and probably the parents are going to arrive tomorrow. How terrible it all is! Boris [his friend] and I have sworn never to get married.'

Aunt Olya returned home in despair. She sent an emissary that evening to try to convince Olga to return to the apartment, and then in the early hours Uncle Vladimir, the opera singer, arrived to persuade the young bride to come back. Olga received little support from Misha, who was appalled by the scandal they had unleashed. The self-absorbed young actor clearly felt sorrier for himself than for his seventeen-year-old bride. 'I said that [Olga] herself should make the decision,' he wrote to Aunt Masha, 'and she decided to go to see her aunt just to calm her down. I decided to allow [Olga] to go back to St Petersburg with her mother in order to prepare her father and tell him the news. Now a few words about myself. I am in such a state, that I cannot write coherently. I won't say anything about the insults and worries that I have undergone. A lot more are still to come my way.'

Aunt Olya, meanwhile, had sent a telegram to her sister-in-law, Lulu Knipper: 'Come at once.' On receiving it, Olga's mother had taken the next train to Moscow and arrived the following evening. Her first question was evidently to find out whether Olga had married because she was pregnant. Olga assured her that was not the case.

'Thank God for the lesser evil,' replied her mother.

The train journey by wagon-lit back to Petrograd took thirteen hours. Before they reached Tsarskoe Selo, her mother told her to go straight to bed and stay there. She would tell her father when he returned from the ministry that she was ill.

Olga clearly needed little encouragement. She stayed in bed for two days, 'crying her eyes out'.

Her mother gave her a good talking-to, emphasizing that she and Misha were married and nothing could now be done about that, but she should not commit a second blunder by having a child with Misha before she had got to know him better. Olga was confined to her bedroom, but she had already seen how she could exploit her position. She threatened suicide if her parents refused to allow her to return to Misha. Even her father in all his anger had to face the fact that the marriage was lawful and could be annulled only by a Church consistory. Olga, no doubt to heighten the pathos, recounted in her memoirs how she was allowed finally to return to Moscow, taking with her no more than a single set of clothes and no jewellery, on her father's insistence.

Misha and his mother met her at the station in Moscow. Apparently, not a word was said in the *drozhky* on the way back to the apartment. It was a most unromantic homecoming. Things, however, must have improved that winter, both in their relationship and in Misha's career. The next year, when Misha came back to Petrograd with the Moscow Art Theatre for the spring season, the young couple appear to have become completely accepted by the parents. 'We're already in Petrograd for a week,' Olga wrote to Aunt Masha in Yalta. 'Misha has given three performances. The success is unbelievable. However, you probably know that already from the newspapers. We're staying with my parents. Papa is treating Misha very very well. There is complete peace.'

'Beautiful Mashechka,' wrote Misha at the same time to his aunt. 'Let your genius nephew greet you and tell you that here in Olya's family he is being received wonderfully . . . Today [Olga's] family are going to see *The Cricket*. I am longing to go home to Mama and if it wasn't so wonderful with [Olga's] family, I would have long ago died from homesickness. Waiting for your honoured reply. Count Mikhail Chekhov.'

Another member of the family recorded: 'I was at the family dinner with [Olga's] parents. I can remember being very surprised seeing Misha wearing a jacket and a collar although the collar was a soft one. [Olga] and he were sitting next to each other at the table, kissing every minute and putting the best bits of food on to each other's plates.'

But the idyll did not last long when they returned to Moscow in the early summer. Misha told her that she would get used to the apartment, but having to share it with an insomniac mother-in-law who hated her made it hard to hide her unhappiness. Meals were a penance, and Olga would try to find an excuse to slip away as soon as possible to escape to their bedroom. Only Mariya, the clumsy old peasant wet nurse, who had 'two left hands', was kind to her. According to Olga, Mariya was treated 'like a slave', with Natalya screaming at her in the kitchen and summoning her in the night when she could not sleep.

Misha, like almost everyone in Russian intellectual circles, wanted to avoid conscription. He later wrote how 'waiting for one's call-up medical examination was agony'. He admitted that he was in a state of total panic as he made his way towards the conscription centre in Moscow. He had confided his fears to an elderly member of the Moscow Art Theatre staff, who had then accompanied him to provide moral support. Misha almost froze when prodded and yelled at by corporals, who ordered these young male civilians to strip off in the filth and cold of the building. It seemed to go on for hours and with no purpose. Anxious relatives peered through the windows, trying to see what was going on. The conscripts stood in line naked for two hours or more as they queued for the doctors. Misha's legs could hardly keep him upright. The exhausted doctor, who finally examined his heart and lungs with his stethoscope, called out: 'Three months!' Misha nearly collapsed in relief. There was some doubt about his state of health, so they would call him back for re-examination later. His sentence was suspended. It took him nearly another hour to recover his clothes, and when he emerged he was deeply touched to find that his confidant from the theatre was still there to ascertain his fate.

Olga's brother, Lev, on the other hand, ran away from his high school at the age of seventeen to volunteer for the army. He later called it a 'surge of false patriotism'. Although frustrated at the time, he was most fortunate. The authorities sent him back to his school to finish his studies. He progressed to the Moscow Higher Technical College, where he was allotted to a reserve unit. Then, almost as soon as he reached the front, he was sent back as an officer candidate at the school of horse artillery at Orel. He would graduate just as the Russian Revolution was about to destroy the world in which they had all grown up.

5. The Beginning of a Revolution

The ability of the theatrical community to exist apart from the terrible reality of the First World War seems slightly bewildering in retrospect. Their letters and personal accounts make few references to the events which were shaking Russia to pieces. They had despised the 'patriotic plays' of 'theatrical pasteboard' put on in the early days of the war and concentrated on their own work.

Stanislavsky later acknowledged that 'art showed that it had nothing in common with tendencies, politics and the topics of the day'. The collapse of the Russian armies in central and southern Poland during the summer of 1915 could have happened on another continent. Among the Knippers, that most Germanic and musical of families, there appears to have been no mention of the anti-German riots of June 1915 in Moscow, when Bechstein pianos were hauled into the street and set on fire.

These disorders were largely inspired by hatred for the Tsarina – 'the German woman'. She was seen, along with ministers bearing Germanic-sounding names, as proof of the enemy within. Rumour-mongers assured everyone that she had a direct telephone line to Berlin to give away the plans of the Russian high command. Her treachery, they claimed, was the reason why so many Russian soldiers were suffering in vain. This growing belief that the incompetence of the Tsarist regime was in fact a smokescreen for corruption and treason did not disturb Misha and his friends in the theatre. Their bohemian world despised politics and politicians as much as military patriotism and futile sacrifice. Some of them, such as Meyerhold, passionately supported the cause of revolution. And even Konstantin Stanislavsky, a patrician merchant as well as actor, looked forward to 'the miraculous liberation of Russia'. He was convinced that it would bring a new era of artistic freedom and enlightenment. He also failed to foresee that his family business, which subsidized the Moscow Art Theatre, would be expropriated.

Apart from officers of the old school, the greatest believers in the war against Germany had been their relatives: the young women of the nobility and upper middle class who had volunteered to roll bandages and serve as nurses for the tragic mass of suffering soldiers – the amputees, the blind, the gangrenous and the shell-shocked. Many of these well-brought-up young ladies regarded this service as much more than a duty. They saw it as a spiritual experience, a homage to Christ washing the feet of the poor. The Tsarina set up her own little hospital, with the young Grand Duchesses suitably attired, but their patients do not appear to have been chosen for the seriousness of their wounds, which suggests something akin to a Petit Trianon version of medicine.

The mainly peasant soldiers, patronized by these earnest women, had never shared the middle class's enthusiasm for the war on its outbreak. They had known that once again the peasantry would be treated as 'meat for the cannon'. Their villages had mourned their departure with the traditional lamentations of a funeral, never expecting to see these sons again. And the fact that they were commanded by young *barins*, members of the landowning class, who in recent years had taken back their land to profit from rising corn prices, had not improved relations between officers and men who felt that they were still treated as little better than serfs.

★

The war did not stop a group from the Moscow Art Theatre, including Stanislavsky, Olya Knipper-Chekhova and the great actor Vasily Kachalov, from touring southern Russia in the late spring of 1916. When it was over, the cast relaxed at the Caucasian spa of Essentuki, which Stanislavsky knew well from previous visits. They enjoyed trips out into the steppe and other diversions, but Stanislavsky himself found it hard to relax. He was in the middle of a row with Nemirovich-Danchenko over the management of the theatre.

Misha had not accompanied them. 'I hope you aren't angry with me for not having written for a long time,' he wrote from Moscow to Aunt Masha that summer. 'It is so nice not to be doing anything, although we are all three in town, but we are still in a very peaceful mood. My *Kapsulka* [my little capsule, i.e. Olga, who was now pregnant] isn't particularly happy to be stuck in the city with Mama. She was dreaming of sketching somewhere in fields and forests. But what can I do? She shouldn't have married me. She could have married Volodya, for example. But she preferred to share my fame with me than to be the wife of a provincial judge.'

For the heavily pregnant Olga, relations with Misha's possessive mother in the shared apartment had become unbearable. To make matters far worse, Misha was drinking again. He poured vodka into his beer for what he called 'deep effect', claiming that he was 'a true Russian', and drank constantly until he collapsed. At night he would wake suddenly and cry out: 'Paper! Pen! Write, Olinka! Write! Great thoughts have come to me.'

As the earlier letter suggested, Misha had fallen out with his cousin, Volodya, who resented the way he was treating Olga. 'My dear Masha,' he wrote to his aunt, 'I love you but please keep that harmful parasite Volodka away from you. I know that he is sitting in your house in Yalta, writing letters to girls in Moscow, saying that you are going to give him a marriage settlement. He can write whatever he wants, but I am sorry for the girls, and your honour also means something to me.' This letter also contained three drawings, a self-portrait signed 'me', a sun with big rays, labelled 'you', and the third, a heap of rubbish with flies buzzing round it, entitled 'Volodka'.

Olga claimed later that she had tried to terminate the pregnancy with hot baths. When she had told Misha that she was expecting a child, he had avoided her gaze, shrugged his shoulders and left the apartment. The marriage was a farce, she realized. One day she returned to the apartment and found their bedroom door closed. She heard a giggle. Misha had brought one of his girlfriends home.

Moscow in the summer was unbearable, so finally Misha rented a dacha. Olga described it as a 'small, utterly primitive little place, which one would only take for the shortest possible time'. She distracted herself painting while Misha, when reasonably sober, played tennis at a nearby court with a succession of girlfriends, one of whom would become his second wife. In August, when the birth approached, she returned to Moscow. Olga was just over eighteen years old when their child, a baby girl, was born on 9 September 1916. They christened her Olga, but she was always known as Ada in this family of confusing names.

Olga suffered a nervous collapse soon after the birth, presumably a form of post-natal depression, exacerbated by the state of her marriage. Another source states that she went down with meningitis. Her romantic illusions were finally crushed by her experiences during the course of that year and the next. Misha showed no interest in their daughter and began drinking even more heavily. Olga had long been treated like a little girl, but now she found that the man she had worshipped was nothing more than a mother-dominated little boy, whatever his undoubted theatrical talents. She found herself forced to reassess everything. Married to a self-destructive drunk, she was trapped by responsibility for a baby daughter. Yet it was not just her own marriage that was collapsing. The whole of Russia and the secure existence that she had known since childhood were starting to disintegrate as fronts collapsed and talk of revolution spread in the streets.

The winter of 1916, the third of the war, was the harshest of them all. Food supplies became increasingly scarce in the rear, while at the front soldiers froze in their makeshift trenches. Their officers did not share their suffering. They lived in requisitioned houses behind the lines. Meanwhile, in Petrograd, the large garrison was becoming increasingly unreliable. Only a few of the officers were regulars. The majority now were recently commissioned civilians, many of whom began to sympathize with the demands of the soldiers to put an end to the war. Even the Tsar's regiments of foot-guards were affected.

The greater the crisis, the more obdurate Tsar Nicholas II became. No politician could persuade him to make changes to save his throne. Once again the deep cultural split in the Russian nation emerged. The mass of the people, especially the rural population, became conscious of their own Russian identity, in contrast to their perception of foreign contamination within the court. And yet that hapless Tsar, crippled by an obsessive wife and his own obstinacy born of weakness, was the most austere, uxorious and Slavophile member of the Romanov dynasty in living memory. He had never liked the imported neo-classical style of Peter the Great's capital. He longed instead for onion domes and massive Muscovite brick walls.

The nobility and the thoughtless rich, sensing that their privileged existence was sliding towards disaster, lost themselves in gambling parties and debauchery, drinking up their wine cellars, buying smoked sturgeon and caviar at wildly inflated prices on the black market and indulging in shamelessly open affairs. In Petrograd, following the Latin American footsteps of the tango, cocaine had also become fashionable in this *danse macabre*. French and British diplomats were shocked at the 'hysterical hedonism' and the careless, apocalyptic mood.

This had spread beyond the idle rich. According to Stanislavsky, it had even affected the Moscow Art Theatre itself. 'The ethical side of the theatre is at present very low,' he had written to Nemirovich-Danchenko from Essentuki. 'Nowhere is there more drinking, more drunkenness than in our theatre, nowhere is there such conceit and disdain for other people and such insulting outbursts.'

6. The End of a Marriage

Stanislavsky, on the urging of Aunt Olya, intervened yet again at the end of 1916 to save Misha Chekhov from conscription. This was no longer a case of unjustified privilege. Not long after the birth of his child, whom he refused to acknowledge, Misha began to suffer a nervous breakdown. Like his father, he was incapable of assuming responsibility for himself, let alone for a young family. He could not cope with the emotional demands of a jealous mother and a miserable young wife. It is hard to imagine that any young woman could have met the approval of this emotional vampire.

'She had been brought up in an orderly German environment,' wrote Sergei Chekhov, 'and could not put up with the breadth of his soul and his indifference towards the conditions in which he lived. She was attuned only to the superficial tone of life and his philosophical mind was alien to her. I think that he never opened his spiritual world to her and apparently she thought him simply insane sometimes. Her relations with her mother-in-law became worse and worse.' This explanation, while basically true, was unsympathetic and also misleading in one sense. Misha really was close to madness and to suicide, as he admitted himself much later. 'In the drawer of my writing table,' he wrote, 'lay a loaded Browning, and I found it very hard to resist the temptation.' Not many eighteen-year-olds, and especially from Olga's sheltered background, could have been expected to cope with Misha and his semi-demented mother.

One also wonders how they coped at a time of acute food

shortages. Misha's old wet nurse, Mariya, had to stand in queues for them while Olga looked after their little daughter and Natalya retired to her bedroom. Misha used black-market contacts to maintain his supplies of vodka, a commodity banned by the Tsar in a show of austere patriotism at the beginning of the war. In fact the bread riots of 1915 and 1916 were partly caused by peasants diverting grain supplies to the far more profitable exercise of making *samogon*, moonshine vodka. As the government took a tougher line with the rural population to secure food supplies, the peasants increasingly held back their grain or fed it to their cattle. Prices rose even more rapidly and food shops in the cities emptied. Queuing for bread now sometimes meant sleeping in the street outside a bakery. And bread queues seethed with rumours and political argument.

Olga's younger brother, Lev Knipper, was by now an officer cadet at an artillery school. He graduated as an ensign of artillery in the early spring of 1917 and, like so many, his fate in the coming civil war was largely dictated by his whereabouts at its outbreak.

Lev and Olga's parents, meanwhile, were fortunate to be living in Tsarskoe Selo rather than in Petrograd itself. Although the spontaneous chaos of the February revolution which overthrew the Romanovs was comparatively good-natured at first, an uglier side appeared within a few days. Gangs looted shops and middle-class houses, looking for alcohol. Women and girls were raped with impunity, since policemen who had escaped lynching were in hiding and trying to escape the city. Any respectably dressed citizen in a collar and tie was likely to be robbed in the street on the grounds that he was a bourgeois. The left-wing writer Maxim Gorky predicted that the revolution 'would probably collapse in ruin worthy of our Asiatic savagery'. Many also remembered Pushkin's phrase: 'the Russian riot, senseless and without mercy'.

The final downfall of the Romanov dynasty came on 3 March, with the renunciation of the throne by the Grand Duke Mikhail, who had been nominated as the Tsar's successor. The news produced scenes of wild rejoicing in the streets of Petrograd and Moscow. Red flags were brandished and hung from windows. Crowds sang a Russian version of the Marseillaise, railwaymen sounded the whistles on locomotives at main-line railway stations, while industrial workers sounded the steam whistles of their factories. No owner or foreman dared object. In many places, enthusiasts broadcast the message of freedom by ringing church bells, whether or not the priest agreed. In Moscow, the monstrous statue of Tsar Alexander III was brought down with dynamite and crowds hauling on ropes, as if the Lilliputians were finally victorious. Red flags were raised at the front and on warships, to the horror of Tsarist officers, and parades were held, with military brass bands booming out the Marseillaise.

The sudden collapse of the autocracy took professional revolutionaries, such as Lenin and Trotsky, completely by surprise. They were exasperated to find themselves so far from the centre of events. But as things turned out, they had not missed their opportunity. The leaders of the Provisional Government, acting out of high-minded liberal naïvety in the case of Prince Lvov, and theatrical vanity in the case of his successor, Aleksandr Kerensky, proved easy to outmanoeuvre. The neck of the new freedom was exposed to the unscrupulous Leninists.

Kerensky was a lawyer. He was small and his starting eyes and curved nose made him look like a very intelligent frog, yet with ringing rhetoric and bursts of emotional energy he could dominate huge crowds. (Olga Chekhova later observed that whenever she saw Dr Goebbels speak, she could not help thinking of Kerensky.) Kerensky managed to convince many highly educated people – Stanislavsky and Nemirovich-Danchenko among them – that he was a political genius, the Napoleon who would bring revolutionary excesses back under control and produce human justice. But historical parallels, especially in times of revolution and war, are often dangerously misleading. The balancing act which he had to undertake between reassuring the bourgeoisie and Russia's Western allies on one hand, while at the same time appeasing the impatience of workers and peasants to take over factories and farmland, would have undermined the credibility of even the greatest leader.

Stanislavsky's family business, the Alekseiev factories, were seized by the workers, and his house, as he admitted to a friend, had been 'done over'. Respect for private property had collapsed with the elastic notion of 'revolutionary expropriation'. Stanislavsky now had nothing more than a salary from the Moscow Art Theatre. He could no longer subsidize it as in the past. Yet his enthusiasm for this new world of freedom did not diminish. He was certain it would lead not only to a fairer world, but to a more beautiful one. On the other hand, he also admitted that he was politically illiterate.

Kerensky was certainly no Napoleon, yet there were, nevertheless, a number of echoes of the French Revolution. Scurrilous, often pornographic pamphlets circulated depicting sexual excesses at court in lurid detail. It was an interesting example of supposedly patriotic prurience. The Tsarina – 'the German woman' – was accused of extraordinary sexual antics with Rasputin, rather as Marie Antoinette – 'the Austrian woman' – had been with her favourite, the Princesse de Lamballe.

A far more important resemblance to 1789, and every other revolution to come, was the abrupt collapse of law and order. Suspects, especially if well-to-do, were lynched, not tried. Citizen militias sprang up everywhere, especially the Red Guards, young workers with captured rifles ready to defend their factories against 'sabotage' by the proprietors. They formed a prototype for the Bolshevik militia later that year.

On 18 June, 400,000 people marched through Petrograd with banners proclaiming 'All Power to the Soviets!', a Bolshevik slogan, even though many did not yet know it. The strikes were endless as the demands of workers mounted and so many political meetings took place that production was continually interrupted anyway. This new attitude spread rapidly to the front, where soldiers refused to be on duty for more than eight hours a day, in line with the demands of the industrial workers. More ominously, the number of mutinies grew as well as the increasingly brutal murder of officers. The military authorities did not dare institute court-martial proceedings.

The more technical side of the civil administration was less threatened. Olga's father, Konstantin Knipper, was fortunate to be a railway engineer as well as an official. His skills were still needed. But if he had been one of the Tsar's ministers, as Olga later claimed in her memoirs, he would not have survived as he did.

The very last performance of the Moscow Art Theatre before the Bolshevik takeover in Moscow was a special guest performance of *The Cherry Orchard* at the Theatre of the Soviet of Workers' Deputies. Stanislavsky remembered 'gray-clad mobs' outside on the street, and 'mysterious preparations' with soldiers 'gathering around the Kremlin'. The atmosphere in the auditorium was feverish and the actors stood behind the curtain listening to the buzz. They wondered what this working-class audience would make of *The Cherry Orchard* at such a moment. 'We won't be able to finish the performance,' Stanislavsky records them saying to each other. 'Either they'll drive us from the stage or they'll attack us.'

In a not entirely convincing account of the evening, Stanislavsky attributed the play's success to 'the lyricism of Chekhov, the eternal beauty of Russian poetry, [and] the life-mood of country gentility in old Russia . . . It seemed to us that all of them wanted to wrap themselves in the atmosphere of poetry and to rest there and bid peaceful farewell forever to the old and beautiful life that now demanded its purifying sacrifices.' Yet the final sound-effect of the axe chopping down a cherry tree was rapidly followed by the distant sound of gunfire. When the audience emerged into the street, wounded revolutionaries and bystanders were already being taken away in trucks. The Moscow Art Theatre soon sent a message to the Moscow Soviet, asking how it could best serve the people. The reply came back telling them to reopen as soon as possible.

The Bolshevik coup was resisted more effectively in Moscow than in Petrograd and the centre of the city suffered during ten days of heavy fighting. St Basil's Cathedral was damaged in the artillery exchanges. This upheaval sent Misha into a hysterical state, but other members of the extended family ran greater risks. Vladimir Knipper, living at 51 Arbat, was seized by officers resisting the Bolshevik takeover after an unbalanced inhabitant on the top floor of their building started lighting different lamps in different rooms. This had provoked suspicions that he was signalling to the enemy. A drunk staff captain put a Nagan pistol to Vladimir's head: 'The Bolsheviks are ruining our capital and you're helping them, you bastards. I'll kill you.' Another officer whispered to him that he was Olga Knipper-Chekhova's brother and he relented.

A real tragedy befell the family less than a month later, on 13 December 1917. Volodya Chekhov, Misha's cousin and former rival in love, somehow managed to take Misha's Browning pistol from the drawer of his writing table and shoot himself.

Just before the funeral, Misha caught sight of his uncle, Ivan Chekhov, Volodya's father. He looked emaciated as well as crushed. Misha never forgot his prominent nose, the suit hanging off him and the crumpled trousers. He looked 'like a carved wooden figure nailed to the floor'. Volodya's mother gently nudged Misha, who was staring at the corpse of their son in its coffin. 'Go to him,' she whispered, 'but I beg you, my dear, don't cry.' Misha gazed at his cousin's face, remembering it with make-up and burnt cork from the charades after Aunt Masha's Sunday night supper parties.

We cannot tell whether Volodya shot himself because he was still in love with Olga, as she suggested later, or because his father was so determined that he should be a lawyer. Perhaps the destruction of their world also played a part in his decision to kill himself. In any case, the effect on Misha was profound. He collapsed completely and was granted a six-month leave of absence from the Moscow Art Theatre. Photographs show that he aged dramatically during this period.

Another member of the family to suffer at this time was Aunt Masha, who came to Moscow from Yalta for Volodya's funeral and contracted typhoid. As was standard practice in this lice-borne disease, her head was shaved immediately. She took that in good heart, but Volodya's death had hit her hard. Aunt Masha, like almost everyone, was so impoverished that she found food very hard to obtain. She had inherited the rights to her brother Anton's plays, but the Moscow Art Theatre could no longer pay royalties. Their mother, Evgenia

Chekhova, who was still alive and living with her in Yalta, was too senile to understand that things had changed and that economies were necessary. Aunt Masha was reduced to taking in sewing.

Olga realized during the course of that tumultuous year of two revolutions that she would have to leave her increasingly unbalanced husband. In May, Misha had to abandon rehearsals of *The Seagull* due to nervous depression exacerbated by drinking.

It appears that Olga had left Misha shortly before Volodya's suicide, but this is not entirely certain. There is as little common ground in the accounts of the end of their marriage as there was about its beginning. Misha wrote later that Olga had been lured away by an adventurer called Ferenc Jaroszi, an officer of the Austro-Hungarian army who had been a prisoner of war in Russia. 'He was,' according to Misha, 'an adventurer of the sort about which my father had recounted many fascinating stories. Elegant, good-looking, charming and talented as he was, he had at his disposal a great inner strength, which made him irresistible.' Misha claimed that when Olga came into the room – 'already in her overcoat' – to say goodbye that December, she remarked: 'How ugly you look! Well, be happy. You'll soon forget it.' She then, apparently, gave him a friendly kiss and left. Not once in his memoirs does Misha mention their daughter.

Olga's account is that she simply could not put up with Misha's drunkenness and obsessions any longer. Her adolescent infatuation for him had clearly turned as much to pity as to anger. She moved her possessions and the baby to the Knipper family's apartment in Moscow at 23 Prechistensky bulvar. But having made the decision to leave, she knew that she could not survive on the small sums of money her mother secretly sent her in defiance of Konstantin Knipper, who was still furious with his favourite daughter. The rampant inflation of the time made each batch of banknotes increasingly worthless. And city-dwellers, even when in possession of money, found that food was increasingly hard to come by. People began to live off barter and contacts. Olga claimed that her daughter's life was saved during that winter of 1917–18 by the great singer Feodor Chaliapin, who gave her milk from the cow which he had brought into Moscow for his family's use.

The shock of being poor for the first time in her life was considerable, and undoubtedly created Olga's determination and ambition for the future. Since she could no longer depend on Misha, she had to forge her own career. Her paintings would not provide a secure income, so she worked for a wine merchant as an office assistant. She also claimed to have carved chess pieces from wood to sell, but perhaps she borrowed this idea from Misha, who used to make them when in his lowest depths of depression.

7. Frost and Famine

Lenin's dissolution of the Constituent Assembly in the first week of January 1918 condemned Russia to the most terrible civil war in history. The Bolsheviks, to their fury, had received no more than 24 per cent of the total vote in the country's first free elections. Lenin was determined to suppress any opposition to his new ministerial committee, the Sovnarkom – an acronym for the Council of People's Commissars. Yet the most immediate threat to the new regime came not from the outraged opposition parties but from a major German advance. The Kaiser's general staff finally decided to exploit the disintegration of the Russian army and the collapse of Trotsky's delaying tactics at the Brest-Litovsk peace negotiations. Petrograd was threatened in February, so the capital of the new Soviet Republic was moved to Moscow. The Bolshevik leadership took over the Kremlin, from the state apartments to the servants' bedrooms.

Olga's parents had also left an increasingly dangerous Petrograd to join her and her sister Ada in Moscow at 23 Prechistensky bulvar. The Knipper family, with the exception of Lev, who was down in the south with his artillery unit, lived together there for a short time with Aunt Olya. Not long afterwards, the Knipper parents set off for Siberia, which Konstantin knew well from his work on the railways. Olga's mother offered to take her little girl with them away from Moscow. She stood a far better chance of escaping starvation in the countryside.

There was a huge exodus from Moscow as well as Petrograd

during that winter. Tens of thousands of industrial workers, finding themselves without food and without work in the expropriated factories, returned to their peasant roots to escape starvation. Members of the nobility and the professional and merchant classes fled the city in various stages of disguise. Some hoped to find refuge on their estates, convinced that their peasants really cared for them. Most were bound for the less revolutionary south of Russia, especially the Crimea and the Don Cossack capital of Novocherkassk, where opposition to the Reds began to consolidate in the form of the Volunteer Army, manned almost entirely by embittered Tsarist officers. Travelling for the first time in their lives with the common people, the dispossessed refugees were shocked to encounter such a visceral hatred for the old order. It was this incoherent anger and desire for revenge which had led to the wanton destruction by peasants of works of art and books in the country houses which they stormed. The Bolsheviks did not hang back from exploiting to the utmost a deep desire among the poor for class warfare. 'Death to the Bourgeoisie!' was a truly popular slogan.

Olga stayed behind in Moscow with Ada. The remains of the winter in early 1918 were still cruelly cold. There was no coal. Foraging for firewood was outlawed, but almost everyone was desperate enough to take the risk of being shot by Red Guard patrols to bring home boughs from a tree or planks from a step. The two sisters were reduced to burning their father's books from his library in a little iron stove. In an attempt to retain some body heat at night, Olga and Ada even built a tent out of a Persian carpet over a mattress on the bedroom floor to keep them warm.

Although much of Olga's time had to be spent searching for food, her ambitions to become an actress had not slackened. She claimed later to have joined a cabaret-theatre group called

Sorokonozhka, or 'The Little Centipede', because there were
only twenty members and they possessed but forty feet. Most
surprisingly of all, considering the circumstances of the time
and her total lack of experience, she had been given a part in
a silent movie, *Anya Kraeva*. Two other parts followed, one
in *Cagliostro* and the other in *The Last Adventure of Arsène
Lupin*. These may seem unexpected titles for Year Zero of the
Leninist revolution, but the semi-amateur movie-makers seem
to have been left to their own devices by the new Bolshevik
authorities.

Theatres, on the other hand, were much more closely
controlled. The Moscow Art Theatre soon had to search for
a repertoire more attuned to the new era, just as Stanislavsky
and Nemirovich-Danchenko had to forget their earlier enthusiasm for Kerensky, who had fled into exile following the
Bolshevik coup in Petrograd. In fact the tall and distinguished
Stanislavsky now strode down Moscow streets with his fur coat
thrown wide open to show a large red bow, demonstrating his
revolutionary loyalty. The actors and stage crew of the Moscow Art Theatre became state employees on pitiful salaries
and answerable to People's Commissar for Enlightenment,
Anatoly Lunacharsky.

Bolshevik agitprop groups brought factory workers into the
much larger Solodovnikovsky Theatre, just across the road,
where Stanislavsky and his colleagues performed as part of
a programme, designated 'Proletkult', to bring culture to the
factory floor. This organization, promoted so strongly by Lunacharsky, was designed through groups of actors, musicians and
singers to create a cultural revolution for the working class,
just as the *encyclopédistes* had produced one for the bourgeoisie
of eighteenth-century France. Lenin, however, was privately
scathing about such efforts, partly because his own tastes owed
more to the *ancien régime*, but also because he knew perfectly

well that this was not real proletarian culture. At best, it was simply an attempt to force-feed the masses on high-minded political correctness. At worst, it was an excuse for cultural nihilists, such as Futurists like Mayakovsky, to call for the destruction of all traditional art works as a shock tactic of cultural liberation.

Some of these workers gaped in bewilderment at the Moscow Art Theatre production or simply ignored the proceedings and just ate, drank, smoked and chatted together. Others, however, shuffled their feet in irritation at what seemed to them a sympathetic portrayal of bourgeois life. Many yelled their opinions. On some occasions, the noise and behaviour struck Stanislavsky as so unseemly that he went front of stage to remonstrate with the audience. The Moscow Art Theatre, which had appeared so revolutionary when it began in 1898, now looked dated, if not reactionary. It was a depressing twentieth anniversary for those who, in Stanislavsky's phrase, 'always served beauty and nobility'. But he also acknowledged rather abjectly that 'we have become the representatives of experience; we have been placed as conservatives with whom it is the holy duty of the innovator to struggle. One must have enemies to attack.'

They were indeed bewildering times. 'Masha my dearest,' Aunt Olya wrote to her sister-in-law in February 1918, 'I so want to write to you and I don't know where to start. There are so many things, new and alien, things that one needs time to grow accustomed to. One's soul needs to digest them and they keep on coming at you. If Anton were alive, he would be wonderful making out what is what . . . From the outside our life still looks the same. I go to rehearsals and to performances.' Yet nothing was really the same.

No theatre, in that time of total poverty, had any heating. Everyone kept on their overcoats. The audience's heads were huddled into their shoulders, the women's wrapped in scarves, the men's with fur or cloth *shapkas* pulled down. The cast, who had to take off their overcoats and hats just before they went on stage, became severely chilled and most fell ill. Many of the costumes had been stolen, and the shortage of wigs meant that Olga Knipper-Chekhova – Aunt Olya – had to dye her hair, which was now quite grey.

The intellectual debates of the early years in the Moscow Art Theatre were now a distant memory. Exhaustion from malnourishment made it hard to concentrate and to act. It often seemed as if the only subject of conversation was food, and where you might find the basic necessities. Horsemeat and dogmeat became vital commodities. Aunt Olya was beside herself with happiness when she obtained an egg, the first she had seen in three months. The revolution in the countryside, with the burning of manor houses which had begun a couple of months after the abdication of the Tsar, had drastically reduced food production. It was to be made far worse when Lenin launched a civil war against the peasantry to force them to hand over their grain to the starving cities. The Bolshevik leaders had a profound contempt for the rural population: what Trotsky famously labelled as the Russia of 'icons and cockroaches'. But the peasants hid their grain and the Red 'food brigades' resorted to terror and torture in an attempt to force them to hand it over. Soon the new Soviet government was having to put down far more peasant rebellions than any Tsar had faced in modern memory. Even the supposed backbone of the movement, the industrial proletariat, was coming out on strike against Leninist authoritarianism and their declining living standards.

Aunt Olya was one of the few members of the Moscow Art Theatre who did not fall ill, but she was utterly dejected by 'the devastation and neglect, the filth and chaos, in which we are living'. Decidedly unpolitical, she could not see the point of the appalling sacrifices to be made in the name of the new order. 'It's not revolution that one wants,' she had written at the time of the 1905 uprising, 'but freedom, room to move, beauty, romanticism', and she deeply regretted the victims 'who belonged neither to one party nor the other'.

There was no middle-ground. You either supported the Bolsheviks or you were an 'enemy of the people'. The population now inhabited a world dominated by commissars in black leather jackets and caps, establishing a discipline of terror at the point of their Mauser pistols. They even became known as 'the leather coats'.

The fate of a human being became utterly arbitrary. In the People's Courts, if the accused had uncalloused hands, he risked an immediate death sentence, whatever the crime. It was also dangerous to have lent anyone money. A debtor could denounce a creditor as 'a blood-sucking bourgeois'. But nothing was as sinister as the new Cheka – the All-Russian Extraordinary Commission for Struggle against Counter-Revolution and Sabotage – which could define whatever it liked as a capital crime and carry out executions on the spot. It was the forerunner of the Stalinist NKVD, which was to play a considerable part in the lives of the Knipper family.

Class war meant encouraging the total subjugation of the *burzhooi*, a term which encompassed the nobility as well as the bourgeois. They were put to work cleaning streets and clearing snow to humiliate them, just as the Nazis did to the Jews less than two decades later. The pleasure for the overseers was to force their former social superiors to accomplish the most menial tasks, then watch those unused to manual labour as they were reduced to a clumsy exhaustion.

As unproductive workers, *burzhooi* were allowed only the most minimal rations. Purely to survive, remnants of the nobility and middle classes were reduced to standing in flea markets, where they tried to barter any possession from icons and bibelots to redundant Tsarist uniforms and diamond rings, in the hope of a small bag of flour or a fragment of a loaf of sugar. Within a year or so, when the civil war further disrupted the food supply, well-brought-up young ladies were reduced to prostituting themselves. A couple of years later it was estimated that 42 per cent of Moscow's prostitutes came from wealthy families 'ruined by the revolution', a social category defined in a revealing Soviet euphemism as 'former people'. Several of these young women became the mistresses of leather-jacketed leaders of the new Bolshevik order. The moral disintegration became almost total.

Privilege had not been abolished. A new form had appeared, as Aunt Olya described in another letter to her sister-in-law. 'I was playing patience late into the night, looking up from time to time at the row of brightly lit confiscated mansions on the opposite side of the *bulvar* and the reflection of brightly lit windows in the liquid mud. It was rather like being in Venice.' The young commissars had wasted little time in expropriating the grand houses of those they had dispossessed in a show of high moral outrage. 'I have received violets in a letter from Gurzuf [the little house in the Crimea given to her by Anton Chekhov],' she went on. 'Such a touching impression in this time of devastation and chaos and hopelessness and dirt in which we are now living.'

The flight of the upper and middle classes from Moscow encouraged the local Bolshevik 'building committees' to reallocate accommodation. Since most of their members came from the former servant class, they relegated property owners to cellars or attics, and took the best rooms for themselves and their friends. Revolution in their view meant literally turning the social order upside down. They were now the new masters.

Olga and Ada soon found more and more strangers billeted on them, with four or five people to a room. The house was also used as a billet for soldiers and the sisters seem to have narrowly escaped rape at the hands of two sailors. 'Every day, my sister Ada and I,' wrote Olga later, 'were prepared for the worst.'

The following winter of 1918–19 was also cruel. There was no fuel for heating inside the houses, so the water pipes froze. The two sisters cleaned their faces with wood ash and cooked frozen potatoes on a small wood-burning stove, known as a *burzhuika* because it was supposed to be like a fat-bellied bourgeois. People chopped up the last of their furniture to provide fuel for their stoves. Very few books were left and hardly a tree remained standing in the city. Not only was there no water available from taps, but the sewerage system had frozen solid, producing unimaginably squalid conditions. The courtyards behind houses had to be used as open-air lavatories. Not long afterwards, Moscow suffered a cholera epidemic.

That winter was a time of even greater famine in the cities than the previous one. So many horses had been slaughtered for meat that carts and *drozhkys* were hauled by women and children. 'Sugar is seventy-five roubles per pound,' Aunt Olya wrote to Aunt Masha in the Crimea. 'Butter is 100 to 120 roubles per pound. They are eating horsemeat everywhere and sell dogmeat as well.' Hardly anybody could afford such prices.

Her niece, Olga Chekhova, bundled in old clothes and a headscarf to keep warm and to avoid looking like a bourgeois, set off by train for Kostroma on the Volga to barter valuables in exchange for potatoes and flour. Hundreds of thousands from the city were attempting to do the same. It was known as 'bagging', from all the bags they carried to fill with food.

Olga suffered the usual squalor of travel at that time in cattle wagons, with only a hole in the floor for a lavatory and insect-infested straw to sleep on. Once they reached Kostroma, she had to evade patrols of Red Guards, and when she finally made a deal with a local peasant, he fell through the ice with the sledge bearing all the provisions she had purchased. Whether or not this was strictly true, she returned to Moscow empty-handed. It would have been a desperate venture in any case, because almost any woman alone was likely to be robbed.

The desperation, especially among demobilized soldiers and deserters, was so great that more and more resorted to robbery. To venture into the street after nightfall was considered extremely dangerous. Rumours multiplied people's fears. One of the most bizarre was that Russian soldiers had captured special German boots with springs in the soles to help them leap over trenches. And at night, dressed in white, they jumped in the street as high as the first floor of houses, causing people to faint in fright, and they then robbed them.

While everybody else suffered, Misha Chekhov, with characteristic perversity, had found 1918 an improvement on the year before. During the depression which followed Volodya's death, he had vowed to give up the theatre. He also resolved never to commit suicide himself. Having spent much of the winter at his writing table scribbling down nightmare descriptions, such as the state of a man crushed by a tram, his nervous state improved during the spring of 1918.

Xenia Karlovna Ziller, the blonde girlfriend and tennis partner who had so provoked Olga during her pregnancy, became his second wife on 3 June. Xenia's family was also German – the Chekhovs seemed to have had a decided bent in that direction – and her father owned, or rather used to own, a factory in Moscow for automobile lubricants. Xenia, by her kindness and calmness, managed to restore Misha's confidence. 'She fell in love with a ruin of man,' wrote Sergei Chekhov, 'and managed to restore this ruin to life.' Misha, with a typical disregard for the political and economic reality of the moment, then set up an acting studio, where his teaching skills attracted a number of young actors. 'Chekhov's Studio' helped restore his professional confidence, even if it did little for his fortunes.

He was still vulnerable, however, to the ravages of alcohol when under stress. His mother, Natalya, died in March 1919 and this triggered another crisis. Misha claims to have travelled across Moscow to find her body among a pile of corpses, all the victims of a typhus epidemic, just before they were thrown into a mass grave.

Other accounts, including that of his cousin Sergei, suggest that he was so drunk and in such a nervous state when he buried his mother that he forgot where her grave was afterwards: an interesting case of psychological suppression, if true. Yet the death of his mother appears to have lifted a huge, menacing presence from his mind, and soon after he rejoined the Moscow Art Theatre. His haunted, tragic clown's face was able to smile again.

Many old people expired in that terrible winter of cold, disease and starvation. Misha also lost his Chekhov grandmother. Aunt Masha had sent news from Yalta that Evgenia Chekhova was dead. And Olga's grandmother, Anna Salza-Knipper, the professor at the conservatoire, also succumbed. It was almost as if the new regime had planned an accelerated removal of those who could not adapt to the harsh realities of Soviet life.

8. Surviving the Civil War

The Russian Civil War, without clear front lines and covering huge distances, became a 'railway war'. Armoured trains provided both the symbol and the reality of conspicuous power and terror. Small armies and irregular bands attacked and counter-attacked from town to town along the endless tracks. There was little alternative. Neither side had more than a handful of motor vehicles and the unsurfaced roads turned to mud during the rainy seasons of spring and autumn – the *rasputitsa*. Konstantin Knipper's expertise as a railway director therefore made him extremely valuable to Admiral Kolchak's White Army when it began to establish itself astride the Trans-Siberian railway during the winter of 1918–19.

The defeat of Germany in November 1918 and the promises of the Entente powers to aid the Whites produced a surge of optimism among anti-Bolsheviks. In fact Bolshevik control appeared to be waning rapidly. The Ukraine, the 'breadbasket' of Russia, became the territory for a triangular, if not a quadrilateral, civil war between Reds, Whites, Anarchists and Ukrainian nationalists. The Volunteer Army, now commanded by General Denikin, which had survived two bitter campaigns in the Caucasus, swelled with Cossack auxiliaries after the savage advance of Red Guards through their villages across the Don steppe. But the Cossacks were a law unto themselves and deliberately uncooperative. The attempt by their so-called Don Army to take Tsaritsyn on the lower Volga at the end of 1918 was an abject failure. The myth of its heroic defence helped Stalin, the commissar there, on his way to power. Later, the expanding city was rebuilt and called Stalingrad in his honour.

The Whites were so short of ordinary soldiers that junior officers had to serve as privates and corporals, while majors and colonels found themselves with the equivalent of a lieutenant's command. There were so many generals from the old Tsarist army that some of them were reduced to commanding battalions or even companies. This frustrated obsession with rank inevitably produced terrible rivalries and constant prima donna outbursts. The White commanders were fixated with their Tsarist uniforms, shoulder-boards, salutes and Peter the Great's 'Table of Ranks', which defined all hierarchy. They had truly learned nothing and forgotten nothing during the revolutionary period of the last two years. Their insistence on attempting to turn back the clock to the days of Tsarist autocracy and erase all hope of land reform deterred even anti-Bolshevik peasants, whose support they badly needed if they were to maintain their armies in rations as well as manpower.

Many commanders were so obsessive in their hatred of Bolshevism that they seem to have become totally unbalanced. Lev Knipper, serving with the Whites in the south, later described their commander, General Khludov. He had a heavy stare and would walk up and down the lines on inspection, paying particular attention to any man forcibly conscripted into their ranks. Sometimes, after a long gaze, he would suddenly say to one of them: 'You've got red devils playing in your head!' and would shoot him on the spot.

Lev in later years rewrote his own history in a shamelessly disingenuous fashion. He claimed that at the time of the revolution he had been staying with relatives in the south of Russia – presumably Aunt Masha in Yalta – and had been conscripted into the White Army. He went on to write that he had found ordinary soldiers to be physically, morally and intellectually superior to him and he had then deserted. In fact Lev had remained with the army of Baron Wrangel right until the end and went into exile with it in 1920.

The Whites' loathing of Bolshevism had started with a burning resentment at their loss of privilege, wealth and power. It was then immeasurably strengthened by the cruelty with which captured officers were treated by left-wing mobs. There were numerous cases of mutilation, including castration and flaying alive. The hated shoulder-boards of captured officers were sometimes nailed into their shoulders. According to White sources, the most notorious torture carried out by local Chekas on captured officers was known as 'the glove treatment', in honour of what soldiers saw as a key item of a Tsarist officer's apparel. The victim's hands and forearms were plunged into boiling water and held there until the skin peeled off. Chekas would compete with each other in the horrifying originality of the tortures they could inflict on their victims.

Red Terror begat White Terror and Russia reverted to the barbarism of Ivan the Terrible and the cruel repression of the Pugachev rebellion. The Whites did not hold back in their revenge on the Antichrist. Even the wives and children of suspected 'red' workers and peasants were bayoneted indiscriminately when a village or town was captured. Similar reprisals would be taken by Red Guards against bourgeois families. In the murderous chaos, Stanislavsky's brother and three nephews were shot in the Crimea. It was not surprising that so many preferred suicide to capture in this politically sadistic conflict.

The Russian civil war was also a war of confusion and misunderstanding. Even those in the Kremlin itself, with access to telephone and telegraph, seldom had a clear idea of what was happening across the great Eurasian landmass. The general public knew far less, in fact nothing beyond rumours and the optimistic communiqués published in *Pravda*.

At the beginning of May 1919, a touring group from the Art Theatre left Moscow for a three-week season in the eastern Ukraine. One of the initial reasons behind this tour was the greater ease of feeding the cast in the south than in Moscow. Nobody had told them that the civil war had erupted again, this time with a three-sided attack on central Russia. Admiral Kolchak, with the grand title of 'Supreme Ruler', was advancing out of Siberia with 100,000 men towards the Volga. General Denikin had started an attack northwards from the anti-Bolshevik heartland of the south, while General Yudenich was to advance later on Petrograd from the Baltic states.

Stanislavsky had no inkling of the 'catastrophe' about to befall his theatre. He went to the station to see off the touring group, led by Olga Knipper-Chekhova and Vasily Kachalov, the leading actor of his time, on their way to Kharkov. There were a number of hangers-on and spouses who accompanied them, including Kachalov's wife and their sixteen-year-old son, Vadim Shverubovich.

The Art Theatre group, in high spirits to be leaving Moscow, travelled south in specially disinfected cattle wagons with their scenery and props. In Kharkov, they were billeted in an abandoned and dilapidated hotel, the Russia, which 'still retained an air of pre-revolutionary elegance'. Their performances began at six to allow audiences home before the curfew, which started at nine. The cast were surprised to find that, despite the confident pronouncements of Soviet newspapers, Kharkov appeared to be on a war footing. One evening, their performance of *The Cherry Orchard* began on time but during the second act there seemed to be an unusual amount of noise on the street outside. The Art Theatre's stage manager went to see what was happening and found that the advance guard of General Denikin's White forces had entered the city unopposed. The Red Guards had fled. The stage manager returned and announced to the audience what had happened. Once the cheering had died down, he added that the play would resume where it had left off.

The rapidity of the city's capture was a far greater mercy than they realized. Usually, a local Cheka detachment would murder all their prisoners before abandoning a city, along with any bourgeois they could find. And the Kharkov Cheka, led by the notorious Saenko, a cocaine-addicted psychopath, was one of the cruellest. Nevertheless, the Kachalov group, as it came to be called after their leading actor, found itself in a quandary. Should they try to cross the lines, abandoning their props and scenery, to rejoin the Art Theatre in Moscow? Or would it be wiser to await events? The Reds seemed to be in full retreat on all fronts. Kachalov's son, Vadim, rushed off to join the White Army in a burst of enthusiasm. His parents were horrified when they discovered what he had done.

On 19 June, Tsaritsyn finally fell to Baron Wrangel's Caucasian Army, supported by British tanks. The White commanders were convinced that the capital was now in their grasp. One actor called Podgorny, desperate to rejoin his wife in Moscow, decided to take his chances. He did manage to get back, but this made all those members of the cast who stayed in White territory suspect in the eyes of the Bolshevik authorities. There were rumours in Moscow about the 'political demonstration' of the Kachalov group, an impression that was not helped when White generals insisted on giving banquets in honour of the Art Theatre actors.

The guest season in Kharkov was extended until the end of June, then the actors took a holiday in the Crimea. They arranged to meet up again in September. Everyone expected that Moscow would have fallen to the Whites by then. Olga

Knipper-Chekhova went straight to Yalta to see her sister-in-law, Masha, now tending the Chekhov house as a museum. She stayed in her own little house not far away at Gurzuf, on the shore of the Black Sea. There, with other members of the touring group, they planned an autumn season, starting in Odessa. Masha, who had seen Lev in good health, completely forgot to tell Aunt Olya, who worried desperately about what might have happened to her favourite nephew. Olga Knipper-Chekhova was overcome with disbelief and exasperation later when she found out that such an important detail had slipped Masha's mind. Vasily Kachalov and his wife, meanwhile, were overjoyed to see Vadim during their holiday in the Crimea. He was fit and well, but still serving in the ranks of a White regiment.

Communications within the diminishing territory of Soviet Russia were so bad that the Art Theatre in Moscow did not hear of the capture of Kharkov by the Whites until early August. An emergency meeting was called and Stanislavsky, who was away from Moscow at the time, had to travel back overnight to the capital. They all knew that the loss of their most experienced actors 'took away all chance of producing any new plays and also of continuing our old repertoire'. There was little choice. 'We had to refill our ranks with actors from the Studios, they with actors who had nothing to do with the Art Theatre.' For some, this was a blessing rather than a disaster. The absence of the theatre's leading actor, Kachalov, was to give Mikhail Chekhov his great opportunity.

Nemirovich-Danchenko's continuing disagreements with Stanislavsky made decision-making exceptionally hard. He felt, with a good deal of justification, that Stanislavsky was a hopeless idealist. In his view, the Moscow Art Theatre had to cut back to survive. Stanislavsky's grandiose plans, including the main theatre and its offshoot studios, had even extended to opening a provincial theatre network. But the argument was soon resolved from above. In December, the whole profession was reorganized under state control. The Art Theatre, along with its former imperial counterparts, became an 'Academic' theatre of the Soviet state, and was subsidized accordingly.

Stanislavsky, despite Nemirovich-Danchenko's suspicions, believed far more passionately in the theatre than in himself. He did everything he could to make sure that other members of the Art Theatre had food and lodging, yet when the local Bolshevik housing committee evicted him from his own house, he told nobody at first. Stanislavsky, who bent over backwards to avoid criticizing the revolution, made no complaint, just as he had never protested when the family factory and all his other wealth were confiscated. He apparently wept in private at the loss of his home, yet made no attempt to contest the eviction order. Fortunately word reached Lunacharsky, the People's Commissar for Enlightenment, who went straight to Lenin.

Lenin had become a great admirer of the Moscow Art Theatre. After all his years of exile, he took every opportunity to catch up on its productions, especially Chekhov's *The Seagull*, *The Cherry Orchard* and *Uncle Vanya*. He was also deeply impressed by Stanislavsky's performance as General Krutitsky in Ostrovsky's *Enough Stupidity in Every Wise Man*. 'Stanislavsky is a real artist,' Lenin wrote afterwards. 'He transformed himself into the General so completely that he lived his life down to the smallest detail. The audience don't need any explanations. They can see for themselves what an idiot this important-looking general is. In my opinion this is the direction the theatre should take.' Lenin had little time for Lunacharsky's doctrine of Proletkult.

The most scathing critic of Chekhov and Stanislavsky at this time was the Futurist poet Mayakovsky, who described their theatre as 'putrescent' and satirized it with lines about 'Auntie Manya, Uncle Vanya, sitting on the sofa whining'. Yet Mayakovsky would be one of the casualties of the brave new world which he had so gladly welcomed. 'We interpreted Mayakovsky's suicide,' the writer Isaac Babel told his NKVD interrogators before he was executed, 'as the poet's conclusion that it was impossible to work under Soviet conditions.'

The early autumn of 1919 proved the critical moment of the Russian Civil War. Admiral Kolchak's forces advancing from Siberia had started to disintegrate under pressure from the Red Army in front and from peasant revolts in the rear, provoked by the Whites' looting and brutality. But the southern front still struck fear into the Bolsheviks. By the end of August, General Denikin's White forces had captured almost all the major cities of the Ukraine. Deep cavalry raids by Cossack commanders such as General Mamontov seized key cities on the road north, including Voronezh on the upper Don.

General Denikin had laid down the plan of attack in his 'Moscow Directive'. On 14 October, one of his armies captured Orel, just 250 miles from Moscow, and stood ready to threaten Tula, the Soviet Republic's centre of arms manufacture. At the same time, General Yudenich's army, advancing out of Estonia, had reached the outskirts of Petrograd, 'the cradle of the Revolution'. In Moscow, escape plans were made for leading Bolsheviks, with the issue of false passports and Tsarist currency. In the Crimea, the upper- and middle-class refugees from the north were convinced that the Bolshevik nightmare was almost over and that they would soon be able to go home. In that early autumn of 1919, the promenade in Yalta was once again full of ladies and girls in long white dresses, with parasols and large straw hats, and even the odd small dog, just as it had been in Anton Chekhov's day.

9. The Dangers of Exile

The collapse of the White armies in the autumn of 1919 was sudden, catastrophic and largely of their own making. They had utterly alienated the peasantry in their rear by arrogance, brutality, looting, rape and the execution of hostages in villages where men evaded conscription. As the Whites advanced on Moscow, even those who loathed the Bolsheviks began attacking their lines of communication, especially in the Ukraine. The White generals had also alienated all those peripheral nations who wanted to loosen their links to Russia. These die-hard imperialists banned the speaking of Ukrainian and refused the slightest degree of independence to their Cossack allies.

Denikin's armies, some 150,000 strong at the start, became increasingly short of supplies. Men had to be sent back to guard the rear from partisan attacks, and at the front their ill-fed conscripts deserted in large numbers. The situation was even more disastrous on their flank, where the Cossack Army of the Don began to melt away. Its advance had already been greatly slowed by the wagon trains of booty acquired on the way. The Cossacks, who saw no reason why they should fight for an ungrateful Russia, wanted to return to the Don steppe with their ill-gotten loot. They utterly failed to foresee the vengeance which the Reds would exact on their villages once the Whites were defeated.

The ranks of the Bolsheviks, on the other hand, were swelling that autumn due to a change of policy. The Kremlin leadership had offered an amnesty to deserters. By mid-October they outnumbered the Whites on the southern front.

They were also helped by the fact that the peasants, who hated them, loathed the idea of a White victory even more. Those who now worked the land seized from the *barins* feared the loss of all their gains in the revolution.

The Reds concentrated their efforts on the defence of Tula and its arms factories. At the same time they prepared their counter-attack, a strike at the flank of the Volunteer Army marching on Tula. This was carried out by the Bolshevik Praetorian Guard, the division of Latvian Riflemen. The Red cavalry, an arm which the Bolsheviks had lacked until then, was thrown against the Cossacks. Meanwhile, just as Petrograd was about to fall to Yudenich's army, Trotsky rushed to the city. In a whirlwind of energy, he revived its defence with rousing speeches and ruthless executions.

The Whites collapsed on all fronts. Kolchak's forces abandoned Omsk in November and, within two months, Admiral Kolchak himself would be handed over to the Reds for execution. The pattern of total disintegration, moral as well as military, was repeated in the south. The *sauve-qui-peut* was rendered even more despicable by massacres of Jews in the retreat. The Whites had become obsessively anti-Semitic, convinced that all Jews must somehow be tainted with Bolshevism simply because Trotsky and a number of other leading commissars were Jews.

The utter corruption and selfishness of most of the Whites had been revealed in the speculation and looting which lay behind their crusade to save Russia. Such self-defeating short-sightedness also contributed to the British government's decision in November to withdraw all support. The nobility and middle class sheltering in the south were thrown into panic. Everyone tried to exchange their Don roubles for foreign currency only to find that they had become worthless virtually overnight. Nobody wanted them. Panic spread as fast as the epidemic of typhus passed on by the lice-ridden troops as they fell back.

Olga's brother, Lev Knipper, who was also lice-infested, was extremely fortunate not to have contracted typhus. He appears to have been better nourished than many, which may have increased his resistance to the disease. Although deprived of a balanced diet, he and his fellow officers had acquired a life-saving source of eggs and lived off *gogol-mogol* – a Russian version of eggnog. He also managed to keep up his spirits at a time when many officers, especially the wounded and ill, had started to shoot themselves. No officer dared to be taken alive by the victorious and avenging Reds. Lev was also fortunate to be part of the forces which withdrew into the easily defended Crimea.

Those forced back into the neck of the Caucasus faced a terrible experience. The scenes at the end of that winter as fear-stricken White refugees fled to the port of Novorossiisk on the Black Sea provide some of the most painful descriptions in modern history.

Unaware of the collapse of Denikin's armies, the Kachalov group had sailed from the safety of the Crimea to Novorossiisk. They were on their way to perform at Rostov-on-Don. There, they found filth, chaos and railways in a state of virtual collapse. The only place left to sleep was on the platform.

Rostov, like most of the region, was suffering a typhoid epidemic and the theatre in which they were supposed to perform had become an improvised hospital. They found another building in which to put on *The Cherry Orchard*. This persistence was partly due to professional pride, but also to financial need at a time of exponential inflation as the Don rouble crashed. Aunt Olya must have wondered constantly about Lev during that disastrous winter and whether their paths had crossed without them knowing it. Yet it was Vasily Kachalov and his wife who experienced a miracle. Quite by chance, a man appeared at one of their performances to tell Kachalov that his son, Vadim Shverubovich, was lying sick with typhus in the railway station.

Vadim was close to death when they found him and brought him back to less squalid surroundings. They brought a doctor, who provided them with medicine and some carbolic acid to clean and sterilize his skin. The doctor warned them that Vadim was approaching the crisis in his fever. During that night, Vadim's mother knew that the crisis must have arrived as his temperature dropped rapidly. She poured what she thought was the medicine down his throat, but in her flustered state she had picked up the carbolic acid. It began to burn his insides. Somebody found some milk once they realized what had happened and that soothed the delirious boy a little. And they then gave him the right medicine. Kachalov maintained his self-control with irony. 'You know, this has the air of a rather vulgar melodrama,' he announced. 'A mother, who has been waiting desperately for her son, poisons him on the very first night of his return. This just isn't possible in real life.' They nursed Vadim back to health, but even after all his experiences, the boy did not want to let go of his pistol.

As the Red armies advanced in February 1920, the Kachalov group had only one route of escape left. It lay south across the Caucasus. They moved first to Ekaterinodar, but that, they realized, would also be attacked before long. Fortunately, the director of the State Theatre in Tiflis, capital of the now independent Georgian Republic, had studied with the Moscow Art Theatre and was delighted to provide an official invitation.

To get to Tiflis they had to return to Novorossiisk in a

goods train. They hoped to find a boat there to take them down the Black Sea coast to Georgia. Vadim Shverubovich, now fully recovered, described Aunt Olya in a coal wagon, sitting erect on a suitcase, reading a book in a gilt morocco binding, oblivious to the dirt, the bitter wind and the sound of gunfire in the distance. Novorossiisk was already filling rapidly with refugees and no ship's captain was keen to take a company of actors with their costumes and props, however much they pleaded. Finally, the master of an Italian steamer took them on as deck passengers and they escaped the growing horrors of the port.

In the course of the next two weeks, abandoned weapons and the corpses of White officers and civilians, killed in their thousands by typhus, cold and starvation, marked the route to Novorossiisk. Survival depended upon getting on one of the French or British ships in the harbour before the Reds surrounded the town and bombarded the port. Some 50,000 troops were evacuated by the end of March 1920, but a further 60,000 military personnel and countless civilians were left behind once the Red forces arrived and brought up artillery. Allied warships fired salvoes of covering fire as the last ships hauled in their gangplanks. Thousands of screaming people on the quayside, including mothers with babies, begged the ships' crews to save them. Cossacks shot their horses down by the harbour as if this would somehow oblige the foreign ships to take them away. Scores committed suicide, either throwing themselves into the icy water or blowing their brains out.

The arrival of the Kachalov group in Georgia, and the welcome accorded them in the delightful city of Tiflis, made their recent experiences seem like a bad dream. It was spring and the Georgians were generous with their excellent food and wines. Aunt Olya was suffering badly from arthritis, especially in her hands. This had not been helped by months of living off horsemeat and no vegetables. The contrast with Bolshevik Russia made Georgia seem a paradise, but she was again afflicted by an acute homesickness for the Art Theatre in Moscow and a longing to revisit her husband's grave in the Novodeviche cemetery. Tiflis had many Russian refugees, and their performances at the State Theatre were eagerly attended. But the Kachalov group knew that they could not stay, nor could they return northwards through the Caucasus. Terrible reprisals were being exacted by the victorious Red Army on the villages of the Terek, Kuban and Don Cossacks.

The hospitable Georgian authorities even arranged for the group to spend a long summer holiday at the Georgian spa of Borzhomi. There the Georgian government put them up in the Likani Palace, a summer retreat built for the Tsar's brother Grand Duke Michael in Riviera Muscovite style, with many neo-classical and Italianate touches. It later became one of Stalin's country houses and he spent some of the happiest times there with his wife, Nadya, before she committed suicide.

For the Kachalov group, their large and empty lodgings provided an awkward splendour, but at least they were left alone to discuss their future. They had to choose between exile and a very uncertain return to Bolshevik Moscow. It was hard, especially for those who found themselves in a minority, because the one thing that they all agreed on was that they could only survive together.

'I have been suffering for a month in Borzhomi,' Aunt Olya wrote to Masha, 'unable to make up my mind whether to go to the west or not. I don't think that I have shed so many tears in my life. I did not want to give the others my consent and I have been expecting from moment to moment to receive a summons back to Moscow . . . We had a crazy day. We had been sitting together from morning to night and could not decide what we had to do . . . How I want to go to Moscow! How tired I am of wandering!'

But with no guarantee from the authorities permitting their free return, even Stanislavsky realized that it was still far too dangerous to intervene on their behalf. The decision of the Kachalov group went against Aunt Olya's longing to return at any price, but she understood Kachalov's need to secure a safe-conduct for Vadim, who as a White Guard could easily face a death sentence despite his youth. 'So it seems as if we're almost certainly leaving, Masha,' she continued her letter. 'We'll travel via Sofia, the Slav countries, Prague – then maybe Berlin, Paris? . . . Masha, try to sense it when we set off across the Black Sea. My God, how revolting and shameful it is to go abroad!'

The dinner parties of the two aunts in Moscow for all their young nephews and nieces must have felt like part of a previous and completely separate life. The last performance of the Kachalov group before departing into European exile was *The Cherry Orchard*. The play's note of valediction haunted her more than ever. Just before leaving she wrote a farewell letter to Stanislavsky. ' "Our life in this house is over", as they said in *The Cherry Orchard*. And God knows where we will be united again and how we will find each other.'

Lev, once again, was on her mind. In her letter to Masha, she remonstrated with her once again for not having told her of his visit. 'You don't understand what a joy it would have been for me to hear that Lev is alive.' But any news of him was by now nearly a year old, a time during which hundreds of thousands of people had died from war, disease and starvation. Despite his later claim to have deserted from the White Army, Lev had in fact remained with Baron Wrangel's forces in the Crimea after the terrible evacuation of Denikin's men from Novorossiisk in March. Wrangel knew that he had neither the men nor the popular support on the mainland of southern Russia to risk an offensive. But in June, when the Poles forced the Red Army on to the defensive with their attacks, he decided to sally forth from the Crimean peninsula. His army managed to seize a large part of the Tauride provinces, but hopes of reuniting the Don and Kuban regions with the White cause were vain. In October, the Soviet regime concluded a ceasefire with the Poles. This allowed them to bring vastly superior forces south-eastwards against Wrangel. The Whites, who had only 35,000 men facing Red armies 130,000 strong, were forced to retreat rapidly back into the Crimea. All Wrangel could hope to do was to hold them back at the landbridge to the mainland, the Perekop isthmus, and prepare for evacuation.

Once again the White currency collapsed in value as civilians scrambled for places on the ships. But Wrangel's withdrawal was at least far better organized, mainly thanks to the geography of the Crimea and the determination of the rearguard to hold the Perekop defence line. Altogether 126 ships, British, French and White Russian, took part in the evacuation, ferrying 150,000 people across the Black Sea to Constantinople and the Bosphorus.

Britain and France arranged for the remains of Wrangel's army to be housed on the Gallipoli peninsula, the site of Britain's painful military disaster five years before. The defeated Turks were not of course consulted. Wrangel's men remained in uniform and in their regiments. The evacuation had forced them to leave horses and artillery in the Crimea, but they had been allowed to retain side arms and personal weapons. Once they were settled in their extremely primitive billets – the headquarters of the Nikolaevskoe military college was a commandeered mosque – Wrangel ordered that military

training should recommence on 21 January 1921 to maintain
morale. But this mainly consisted of endless parades, either to
celebrate regimental days or in honour of visiting White
Russian dignitaries.

Lev was evidently among those young officers who wanted
to leave, but it was not easy. A special commission considered
the applications of those wishing to be dismissed because of
illness or injury. Those who fell into this category were moved
to a camp for refugees. Those who wanted to quit the army
for other reasons encountered various obstacles. A common
practice was to stop giving them their rations, taking away
their warm clothes and blankets. Lev wanted to leave, but
without money he did not stand a chance. He feared that if
he stayed, he would die. His only hope was Aunt Olya, but
he had no idea where she was.

Lev was indeed fortunate that his aunt had not been able to
return to Moscow as she had hoped. The Kachalov group
had been in Constantinople but encountered no success in
arranging a season of performances. The shortage of money
had forced them to move from a modest hotel to a virtual
dosshouse, before taking ship for the Balkans.

Aunt Olya's brother, Konstantin Knipper, was much luckier
in his attempts to return to Moscow. After the collapse of
Admiral Kolchak's forces, he somehow managed to get back
from Siberia with his wife and Olga's child. The importance
of his skills as a railway engineer saved him. The Bolshevik
government was prepared to make temporary concessions to
get the right expertise at that time, and repairing the railroad
system was vital if the starving cities were to be fed. On their
return to the family apartment at 23 Prechistensky bulvar,
Olga's little daughter did not recognize her mother after so
long. She refused to allow Olga to kiss her or to hold her

hand, because she did not consider her to be her 'real mother'.

This was to be the last time that Olga ever saw her father. She was thinking of leaving Russia, at least for a while. In those 'hunger years', survival itself was degrading. Most young actresses were forced to resort to part-time prostitution and venereal disease was rife. Olga wanted to try her luck in Berlin, leaving her daughter, Ada, once again with her mother. She was greatly encouraged in this plan by Ferenc Jaroszi, the Austro-Hungarian cavalry captain described by Misha. He and other members of the family were certain that she married him. Olga applied for a six-week exit permit. Later, in a typical example of compulsive embroidery for her movie memoirs, she claimed in one volume that permission had been given by Lunacharsky himself, thanks to the intervention of Aunt Olya (this was most unlikely, since she was still abroad as an illegal émigrée); and elsewhere that her exit pass had been signed by Lenin's wife, Krupskaya.

According to her own account, the twenty-three-year-old Olga set out in January 1921 from Moscow's Belorussky station looking like a young peasant woman. Her head was wrapped in a large headscarf and she wore *valenki* felt boots and a bulky overcoat. Her few belongings were stowed in a bag made out of an old piece of carpet. She claimed to have concealed her most valuable item, a diamond ring to turn into cash in Berlin, under her tongue while pretending to be semi-mute. She would have been arrested if the ring had been found at one of the many control points. The export of jewellery was strictly forbidden to prevent 'former people' taking anything of value out of the Soviet Republic, where all such items were now forfeit to the state. Passengers were searched at the Belorussky station by Red Guards in their strange *budyonovka* – pointed hats with earflaps, shaped like an Asiatic helmet, but with a large red star on the front.

But the date which Olga Chekhova gives for her departure seems highly unlikely. In her letter of 11 September 1920, Aunt Olya wrote to Masha: 'They have written to me that my Olya has gone abroad with a new husband.' This would indicate, when one considers the bad communications, that Olga had left for Berlin in August 1920 at the latest. Olga Chekhova's claim that she thought that she was leaving Soviet Russia for just six weeks is also unconvincing. But she could never have foreseen the manner of her only return to the city, when, at the end of April 1945, she was to be flown back from Germany by special aeroplane on the orders of the chief of SMERSh.

Both brother and sister had, within a few months of each other, become émigrés, one of the key words in the Bolshevik lexicon of hate. Lev ranked even higher in the order of enmity as a 'White Guardist'. Yet both became valued agents of the Soviet intelligence services at a key moment in history.

10. The Far-Flung Family

In that time of civil war and chaotic communications, it seems miraculous that any letters managed to reach their intended recipient. Yet Lev, stranded and penniless on the Gallipoli peninsula with a miserable mass of other White officers from the Wrangel army, somehow made contact with his exiled Aunt Olya, touring in the Balkans with the Kachalov group. As soon as she heard of her favourite nephew's plight, she immediately sent money and told him to join her.

Aunt Olya had the funds to send to him only because a Russian émigré organization, planning to start a movie studio in Milan, had paid the Kachalov group a large advance to take part in an adaptation of a novel by Knut Hamsun. The project collapsed, but the group did not have to pay back anything. They had by then reached Bulgaria, and this financed their first foreign season in the capital, Sofia.

Vadim Shverubovich later described the complications of touring abroad. The group had brought *The Three Sisters* into their repertoire in Sofia and they needed a band to play the Skobelev March when Masha is saying goodbye to Vershinin in the last act, the most moving scene of the whole play. A Bulgarian military band was found, but the bandmaster, corseted with gold braid and sporting a huge moustache, did not know the Skobelev March, so he launched his men into a thumping Prussian alternative. Aunt Olya, whose definitive version of Masha had always been played with the Skobelev, 'rushed towards the orchestra pit, looking like some wounded bird in Masha's long black dress'. She screamed at the bandsmen and fled to her dressing room, completely distraught. Aunt Olya, like Masha in *The Three Sisters*, was pining for Moscow. She was close to nervous collapse, longing for a message from Stanislavsky to say that the authorities had forgiven them and that they were needed back at the Art Theatre.

The Kachalov group proceeded north-westwards through the Balkans to the newly created kingdom of Yugoslavia. Aunt Olya wrote to Stanislavsky from Zagreb, describing their celebration of the New Year of 1921, according to the old Russian calendar. 'We lit candles in a fir tree, and several of the young ladies told fortunes. Then everyone got carried away with memories of the theatre. A lot of stories were told. We spoke a lot about you and the performances, marvelled at them, and remembered Anton Pavlovich, and I recounted his last days in Badenweiler. It was quiet and everyone softened. Our performances are going well. The Croats are in love with us. If we have succeeded and if we are popular is all thanks to you and Vladimir Ivanovich [Nemirovich-Danchenko]. You are with us always and everywhere, invisible and untouchable but inseparable from us. We always talk of you at rehearsals. How would you have done this or that and what you would have said.'

When Lev joined them in Zagreb, his gratitude to his saviour was so great that Kachalov called Olga Knipper-Chekhova 'the aunt who gave birth to her nephew'. Lev adopted the remark and it became a catch-phrase in their relationship. He continued on with the group and became friends with young Vadim Shverubovich, whose life was also to take some strange and dangerous turns. The two young men and their likely fate at the hands of the Cheka if they returned home greatly complicated the return to Moscow for which Aunt Olya so yearned.

★

While Aunt Olya dreamed of returning to Moscow, her niece Olga had abandoned it. If one leaves aside the questions of date and her relationship with the Hungarian cavalry captain, Ferenc Jaroszi, the basis of Olga's version may still have elements of truth. She claims to have been the only young woman on a train full of German, Austrian and Hungarian prisoners of war. The journey from Moscow in that January of 1921 via Riga to Berlin was long and exasperatingly slow. At the Schlesischer Bahnhof, a schoolfriend from Petersburg came to meet her.

The schoolfriend utterly failed to recognize the figure bundled in overcoat and boots until Olga took off her head-scarf. With words of sympathy for the exhausted and famished traveller, she insisted on taking her to a nearby Café-Konditorei for coffee and cakes with whipped cream.

'Are you staying for good?' the schoolfriend asked.

'No, six weeks.'

The coffee and cakes were too much for a stomach reduced by the hunger years in Moscow. She was violently sick and remained unwell for several days.

Olga's schoolfriend found her a room in a dilapidated house in Gross-Beeren-Strasse. The place, run as a pension, belonged to the widow of an officer killed in the war. Olga, despite her claims that the family had spoken German at meals on alternate days, hardly spoke the language at all. Her friend told the maid to keep bringing her camomile tea. After a few days, Olga recovered and the two young women went to a jeweller to sell the ring supposedly smuggled under her tongue. (In another version of her own story it was sewn into her overcoat.) The jeweller named a price which made her friend go pale. Olga, who did not understand his exact words, realized that he was offering far less than it was worth. The two of them rose to leave. Finally, he improved his offer with a lot of protestations about the difficult times. Olga accepted and went straight to buy some proper shoes to replace her felt boots.

On the other hand, one wonders about her short-lived relationship with Jaroszi. One account indicates that she abandoned him almost as soon as she reached Berlin and that he became a doctor. To survive in Berlin, Olga again claimed that she carved and sold chess pieces. She also did any odd jobs that she could find and tried to sell her drawings and small sculptures. No doubt helped by the Chekhov name, she quickly made friends in Berlin's large Russian community. She soon met people in films and, through them, the producer Erich Pommer, who became the leading figure at the UFA (Universum-Film AG) movie studios at Babelsberg, just outside Berlin, next to Potsdam.

Pommer had brought Fritz Lang from Vienna, but Olga Chekhova's first director was to be Friedrich Wilhelm Murnau. Murnau had not found anyone for the part of 'the young châtelaine' in his silent movie *Schloß Vogelöd*. Olga's account of meeting Murnau has, as usual, novelettish touches which may well be a complete invention. She claims that a Russian Grand Duke who had commissioned her to do some sculpture told her 'that she had the quintessential face for the cinema'. He apparently dabbled on the fringes of the movie business and invited her to lunch at the Hotel Bristol, arranging for them to sit at the table next to Pommer and Murnau. The producer and the director began to look at her. Knowing her host slightly, they joined him and Olga at their table. The Grand Duke told them she was an actress.

'Have you ever done any filmwork?' Pommer asked her.

'Unfortunately not in Germany,' she answered. 'Only in Russia.'

It was one of the very few times when she acknowledged her small Russian film parts. In future, they would be written out of her life. Pommer invited her to come to their studio at Babelsberg the next morning for some test shots.

Olga spent the rest of the day borrowing clothes and polishing herself up. Murnau obviously liked what he saw and she was given the part. Over the next few days, acutely aware that she had hardly ever seen a movie, she tried to catch up by visiting just about every cinema she could.

The other members of the cast were German and Austrian stage actors. She kept quiet about her three little film parts in Moscow, but more than made up for it by claiming to have been a member of the Moscow Art Theatre and to have been trained in person by the great Stanislavsky. This, of course, was totally untrue. A few years later, when she obtained her first theatre part, Olga admitted that it was her very first stage role in a letter to Aunt Olya in Moscow, who knew that she had never had anything to do with the Art Theatre. 'I could not imagine what I would feel before I stepped on the stage, because I never had any acting training except for studying with Misha. There was just the influence from his studio where we used to spend days and nights.'

She was also safe from close inquiry about her acting experience because her German was so bad. In fact she had to work from a script translated into Russian for her. Olga described the filmset as a madhouse. In those days of German silent film, there was a piano player trying to put the actors in the right mood as they mimed their lines. Not understanding what anyone was saying and with working conditions totally confusing, Olga found it very hard to concentrate.

Schloß Vogelöd opened in a cinema on the Kurfürstendamm called the Marmorhaus, or Marble House, an extravagant mixture of ancient Egyptian and Greek architecture. The première took place on 7 April 1921. The date alone is enough to cast the most serious doubts on Olga Chekhova's story that she had left Moscow in January 1921. Clearly she must have left the previous summer, as Aunt Olya indicated in her letter from Tiflis.

Olga hated her performance when she saw the final cut, but the press liked it – one critic even compared her to the great Eleanora Duse – and she found herself being promoted as 'Die Tschechowa'. The demand for interviews and her very limited capacity to speak German forced her to start learning the language properly. But even as a supposed 'star', everything was so terrifyingly expensive in this time of hyper-inflation that she had scarcely enough money for the rent.

In September 1921, the Kachalov group had still not yet heard from Moscow, so they began a season in Prague after a summer break in the mountains. The group was rehearsing *Hamlet* to broaden their repertoire, with Kachalov in the title role. 'We will be playing *Hamlet* in a week's time. God help us!' Aunt Olya wrote to an old friend. 'Kachalov was looking beautiful,' she wrote to Stanislavsky. 'He was looking younger and more supple than before.'

Vadim Shverubovich, who became Lev's friend during this émigré year, described how a banker from Prague, 'with a family name like either Rosenkrantz or Guildenstern', took them up and gave parties for them. 'We spent a lot of time with him and drank a lot. Soon we started addressing our host as Herr Rosenkrantz or Herr Guildenstern.' But despite such levity, his father began to suffer from serious depressions. They had heard from a young Polish actor who had been with the Moscow Art Theatre that it was faring badly in their absence. Aunt Olya too was still suffering from acute homesickness. 'I have been ill recently,' she wrote to a friend. 'I had a temperature of about 40 and was delirious. I saw a Valkyrie flying to Moscow and how I suffered not being able to fly with it. I saw little lamps on the graves of the Novodeviche monastery. I felt that the Last Judgement was drawing close, and saw an archangel blowing a trumpet!'

'You mustn't think that we don't want a reunion,' she wrote to Stanislavsky that September. 'It is my dream that Stanislavsky will spread his wings and create the kind of theatre that is needed now, and that it will be in Russia!' However heartfelt, perhaps she chose her words knowing that they might be seen by other eyes. After Prague, the group travelled on to Germany that winter. Following a short season in Leipzig, they reached Berlin at the beginning of February 1922.

On 14 February, Kachalov received a letter from Nemirovich-Danchenko. At last it looked as if they were to be recalled to Moscow. Aunt Olya sat down to write to him as soon as she heard the news. Yet there is a hint of repressed anger at the start of this letter to her old lover. The fact that Nemirovich-Danchenko had not written during all their time abroad had clearly hurt her. 'I have just come back from playing in *The Cherry Orchard* and read your letter to Vasily Ivanovich [Kachalov] and for the first time I felt the desire to write to you.' But the thought of Moscow was too exhilarating to permit such resentments to fester. 'Your letter has finally told me what I have been dreaming secretly about all the time. That our return is needed.' Perhaps her heart had softened towards him, influenced by the fact that she had just been playing Ranyevskaya, who could not resist forgiving her heartless lover in Paris. 'Maybe when we are close and we are looking into each other's eyes, we will understand without saying anything how dear we still are to each other . . . what I am looking forward to most of all is to see you again, you and no one else.' On the other hand, Aunt Olya, who was so generous and kind towards her own family, had a reputation for scheming within the Moscow Art Theatre. She knew she needed help at this moment, and she was certainly prepared to exploit any lingering loyalty from an old flame.

11. The Early 1920s in Moscow and Berlin

The Moscow Art Theatre was indeed in a sorry state during the absence of the Kachalov group. Despite the appreciation of Lenin, it felt embattled under the new regime. Proletkult had been calling for the abolition of all pre-revolutionary theatre, and the most influential new critic, Vladimir Blum, referred to the Moscow Art Theatre as the 'standard-bearer of the bourgeoisie'. Even Stanislavsky himself had very mixed feelings about Chekhov's work after the horrors of the civil war. 'When we play the farewell to Masha in *The Three Sisters* I am embarrassed,' he wrote to Nemirovich-Danchenko. 'After all that we have lived through it is impossible to weep over the fact that an officer is going away and leaving his lady behind.'

The only new production during the years of revolution and civil war had been a disastrous attempt by Stanislavsky to stage Byron's *Cain*. Meyerhold, the most avant-garde director of all, came to Stanislavsky's defence, praising his courage to stage such an ambitious work, but he was a lone voice.

The Art Theatre's artistic fortunes only started to improve in the early spring of 1921. Since their leading actor, Kachalov, was still abroad, the decision was made to give the lead in Strindberg's *Erik XIV* to Mikhail Chekhov. The play opened on 29 March to a storm of controversy. The most obsessive opponent of the Moscow Art Theatre attacked Misha's performance as 'the same old snub-nosed little idiot Petrushka'. But most reviews were adulatory. Misha had risen to the challenge with a performance of genius.

That autumn Stanislavsky gave Misha the lead role in

Gogol's *Government Inspector*, and another opportunity to develop the theatre of the grotesque – what Stanislavsky defined as 'the vivid, external, audacious justification of enormous inner content, which is so all-embracing as to verge on exaggeration'. Misha had found his forte. His Hamlet, which followed, was a truly original interpretation and produced an even greater success.

Misha's cousin Sergei Chekhov found his performance 'unforgettable'. He later described how he met up again with him. 'As the play finished, I stood up to applaud with everyone else. When [Misha] was taking his bow, he saw and recognized me and smiled through Hamlet's make-up with that sweet Misha smile. He invited me afterwards to come and see him.' Sergei was happy to find that, in marked contrast to the last time he had seen his cousin, at Volodya's funeral, he was 'well-groomed, nicely dressed and looking well'.

Backstage, Misha discovered that Sergei had just arrived back in Moscow from the Chekhov home town of Taganrog and had nowhere to live. Longing to talk about members of the family, such as Aunt Masha, and to reminisce about their youth before the revolution, Misha immediately invited him to stay with him and his wife, Xenia, in their large apartment off the Arbat. Apart from the bedrooms, it had a dining room, where Sergei slept on a sofa behind a screen, and a round sitting room, where there was a small stage with a canvas curtain. Here the Chekhov Studio had held lessons and now it served as a workspace for the young actors who gravitated towards Misha. There was even a housekeeper-cum-cook to look after them, which was typical of Misha at such a time of anti-bourgeois agitation.

'I am staying with Misha, whose hospitality exceeds all limits,' Sergei wrote to his parents in March 1922. 'His wife is very sweet and kind. Apart from us, another six young people

are living here as a commune. I became part of the family at
once. I am already much less thin.'

Sergei had reached Moscow half-starved. The region of
Taganrog had suffered cruelly during the Red Terror that
followed the collapse of Denikin's armies. Sergei, compulsively hungry all the time, simply stared at butter or anything
sweet on the table. Misha and Xenia noticed this and pushed
them closer, but the biggest treat, he found, was black bread.
The bread was kept in a stove near where he slept in the
dining room and at night he could smell it. He could not resist
his craving and broke off pieces to eat, riddled with guilt even
though he knew he would be forgiven. Misha, with his own
addiction to alcohol still unconquered, was no doubt the first
to understand.

'Xenia Karlovna simply adored Misha,' wrote Sergei. 'Once
Misha took a bath. I heard him go to his bedroom afterwards.
Several minutes later the door to my room opened and Xenia
Karlovna summoned me. "Sergei," she said, "just come and
see this charming picture." Misha was lying in bed covered
by a quilt. His dark hair was very distinct against the white
pillow. He was smiling in an arch way and Xenia Karlovna
stood by the bed, her hands folded almost as if in prayer,
marvelling at her husband.'

Misha enjoyed teasing his wife. He would sometimes bring
out a picture of Olga and show it to her. 'Xenia,' he would
say, making succulent noises, 'just look what a beauty my first
wife was.' An embarrassed Xenia would then try to snatch the
photo from Misha's hands, and kept saying: 'Mishka, don't
you dare. Mishka, give it to me.'

On a beautiful spring day in Moscow, Misha and Xenia
decided to go for a walk. They invited Sergei to come with
them. He remembered how passers-by turned to look at
Misha, with a smile of recognition. 'Well, it's not surprising,'

Xenia said, so happy for him. 'You are now the most famous actor of all.'

Misha may have become famous in Moscow, but his first wife, Olga, was unlikely to have kept a photograph of him. Her main preoccupation, apart from her career, was how to get her mother and her daughter out of the newly constituted Soviet Union. In the meantime, she concentrated on learning German and on her work at the UFA studios at Babelsberg.

Universum-Film AG had been conceived in 1917 under military auspices to provide propaganda films, both newsreel and feature, for German army *Feldkinos* set up behind the front line for resting troops. Field Marshal Ludendorff had greatly encouraged the project, which would depend on private capital from major industrialists. Even defeat in 1918 did little more than interrupt a studio production line that started with Ernst Lubitsch's films starring Pola Negri. *Madame Dubarry*, made in 1919, was such a success abroad as well as in Germany that Pola Negri was enticed over to the United States by Hollywood.

For Olga Chekhova to have been taken up by Pommer and to have had a success in her first film with Murnau just as the UFA studios were in full expansion was a remarkable stroke of fortune. Pommer soon built the largest studio complex in Europe, employing at its height some 4,000 people. And with directors like Lubitsch, Murnau and Fritz Lang, who made *Metropolis* there in 1925 and 1926, German cinema attracted the interest of the world. Both stars and directors were sought by Hollywood, and the American cinema of the time was greatly influenced by what Pommer had started.

Aunt Olya and Lev returned finally to Moscow via Scandinavia with the Kachalov group in May 1922. There is no mention in any of their letters that they had met Olga in Berlin, yet they did make contact. The Russian émigré grapevine was far too effective for Olga not to have known of her aunt's arrival. It also appears that Sergei Bertensson, the Moscow Art Theatre stage manager on the tour, met her and fell hopelessly in love.

In Moscow, on the other hand, the slightest whisper of the word émigré put people on their guard. The Kachalov group, to their dismay, found that nobody had come to the Belorussky station to welcome them back. And when the two parts of the Moscow Art Theatre met up again, there appears to have been a good deal of unease on both sides. Lenin, on the other hand, could afford to ignore such political squeamishness. 'At last!' he is said to have exclaimed on hearing of the Kachalov group's return. 'It will be very interesting to discover their reaction to the new Russia, to the new Moscow. They are a sensitive lot. In any case, our audiences will be very happy to see them again.' Lenin certainly spoke for himself. He far preferred the old productions of the Moscow Art Theatre to the hectoring Proletkult worthiness espoused by Lunacharsky. It was an interesting paradox that Lenin, who wanted to exterminate the bourgeoisie, should have been so fond of Anton Chekhov's plays. And less than a decade later, Stalin adored Mikhail Bulgakov's play *Days of the Turbins*, which was condemned as reactionary, if not counter-revolutionary, by his culture commissars. The Soviet leader went to see it no fewer than fifteen times at the Moscow Art Theatre.

Aunt Olya was careful when expressing her reaction to the new Russia. Clearly the reality of Moscow had not lived up to her longings from abroad, but above all she had been shocked to find that so many friends had died in her absence. 'Here I am in Moscow after three years of wandering,' she wrote to her sister-in-law Masha in the Crimea, 'and so far I am happy to be in Russia. I don't know how I am going to feel afterwards.'

The main purpose of this hurriedly written letter was to take advantage of a reliable courier, the brother of the poet Osip Mandelstam, who could take Masha earnings from Chekhov plays staged abroad. 'I only learned late yesterday evening that Yevgeny Emilevich [Mandelstam] is going to the Crimea today. In August we are leaving for America with the theatre for a year.' Mandelstam was asked to deliver part of the Chekhov royalties from the earnings of the Kachalov group, most of it in German marks, the rest in 'lemons', the joke-name for inflated Soviet banknotes at the time, because million sounded like *limon*.

For Aunt Olya, part of the pleasure of her return to 23 Prechistensky bulvar was to see her two great-nieces – Olga and Ada's little daughters. Although it was a large apartment by Soviet standards, the compulsively generous Aunt Olya shared it with many members of the extended family.

Aunt Olya was the only one to have a whole room to herself. Her nephew Vova, Vladimir's son, described it: 'There was a small bed in the far corner behind a silk screen, with a coverlet of red fox fur, a marble washstand and a wardrobe with a mirror. By the window there was a small desk and an antique little round table with several armchairs.' It must have been quite a large room, because it also contained a grand piano, where Lev later wrote his music, and the pelt of a polar bear spread-eagled on the floor. Two glass-fronted bookcases on another wall were filled with publications presented to her by friends. Gorky had written the following dedication in one of them: 'For you, Olga Leonardovna. I would like to have bound this book with the skin of my heart, but my wife would bark at me. You are nice, you are good, you are a sweet person and you are talented. I could say a lot more to you but it would be better if I just silently shake your hand with all my heart.'

She invited Sofya Chekhova, the mother of Volodya, who had shot himself in 1917, to move in after her husband died. There were also her brother Konstantin, now too sick to return to work as a railway engineer, his wife, Lulu, Ada and the two little girls. Lev turned up from time to time to stay as well. Aunt Olya, however, appears to have known about only one side of her adored nephew's life.

'On my return to Moscow,' wrote Lev many years later, 'I could not fight my passion for music any more.' He was twenty-three. At first, his family was highly sceptical. His aunt, his father and his uncle Vladimir, the opera singer, sat as a jury to hear whether he had any talent, both as a pianist and as a composer. Their verdict was 'very discouraging' and they tried to persuade him to give up his plans. Lev, however, was adamant.

Aunt Olya, despite her participation in the unfavourable verdict, could not resist wanting to help. She introduced Lev to Yelena Gnesina, the director of the best-known music school in Moscow. Gnesina employed him as the administrator of the school building. Lev claimed later that, as a 'White Guardist', he could not be taken on officially as a pupil, so Gnesina gave him a job and private lessons. In fact the only problem was that Lev, at twenty-three, was far too old in a school for students between the ages of seven and seventeen. 'Those were hard years,' Lev wrote towards the end of his life, but his memoirs are just as disingenuous as those of his sister Olga, even if he did not indulge himself with fantasies.

According to the spymaster General Pavel Sudoplatov and other Soviet sources, Lev Knipper, 'after he returned to Moscow in 1922, was interviewed many times by state security organs' (at that stage the newly constituted OGPU, the forerunner to the NKVD and later KGB). Lev's status as a 'former

White Guard officer' left him little option but to comply. Whether he was forced to recruit his sister in Berlin straight away or later is impossible to tell without access to the relevant files, which remain firmly closed, but according to General Sudoplatov's son, Professor Anatoly Sudoplatov, who knew Lev's controllers, 'in the 1920s [Olga Chekhova] was a key figure, instrumental in arranging all sorts of meetings among Russian émigrés in Germany'. In any case, Lev was to visit her in Berlin quite frequently, a link neither of them ever mentioned, even to their relatives. Apparently Lev Knipper, 'assisted by the NKVD, maintained regular communications with Olga Chekhova during the 1930s'.

In the beginning, Lev may have seen his relationship with the OGPU as an intriguingly dangerous game. He seems to have enjoyed a surge of self-confidence at this time. He had conquered his childhood weakness, he had survived the civil war, he was extremely good-looking and enjoyed the admiration of many women, and especially of his aunt, one of the most respected figures in Russian cultural life. Perhaps his new secret life encouraged him to think that he could flaunt Western ways and new artistic ideas and ignore the dreary dictates of Proletkult. Yet in his youthful arrogance, he must have also underestimated the dangers. As a former White Guard, he was forever in their power and might have to denounce friends and colleagues in the arts. It was probably a classic case of refusing to see that he was selling his soul, and then having to persuade himself of higher motives later, once the bitter truth became clear. One side of his character might also have been attracted to the work. Lev was extremely touchy and he did not forget a slight, whether perceived or real. His highly controlled exterior, according to some of those who knew him, concealed some deep resentments.

Aunt Olya, meanwhile, was impressed and worried by Lev's

dedication to his musical studies. 'Lev has just turned up,' she wrote to a friend that August. 'He has completely plunged into his music. He was working so hard that he utterly exhausted himself. He has lost fourteen pounds and the doctor has forbidden him to do any work and to rest and put those pounds back on.'

According to Lev, having learned the basics of theory, he started on harmony in that same month of August. He was also composing in any spare moment. The pressure of over-work, he claimed, led to a recurrence of his childhood osteo-tuberculosis and 'a committee of professors decided that it would not be possible to cure me'. Next month, a large group from the Moscow Art Theatre was about to go on tour abroad, first to Western Europe and then to the United States. It was part of the Bolshevik regime's attempts to normalize relations and re-establish trade links after the civil war. Aunt Olya was able to arrange for Lev 'to join the theatre on paper' so that he could be treated by specialists in Berlin.

That a recently returned White Guardist should be allowed back to Berlin within such a short time would have been surprising to say the least. But as a cover story for a mission, it could hardly have been bettered. Lev was to re-establish contact with his sister Olga and report on any White Russian émigré activities in Germany, while he pursued his musical studies there as a cover. 'From time to time,' General Sudo-platov cryptically wrote later, 'we used Lev Knipper's contacts with the émigrés.'

This period was one of intense secret operations abroad mounted by INO (Inostrannyi Otdel), the Foreign Intelli-gence Department of the OGPU. Even after the destruction of the White armies, Lenin was determined to pursue counter-revolution abroad. In December 1920, Feliks Dzerzhinsky, the founder of the Cheka, had begun to organize operations against émigré groups in France and Germany. Berlin alone contained 200,000 White Russian refugees.

Relatives of prominent émigrés were seized as hostages at home and agents were rapidly recruited for operations abroad to infiltrate émigré organizations and arrange the kidnapping of their leaders. A sophisticated development was to create fake White Guard organizations within Russia to trap the regime's enemies. These activities were given the highest priority. For the first dozen years of its life, INO's 'main foreign target remained the White Guard movement'.

The White Guard movement was directed from Paris by the Russian Combined Services Union (ROVS), led by General Kutepov, who was kidnapped in Paris by OGPU agents in January 1930. A successor, General Miller, was also kidnapped in December 1936. He was taken back to the Soviet Union drugged inside a trunk, interrogated, tortured and then shot. The émigré world of White Russians in the early 1920s was a political demi-monde of agents and double agents, mostly working for the OGPU. Homesick White Russians in Paris and Berlin, many of them well-born officers working at night as taxi drivers, were prepared to betray their closest friends for the chance of what they thought was a guarantee of safe conduct home.

Lev, however, was not expected to take part in kidnappings. His task was to identify those émigrés, especially intellectuals, who could be persuaded to return to the Soviet homeland as obedient citizens. He apparently played a quiet but important role in providing information for the OGPU on writers like Aleksei Tolstoy, a former White officer like Lev and the author of the Moscow Art Theatre's early success *Tsar Feodor*, in which Olga Knipper-Chekhova made her name and attracted the interest of Anton Chekhov. Tolstoy, who became known as 'the Red Count', was allowed back in 1923 as a 'repentant expatriate' and never disappointed the Kremlin. He was raised to the status of grand old man of Soviet letters after Gorky's death.

The Russian émigré community in Berlin was more like a colony, largely because it was so concentrated on the western centre of the city. Berliners jokingly called the Kurfürstendamm the 'Nöpski Prospekt', and Charlottenburg was known as 'Charlottengrad'. Writers including Vladimir Nabokov, Ilya Ehrenburg and Boris Pasternak treated the cafés of the area, such as the Prager Diele, in the same way as French existentialists later used the cafés of Saint-Germain. There were around 200 Russian-language newspapers, magazines and journals in Berlin, a number of publishing houses and even a Russian high school. But this already precarious community was to be devastated and scattered within a decade by the economic crisis and unemployment triggered by the Wall Street Crash.

The Moscow Art Theatre touring group, some sixty strong, with Lev discreetly in attendance, reached Berlin at the end of September 1922. They had sailed from Petrograd down the Baltic to Stettin, encountering heavy storms on the way. Most of them felt very sick and battered when they took their train to Berlin, arriving a week after Stanislavsky.

Stanislavsky was very nervous. He could relax even less in foreign countries than at home in Moscow. Every arrangement for the tour had been made by the impresario Morris Gest, who was also a great publicist. As a result, Stanislavsky, already ashamed of his shabby overcoat, found himself, as he stepped from his carriage in the Friedrichstrasse station, ambushed with flashbulbs and moving-picture cameras. He even had to repeat his departure from the station for their benefit.

The tour, as he knew only too well, was an immense

undertaking and politically fraught. Outside Russia they were likely to be seen as representatives of the regime which had butchered the Tsar and his children, while any soothing remarks they made abroad could be interpreted at home as 'counter-revolutionary'. The fact that Lenin and Lunacharsky had given permission for this foreign tour was not a guarantee of their safety on return.

The tour did not start well in Berlin. Stanislavsky was trying to lick the cast into shape for *Tsar Feodor*, only to find that they could not rehearse properly at their theatre, because they were sharing it with another company. Max Reinhardt, the great impresario of the period, stepped in to help with the offer of his own company's workshops. Stanislavsky insisted that not a minute should be wasted. Although nearly a quarter of a century in the Art Theatre's repertoire, *Tsar Feodor* had not been performed for some time and needed a good dusting.

At the technical rehearsal on 24 September Stanislavsky was sitting in the auditorium. The dramatic moment came when the bells of the Kremlin were to ring out, but the sound was tinny. 'And when are we going to hear the real chimes?' Stanislavsky called out from the darkness of the deserted rows. Somebody in Moscow, without telling Stanislavsky, had decided to leave the main bell behind because it weighed one and a half tons and was thus far too heavy for a European and American tour. Stanislavsky's pent-up nerves exploded in a magisterial tantrum. He insisted that the performance must be cancelled. Eventually, a stagehand suggested that a large circular saw, if suspended, could prove a reasonable substitute if struck in the correct way. Circular saws were summoned for a trial from a nearby workshop, Stanislavsky was finally convinced and the play went ahead.

While the real members of the Moscow Art Theatre concentrated on *Tsar Feodor*, Lev Knipper slipped away for his 'intensive treatment'. He certainly saw his sister Olga at this period and later, during his fifteen-month stay in Germany. Some of the time he spent in Freiburg at a sanatorium, where he had a piano in his room and composed; the rest he spent in Berlin. There can be no doubt at all about Lev's driving musical passion. And thanks to the OGPU he had the rare opportunity of being allowed to live in Germany and study modern composition. How much spying he managed to do on the émigré community in Berlin is impossible to tell, yet he must surely have achieved some results, because the OGPU and then the NKVD allowed him to go abroad again and again.

12. Home Thoughts from Abroad

The contrast between life at home in Soviet Russia and life abroad could be very disorientating for members of the Moscow Art Theatre. 'My fate has torn me away from Russia and from the life I had been dreaming of,' Aunt Olya wrote to a friend from Paris. 'And with a kind of anger I have plunged into the easy life, feeling satisfied with momentary impressions. This city is unbelievably beautiful. It is a joy to walk in the streets.'

It was also unsettling for White Russians in Paris when the Moscow Art Theatre arrived to perform *The Cherry Orchard*. 'This must have been so disturbing for our former fellow countrymen,' she added. Many White Russian émigrés were reduced to tears, seeing the re-creation of the country they still longed for and loved, and experiencing once again its poignant, painful ending, with Ranyevskaya leaving for Paris and the lover who she knew was faithless.

Aunt Olya dreaded the next and largest stage of their tour, the United States. 'Please think of me on the 27th when we sail from Europe's shore,' she wrote in the same letter of December 1922. Her misgivings were rapidly confirmed by the restlessness and brashness of the New World. 'It's so noisy here. Everything is catching up and overtaking. There's a dance-hall for every three houses. There are movie theatres, restaurants and concerts, but the nation itself does not have a drop of artistic blood in it. It's a kingdom of incredible advertising. You go out in the evening and you don't believe your own eyes. One doesn't know where to look. There's a sea of light, everything is jumping, moving, shimmering, with words written in light . . . We are a huge success, but to be honest with you, it does not please us.'

The reputation of the Moscow Art Theatre was so great that the Friday matinées were packed with actors, treating the performance as a master class. And the general effect on the theatrical profession in the United States was inestimable. But even that was little consolation for Aunt Olya. She was homesick for the potholed road which led from her apartment building on the Prechistensky bulvar to the Moscow Art Theatre on Kamergersky pereulok. She could not understand the United States. 'It's like some wind-up clockwork machine. It's impossible to read anything in people's faces. It's as if everything is always all right. This is the expression they wear in the street and when they go about their business.' On the other hand, she was honest enough to admit that she loved the en-suite bathrooms in the hotels and the constant hot water.

The Moscow Art Theatre was clearly not prepared for the contrast in New York between well-heated hotels and freezing rehearsal rooms. Many of them fell ill with flu and even bronchitis. Aunt Olya was amazed by the luxurious fur coats of American women worn over (by Soviet standards) revealing little dresses. In her eyes, the dresses of the 1920s left women almost naked.

She received a letter from her brothers Konstantin and Vladimir in Moscow and burst into tears. She could not put on her make-up for the performance. Her homesickness cannot have been improved by Rachmaninov, Anton Chekhov's old friend, coming to see them. 'He's thin and angular,' she wrote after a late dinner with him on 5 March 1923, following a performance. 'There's suffering in his face and incredible tiredness.' After another meeting with Rachmaninov, she wrote: 'It is so touching when he speaks of Anton Pavlovich [Chekhov] and asks me to talk about him. His face lights up.' For all émigrés, Chekhov was the essence of the Russia which they had loved and lost.

Lev, on the other hand, rejoiced in the stimulus of foreign culture. From Freiburg, he went deep into the Black Forest for the festival of modern music at Donaueschingen, where he met Paul Hindemith. Hindemith and Arnold Schoenberg were great influences on him at this time. He was in a whirl of new discoveries. 'I'm plunged into expressionism,' he wrote to Aunt Olya on her return to Europe. He urged her to bring his sister Olga down with her from Berlin, because she needed rest.

In that summer of 1923, his adopted mother rejoined him there after the first part of their American tour. 'I spent only three days in Berlin,' wrote Aunt Olya to her brother Vladimir. 'After the hellish work in America I arrived after a twelve day sea trip, scatter-brained and not knowing what to do with myself.' She stayed in Berlin with Olga and was most impressed by the way she had decorated her apartment. After America, even the hated Berlin – 'all green and almost beautiful' – appealed to her. Germany seemed 'almost small, sweet and cosy' after New York.

'I decided to move south to join Lyova [Lev]. The Stanislav-skys are here too. At the moment I am staying with Lyova, who has moved from the sanatorium to a private house [in Freiburg]. I am thinking of wandering in the mountains [of the Black Forest] to return to my senses. Lyova has got his own room with a grand piano. He is writing music, but very advanced music. I haven't yet heard enough of it to make it out.' Stanislavsky was also taking a break from the American tour to write his book *My Life in Art*. Maxim Gorky was in the area as well, so Aunt Olya and Stanislavsky went over to visit him.

Olga came down a little later from Berlin to join them and, while Lev composed, she and Aunt Olya walked and sat together chatting. Olga told her about her life in Berlin and also about Sergei Bertensson, the stage manager of the Moscow Art Theatre who had fallen in love with her. 'I know that our Bertensson had serious intentions,' Aunt Olya wrote to Vladimir in Moscow, 'and that he had proposed to her, but nothing came of it, and she keeps him by her side as a friend. He is very much in love with her and he does everything that she commands him to do. She has told him that she is not going to have any more ties in her life without strong feelings.'

At the end of August, when 'more slave labour in America' appeared on the autumn horizon, she wrote again. 'It looks as if Lyova is going to become someone very interesting. In my opinion, his compositions are intriguing. I feel that it is not nonsense. He has met many young composers and was beyond himself with awe at this artistic environment. He is very confident of his talents.'

Lev and Olga, accompanied by Aunt Olya, soon returned to Berlin. Lev began studying with Philip Jarnach and spent much time at the Society of Modern Music. While Olga returned to work in the studios at Babelsberg, Aunt Olya had to embark on the second part of the American tour, which she so dreaded. But it was Stanislavsky who suffered the most in the United States. He received a telegram from Nemirovich-Danchenko in Moscow warning him that the Communist satirical magazine *Krokodil* had quoted him in an interview in America describing the results of the Russian Revolution. 'What was our horror,' he was reported as having said, 'when the workers invaded the theatre with dirty clothes, uncombed, unwashed, with dirty boots, demanding the performance of revolutionary plays.'

Stanislavsky immediately sent back a rebuttal to be printed in *Pravda*, claiming that this interview was 'lies from beginning to end'. He had in fact said the very opposite, boasting of the Art Theatre's great success with proletarian audiences. This was some way from the truth, but Stanislavsky was outraged at the position he found himself in. 'Moscow accuses us of disloyalty,' he wrote to Nemirovich-Danchenko, 'but we get even blacker looks abroad . . . In Paris a considerable number of people, both French and Russian, boycotted us because we came from Soviet Russia and therefore were Communists. Now they won't let us into Canada, officially declaring us Bolsheviks.' Not long afterwards, *Prozhektor*, another satirical magazine, published a photograph of Stanislavsky and Olga Knipper-Chekhova with Prince Feliks Yousupov, the assassin of Rasputin. The obvious implication was that the Moscow Art Theatre mixed with émigrés whenever it was abroad.

In Germany, Olga Chekhova had to be even more discreet about politics. In the absence of accessible records, one can only speculate about the details of her recruitment by Lev, but the most obvious incentive presented would have been exit visas for members of her family, especially her mother and little daughter. These were indeed delivered the following year, again an unusual gesture to assist a Soviet citizen who had failed to return after the expiry of her own exit permit.

According to General Sudoplatov, who was later in charge of Soviet intelligence in Germany, the basis for Olga Chekhova's collaboration consisted of 'a trustful relationship with us and the obligations imposed by recruitment'. This rather Delphic but standard phrase in Soviet intelligence circles denotes that although she signed a paper (probably under pressure), she was a voluntary, unpaid agent. Professor Anatoly Sudoplatov, who worked with his father on every aspect of his book, said that the main interest in Olga Chekhova was as a 'sleeper', to be activated when her contacts in high places might be useful. She was not considered the right material to be an active agent.

Olga Chekhova was indeed unsuited for imminent operational needs in that autumn of 1923. It was a period of intense OGPU and Comintern activity in Germany. A self-deluding myth had gripped the Politburo in Moscow that an uprising by Communist workers could trigger a German revolution. They were desperate for this momentous event to take place before the death of Lenin, who had suffered a series of strokes. Zinoviev had given the order to the German Communist Party in August. Trotsky could hardly contain himself with excitement. 'Here at last, Comrades,' he told fellow members of the Politburo, 'is the tempest we have been expecting impatiently for so many years . . . The German revolution means the collapse of world capitalism.'

Experts to direct this revolution were sent from Moscow, including the deputy chief of the OGPU, who was to set up a similar organization in Germany to crush the counter-revolution. But all the Politburo's hopes were in vain. The German Communists represented a small minority of the working class, and when the order went out for a rising on 23 October, it was ignored everywhere except among the Hamburg dockers, who had unloaded weapons secretly shipped to them from Petrograd. They were rapidly crushed. Lenin had to be told that his favourite prediction had not come to pass. Although incapable of coherent speech, he was still mentally alert and the news must have been another heavy blow.

★

Olga Chekhova, meanwhile, concentrated on her career. Following her success as the Baroness Safferstädt in Murnau's *Schloß Vogelöd*, she played in over forty silent movies during the 1920s. She also worked hard to perfect her German and lose her rather heavy Russian accent. This would enable her to take on stage roles as well, but it also meant that she was well prepared for her first talkie in 1930.

The most controversial movies of her early career were *Der Todesreigen* (*Dance of Death*) and *Tatyana*. Both were made in 1922 and both were set in the Russian Revolution. In *Der Todesreigen* Olga Chekhova played a young Russian aristocrat who falls in love with a revolutionary and the revolution, but the horrors, the squalor and the misery depicted in the film were far too vivid for German Communists. In one notorious scene, Olga was seized and mauled by Red Guards. German left-wingers attacked the theatre where it was premièred, chanting 'Down with anti-Bolshevism!' and a riot developed. Olga avoided any comment on these events and this interesting moment in her career naturally raises the question of her agreement to help Lev and Soviet intelligence.

Olga wanted to help her family back in Russia, and particularly Lev, who needed it most after his time as a White Guard. She had also decided to get her daughter out, having created a far better life for herself in Germany. In her new country, she was admired and taken seriously, a very welcome change for her after the patronizing attitude of Misha and the Moscow Art Theatre circle. Her political instincts, as Soviet intelligence recognized in 1945, were basically those of an old-fashioned conservative. But for purely pragmatic reasons she was ready to be a 'fellow-traveller'.

After filming *Der verlorene Schuh*, based on the fairy tale *The Lost Shoe*, Olga Chekhova then played a young fishwife in *Das Meer*, set on a Breton island off Brest. She also played the part of *Nora* in an adaptation of Ibsen's *Doll's House*. This received excellent reviews. But soon afterwards, in December 1923, she and Lev heard from Moscow that their father was extremely ill. Lev decided to return immediately. He was only just in time. Konstantin Knipper died on 6 January 1924. Lev sent a telegram in German to Aunt Olya in New York: 'Papa gestorben 6 Januar. Leo'.

Lev wrote a long letter to Aunt Olya describing her brother's end. Konstantin Knipper had been delirious, talking about his work and making speeches. But the death itself was peaceful. Lev had then clearly been irritated when his Uncle Vladimir arrived and 'sobbed like a child', which 'broke our harmony'. As well as Lulu Knipper and Lev, Olga's former husband Misha joined them at the deathbed. 'I was living through the most beautiful moment of my life,' Lev continued in his letter. 'I sensed Papa's presence all the time. I feel no pain. I am happy for him. There aren't many people who die in such a good and <u>pure</u> way. Misha and I washed and dressed him. We did it all with our own hands. I didn't let Mama do anything. He seemed alive, he was still warm. It seemed to me as if he were still breathing. I am endlessly grateful to Misha for the colossal moral support that he's given us. I will never forget this. He's got such a generous and complete soul.'

After Misha left, Lev stayed with his mother. Lulu felt that all she had left after her husband's death was Olga's little girl. She did not want to go to Berlin, but at the same time she did not want to be parted from her granddaughter, whom Olga now wanted with her. Lev told their mother that she had to go to Germany.

In the same letter to Aunt Olya, he started talking of the future without wasting any time. 'Now, on quite a different subject. You know what I mean. Money . . . My happiness lies in my art, in my work. I've made a huge step forward in the last two months. One more year, and I will stand on my own two feet. But now I don't really want to work for money. I've written a foxtrot and sold it for fifty roubles, but it was so hard and unpleasant. My darling Aunt Olya, please forgive me for approaching you like this. You don't like this. But you know me. I need money very, very much. Because the funeral is going to cost us (a very modest one) 200–250 dollars. I will take a break from my lessons and try to raise some money, but the problem isn't so much mine, but Mama's. [Olga], of course, will send us some money, but it won't be much. Please don't cry, don't grieve. Death is beautiful, I've understood it clearly now for the first time. It is a great, mysterious celebration.' And so ended Lev's rather chilling letter.

Once family matters were attended to, Lev wasted little time in trying to establish his supremacy in modern music in a city cut off from all new developments abroad. Composers, conductors and musicians were indeed bowled over by this young apparition from abroad. His opinions, to say nothing of his plus fours and golfing shoes, left them open-mouthed. 'Everyone was such a formalist in those days,' wrote the conductor E. A. Akulov almost seventy years later. 'I remember Lyovushka Knipper's return from Berlin. We were all penniless and looking like shabby alley cats after a fight, and he came back wearing some incredible shoes. So, anyway, Knipper said to us: "One really can't write music in this way." We were looking at his incredible shoes with leather festoons, his unbelievable trousers, and we believed that major chords with three notes had actually been cancelled all over the world.'

In Berlin, meanwhile, Olga's career had become exhaustingly successful. Germany was in an appalling economic crisis, and thus in desperate need to forget its present worries and the trauma of defeat in the First World War. The studios at Babelsberg were initially working flat out, but soon the financial situation reduced the output by half as inflation destroyed the value of money. Fortunately, in spite of the demand for escapism, the new industry attracted some brilliant directors from the theatre who were longing to experiment. Many came from Vienna. There were few prospects for them in that beautiful shell, emptied of meaning by the collapse of the Austro-Hungarian empire.

After playing the title role in *Nora*, Olga Chekhova tried to produce her own film, *Die Pagode*, but this was not a commercial success. Her determination to seize every opportunity pushed her into accepting almost any part going, to the point where she was making up to five or even more films a year. Most of these roles stereotyped her as a society lady, but where she was extremely clever was in the way she could almost change her face at will for each part. One can compare photographs of Olga Chekhova in a dozen different movies, and even when you know it is the same actress, it is very hard to see. This did not just come with changing the style or colour of her hair; it seems that she even managed to change the shape of her face.

She also made every effort to play the publicity game, with interviews, articles and photographic sessions. She had moved to a slightly larger apartment at 21 Berchtesgadener Strasse in Berlin-Schöneberg, but, as Aunt Olya had remarked in one of her letters, Olga had no time for relationships and was exhausting herself with work. There can be little doubt that after her feeling of helplessness when her marriage to Misha fell apart during the Russian Revolution, she never wanted to depend on a man again. This made her extremely circumspect in her relations with suitors beyond the usual good-mannered flirting. She was determined to earn enough money to avoid any such vulnerability, a feeling which must have been greatly strengthened by everyone's sense of powerlessness during the raging inflation of 1923.

The collapse of savings during the inflation had deeply damaged the middle classes, psychologically as well as financially. The west end of Berlin became famous for large, gloomy apartments turned into boarding houses by ruined war widows. But once the currency was stabilized in a bold move by the Weimar government, economic prospects began to revive, at least for those who were employable.

Alongside the terrible unemployment and misery, the febrile gaiety of the 1920s was something of a *danse macabre* to banish any memory of what the world had just been through. The revealing short dresses which had so shocked Aunt Olya in New York were eagerly bought in Berlin by those women who could afford them. Olga Chekhova, now beyond the stage of needing to borrow clothes, had also had her hair bobbed, a style which the Germans called the Bubikopf, because it made a woman's head look like a boy's.

Once her German was good enough, she managed to obtain a one-year contract at the Berliner Renaissance-Theater. No doubt the theatre management was taken in by her totally false claims to have been a member of the famous Moscow Art Theatre. Yet she still drove out early to Babelsberg every morning for filming, which made it a very long day. The compensation, of course, was that her spending power was increased considerably. Soon she bought a smart new Talbot convertible with the enormous running boards of the period. She even had a chauffeur, but often preferred to drive the car herself. Olga Chekhova clearly revelled in the idea that she was at last in control of her life.

13. The End of Political Innocence

Misha Chekhov came back into the lives of the Knipper family again in 1924. Aunt Olya told Nemirovich-Danchenko that she would 'be happy to play the mayor's wife' in *The Government Inspector*, the Gogol play in which Misha was now the star. He was about to be made the first Honoured Actor of the USSR. The drama of Olga's elopement with Misha must by then have seemed almost as distant a memory as a crisis in childhood.

Misha was certainly ambitious, yet all the time he held passionately to his ideals. Lev Knipper, on the other hand, seems to have harnessed his artistic credo to his driving ambition, yet he believed in himself so intensely that he felt he could follow any unconventional path which took his fancy. A month after his father's death, Lev proudly sent Aunt Olya, then back in New York, a newspaper clipping which stated: 'Intensive work is going on to prepare a new programme of plastic compositions based on the music by Liszt and L. Knipper – a young composer who has arrived from Berlin.'

The letter which accompanied it was briskly energetic in its descriptions of what he was up to. 'I have left the Gnesina school and now I am studying on my own, preparing for the Conservatoire, for its conductors' faculty. I am studying hard. At the same time, I am writing a ballet. It is going to be staged this autumn . . . I am already being spoken of in Moscow music circles . . . The ballet is based on an absolutely new concept – a harmonious combination of music, eurhythmics and light, because I have concluded after studying them that the attempts of Wagner and Scriabin were erroneous from the start.' He finally turned to the subject of the family. 'I need to send Mama abroad as soon as possible, she is falling to bits from her illness. And I can't leave [Sofya Chekhova, the mother of the suicide Volodya] in charge of our apartment, it would ruin the place.'

Lev must have been in touch with Olga about exit permits, warning her to prepare for the arrival in Berlin of their mother and her two granddaughters. Olga herself was also flushed with success at this time and could not resist boasting to their aunt. 'Darling and dearest Aunt Olya,' she wrote triumphantly of her first experience of the stage at the Renaissance-Theater. 'I have just been baptized. Posters of me are everywhere and newspapers are writing about me.' She was playing an aristocrat in a drama set in the French Revolution. 'I could not understand what I would feel before I stepped on the stage, because I never had any acting training except for studying with Misha. There was just the influence from his studio, where we used to spend days and nights.' This is the clearest possible admission from her own pen that she had not acted in the Moscow Art Theatre, as she had claimed on her arrival in Germany. It was a fiction she shamelessly maintained throughout her life. In her 1973 memoirs she lists 'The Most Important Theatrical Pieces in which I Played a Leading Role'. They include Russian productions of *The Cherry Orchard*, *The Three Sisters* and *Hamlet*, plays in which Misha had acted.

'The theatre is full all the time,' she wrote six days later, 16 March 1924. 'They are predicting that I will be a very good actress. It is hard for me to write to you about this because I find it so funny that I have become famous here and that people go to the theatre just to see me and that they believe in me.' She then made an interesting admission. 'I find that what I am able to give people in the theatre is simpler for me than life outside the theatre.'

She acted in three plays in four weeks, then left for ten days' filming in Rome and Florence. She returned to Berlin on 4 May and took up again the punishing routine of making films by day, then leaving the studio at Babelsberg to drive to the theatre for her evening performance. 'Of course it is very tiring to be filmed,' she told her aunt, who had never strayed from the stage, 'but one's got to get along.' In her case, this meant making as much money as possible. She now knew for certain that her mother, her daughter, Ada, and her niece, Marina Ried, were to arrive on 10 May. 'I've got to buy them clothes and find a place to live.' Olga wanted 'to earn a lot of money this summer', to take Ada and Marina 'to the south of France or Italy for six weeks'.

Before leaving Russia for the last time, Olga's mother, Lulu Knipper, took the seven-year-old Ada round to Misha's apartment to say goodbye. Misha, then at the height of his success in Moscow, never imagined that he too would soon follow the path of exile.

Aunt Olya went back with Lev to Germany that summer, visiting both Freiburg and Berlin. On their return to Russia, they went down to Yalta to see Aunt Masha, who was still guarding her brother's house as a shrine to his memory. After Moscow, the tall cypresses and the meridional warmth of the Crimea exerted an irresistible appeal. Aunt Olya, almost like a child, had a ritual on first catching sight of the sea. She would stand up in the railway carriage and bow to it, 'with a slightly guilty smile'.

They first visited Masha at the Chekhov house in Yalta. The local young ladies, hearing of their arrival, came over, ostensibly to pay their respects to Chekhov's widow, but also, it would appear, to make the acquaintance of her good-looking nephew. Lev was evidently an effective seducer, but one suspects that he gave little away emotionally.

After the visit to Yalta, the two holidaymakers from Moscow spent most of the time at Gurzuf, where Aunt Olya had the small seaside house left to her by Anton Chekhov. This simple house of whitewashed walls, terracotta tiles and pale green shutters was situated at the base of a promontory formed by dramatic rocks overlooking a small bay. The house had a handful of cypresses to provide a little shade from the blinding sunlight.

Soon after their return to Moscow, Aunt Olya received a letter from Masha in Yalta. 'I am now working for the Soviet state,' she wrote with a mixture of amusement and pride. 'I am now officially director of the Chekhov house-museum. Give my greetings to Lyova and tell him that he has put splinters into the hearts of local ladies. They are unable to forget him.' But the real reason for the letter came at the end: 1924 marked the twentieth anniversary of Chekhov's death and there was to be a celebration in the Kremlin to mark it. 'Tell me,' she wrote, 'how Lunacharsky sees Anton Pavlovich in the light of the present situation.'

Aunt Olya reported back a fortnight later. 'The commemoration of Anton Pavlovich did not go very well in my view,' she wrote. It had taken place in the Kremlin in the Hall of Columns. The audience consisted of two sharply opposite worlds, the lovers of the theatre and of Chekhov on the one hand, and hard-line Bolsheviks on the other. Aunt Olya had not enjoyed reading her memories of life with Chekhov to such a divided crowd. 'What was liked by one made the other sceptical . . . My memories could only be understood by an audience used to literary life. Lunacharsky spoke for a long time, but I did not listen and I told him so. He seemed to be talking about a "Chekhovist movement" which had not been understood correctly.'

In Berlin, Olga eagerly awaited the arrival of all her surviving family, save Lev. Her sister Ada was going to follow later. Olga had rented a new apartment with fifteen rooms at Klopstock Strasse 20 in the Tiergarten district of Berlin. There had been no problem with exit visas. Lulu Knipper arrived safely with the two little girls. They had taken the same sea route as Aunt Olya, down the Baltic from Leningrad to Stettin, but they were spared from dreadful weather.

The Klopstock Strasse apartment soon looked partially lived in, with icons and family photographs brought out of Russia by Lulu. But the walls seemed strangely bare in the principal living rooms, as if they were about to move on again. The revolution, the civil war and the death of her husband, Konstantin, had changed Lulu, now known to the whole family as Baba. From the musical young mother, she had become an imposing grey-haired, stout woman. She was also a very heavy smoker, with a gruff voice and manner, although her heart was warm.

Baba ran the household and dealt with the staff, while Olga earned the money in her punishing regime of work. As well as the cook, Baba oversaw the parlour maid, Olga's lady's maid, the chauffeur and an English governess for the two girls. The household – and the chaos – increased later with the arrival of Lux, a large white dog resembling a half-grown polar bear. The Knipper family, which Anton Chekhov had considered so very German in Moscow, seemed to become increasingly Russian during their exile in Berlin.

The Knipper matriarchy was, of course, surrounded by other Russian émigrés in the western part of Berlin. But Olga's social life revolved around her work, especially the theatre. She would go occasionally to grand receptions, where she could meet interesting and useful people. At the Ullstein Villa in the Grünewald, she met the foreign minister, Gustav Stresemann. In typical style, she claims not only to have become great friends with him, but that he arranged for her German citizenship.

She travelled frequently, sometimes making movies abroad, but always at a hectic pace. 'Dear Aunt Olya!' she wrote in April 1926. 'As you see, I am in Paris. I've come here to rest for ten days in between two films.' One of them was René Clair's *The Italian Straw Hat.* 'The most important thing is to get a breath of a different pace of life for the new film . . . Next winter I'll be playing with Reinhardt.'

That year she also had a role in a very German film, *Die Mühle von Sanssouci* (*The Mill of Sans Souci*). It was the first of several films glorifying Frederick the Great. The story in this case was impeccably democratic – Frederick wanted to pull down a mill overlooking his new palace of Sans Souci at Potsdam, but was thwarted by his own law courts. Yet almost anything about the Prussian king and legendary strategist held an almost sacred appeal to nationalists embittered by the Treaty of Versailles. Hitler, a fanatic of the cinema, would almost certainly have seen it, having already greatly admired Olga Chekhova in a movie earlier that year, *Brennende Grenze* or *Burning Frontiers.* Olga Chekhova, on the other hand, would probably have been barely aware of the future Führer's existence at this stage.

In July Olga wrote from Italy to her aunt, who was then staying with Masha in Yalta. 'I am stuck here again with filming. Yesterday we visited new archaeological works at Pompeii. My God, how interesting! Yesterday there was a little eruption of Vesuvius – the sight was grandiose. Did you get my [money] transfer? I will write again at the end of the month. Kisses and greetings to everyone.'

Having never been taken seriously by her aunt, especially after her disastrous marriage to Misha, it was hardly surprising that Olga could not resist alluding to her success. 'I will be here [in Berlin] until 15–20 October,' she wrote the following year, 'then off to London, and back here only at Christmas. Karenina is a big and beautiful role . . . In this film world every other word is "money", and every day away from here costs money. Sometimes it is so hard to live like this, like a gypsy. I have to travel because of my work, but what can one do? . . . They keep inviting me to America, but I am not going, I cannot work among people who have no heart and soul.' What she did not mention in the letter was that the movie she was making in Paris and London at that time was *Moulin Rouge*, which became a great *succès de scandale*.

Olga Chekhova was still trying to broaden her range of parts away from the typecasting of baroness and society beauty. In the French version of *Moulin Rouge*, she performed an erotic dance with a python wrapped round her, and the chorus line included many bare breasts. Even though *Moulin Rouge* proved a huge success all over Europe and in the United States, and at last made her an international star, it was one of the films which she failed to mention in her letters to Aunt Olya, in case it shocked her.

Olga was now thirty years old and playing the *grande dame* in real life, even if she tried to avoid it in front of the cameras. She commissioned a very expensive stained-glass panel with the Knipper coat of arms and her writing paper was embossed with a specially designed monogram, consisting of her initials in German, OT for Olga Tschechowa. She used it in her letters to her aunt, written always in pre-revolutionary style. She even insisted on referring to her aunt's address in its old form of Prechistensky bulvar, rather than its new name, Gogolevsky bulvar. Above all, she enjoyed inviting her aunt to stay in Berlin, insisting that she would pay for everything.

In September 1929, she wrote to her aunt from a film set in Bavaria. 'I am studying singing and learning to breathe properly, and studying English too. I am surprised at myself.' She was learning English because Hollywood, fascinated by European actresses such as Greta Garbo and Marlene Dietrich, felt compelled, as always, to try to replicate a winning formula.

The comedy *Die Drei von der Tankstelle* (*Three from the Filling Station*), her first 'talkie' in 1930, had also achieved international success. Later that year, Olga Chekhova sailed for New York from Cuxhaven on the transatlantic liner *Europa*. She was under contract to Universal to make a romantic comedy, *Love on Command*. In Hollywood, she went to parties with Greta Garbo, Douglas Fairbanks, Harold Lloyd and Charlie Chaplin. Chaplin asked her to teach him how to chew sunflower seeds in the true Russian style, spitting out the husks.

Olga Chekhova was deeply impressed by the technical advances which she encountered in American film-making. It was the first time that she had seen a camera able to move around, following the actors and the action. No longer did the actor have to play as if on a tiny stage. Yet her brief time in Hollywood was not a great success. In *Love on Command*, another talkie, Olga Chekhova's Russo-German accent proved rather too strong for American tastes. This was a major disadvantage, since Greta Garbo and Marlene Dietrich had already cornered the sophisticated Nordic market. The studio bosses also made it clear to her that she was overweight and demanded that she lose up to twenty pounds. Perhaps not surprisingly, Olga Chekhova strongly echoed her aunt's dislike of the United States when she returned home.

★

In Moscow, Lev had started to make a mark, but he had not yet achieved anything like the fame of his sister. The first public performance of his music took place in 1925 in the Revolution Theatre. The piece bore the slightly pretentious title 'Fairy Tales of a Plaster Idol'.

'It was shameful and scary,' Lev wrote many years later, 'because my music was disgusting. It must be the usual thing for any young composer when his music is played for the first time.' During a rehearsal, a famous critic had come in wearing an expensive coat open down the front and wearing a fur hat.

'"What are you playing there?" he asked.

'"It's my own composition."

'"Ah, it sounds very interesting."

'The next day this critic published a laudatory review of my music, which he did not really listen to. Others praised me too. Others warned me of "dangerous tendencies". I should give up a lot of clever inventions. I had to look for a simple and understandable musical language.'

Lev did not waste time consolidating a reputation, he wanted to move on. The following year he began work on an opera based on Voltaire's *Candide*. 'My dream was to perform it in the Leningrad Opera Theatre,' he wrote. Initially, the reaction to his work in Leningrad was clearly encouraging. 'They are making such a fuss about me here,' he wrote to Aunt Olya. 'I won't say it's unpleasant, but I don't swell up. I modestly oppose exaggerations and say that one shouldn't get carried away if the first act has been a success. This does not automatically mean that all the following acts would be as good.'

Perhaps they were not as good, or perhaps his overall scheme failed. He aimed to combine symphony music, opera, dancing and speaking. 'Even Radlov, who was a very daring producer,' Lev had to admit in later years, 'got scared by the complication of the whole performance and never staged it.'

That summer Lev spent as usual in the Crimea in Aunt Olya's house at Gurzuf. 'My life is still much the same: I see no one, go out only to play tennis. I am extremely well.' The competitive Lev was soon the tennis champion of the Crimea.

Then, like the rest of the family, he gravitated towards the complex of the Moscow Art Theatre. Nemirovich-Danchenko employed him as a consultant to its Music Theatre for opera in 1929, which suited Lev perfectly as he was determined to write a piece by which he would always be remembered. Nemirovich-Danchenko advised him on the first version of his adaptation of a play about a notorious incident during the civil war – the killing by the British of twenty-six commissars from Baku. In its final form as *North Wind*, the opera proved a considerable success.

A more sinister explanation has also been advanced for Lev's work with the Moscow Art Theatre. As an institution it was increasingly seen as 'politically unreliable' and Lev may well have been expected by his OGPU masters to report on his colleagues. There are even rumours that Aunt Olya was suspected of denouncing rivals and that she had promised young lovers in the cast that she would save them from arrest. Such stories are probably more indicative of the back-stabbing within the theatre than anything else. There is no evidence that either Lev or Aunt Olya denounced anybody, nor that any members of the company were arrested at this time. Lev may even have used his influence with the 'security organs', as he did later, to help friends.

Lev's controller at this time was Major of State Security, later Commissar of State Security, Viktor Ilin. Ilin worked in the secret political department and was in charge of running informers among the intelligentsia, 'and, more importantly, with persons among the intelligentsia and political figures who had relatives abroad'. During the 1920s, Lev's primary task for the OGPU had been to provide intelligence on émigré intellectuals, but he was also expected to report on Russians of German origin within the Soviet Union. Under Stalin, a new mood of xenophobia was developing along with the hunt for Trotskyists.

Misha Chekhov's greatest achievement on the Moscow stage was almost certainly his *Hamlet* of 1924 with the Second Studio of the Moscow Art Theatre. As well as the title Honoured Actor of the USSR, he was elected to the Moscow Soviet. But over the next three years he fell foul of the Soviet cultural authorities, including Lunacharsky. According to Misha's loyal cousin Sergei, 'his enemies spread a rumour that Misha's philosophy was counter-revolutionary'. His views, especially on dramatic art, were indeed counter-revolutionary, because Misha believed in artistic truth rather than Communist political correctness.

Opportunists began to create trouble for him at the theatre and he made a bad situation even worse for himself. During the winter of 1927–8, he did not create a single new role and in the following spring he and his wife, Xenia, went abroad. One rather tall tale claims that Misha had played chess with the notorious OGPU chief Yagoda and won, thus gaining an exit visa. Whether or not he had made up his mind before they left, it was soon clear that they would not return to the Soviet Union. Almost as soon as he had departed, rumours began to circulate that he was working in Vienna with Max Reinhardt. This later proved to be true. It could not have been a wiser decision. Misha would never have been able to stand the regime of Socialist Realism which began six years later. And he might well have suffered the same fate of torture and execution as Meyerhold.

When Misha and Xenia reached Berlin in 1928, his former wife, Olga, came to their rescue. She found them a small apartment near to her own so that eleven-year-old Ada could visit her father easily. But perhaps the most piquant part for her of this gentle reversal of fortunes was to direct Misha in her own film called *Der Narr seiner Liebe* (*The Fool of Love*). Shortly after Misha played the village idiot in the movie *Troika*, in which Olga starred.

Misha moved to Paris in 1931, where he played several of his most famous roles: Hamlet, Malvolio in *As You Like It* and Strindberg's *Erik XIV* in the Théâtre de Montmartre. Then, under the encouragement of a new Swiss admirer, Georgette Boner, he set up a company called the Théâtre de l'Avenue. They created a play, *Le Château s'éveille* (*The Castle Awakes*), based on the fairy tale of Prince Ivan.

Olga's sister, Ada, who had never enjoyed anything like her sister's success, joined her former brother-in-law's cast as '1st Witch'. Ada had clearly not accustomed herself to life outside Russia as easily as Olga. 'I both accept the West and push it away with all my force,' she wrote to Aunt Olya. 'I am avoiding people here, they are all strangers . . . I've enrolled as an actress here, and can you imagine, it's all going very successfully from the first play . . . Misha is content, he says I'm a good actress.'

In her letter, Ada recounted that everybody at home in Berlin was fine, but they were hard up. 'Olga only played in one film, in June.' This comparatively lean period would not last long, and soon Olga was working again as hard as ever. Her most successful movie at this time, *Liebelei*, directed by Max Ophüls, was a tragic romance based on Arthur Schnitzler's famous play about codes of honour in late-nineteenth-century Vienna. The storyline was typical of those inter-war years. A good-looking officer falls in love with a violinist's daughter, but a past love affair with a baroness comes back to haunt him.

Yet even during the six-month period of little work, Olga had shown hardly any inclination to become seriously involved with a man. Perhaps seeing Misha again had reminded her of the disadvantages of men trying to run her life.

Her brother, Lev, on the other hand, had married quite suddenly the previous year. His choice of partner was surprising for a supposedly penitent White Guardist. His wife, Lyubov Sergeevna Zalesskaya, was the daughter of a famous architect of noble family. She was daring, intelligent and avant-garde, and looked the part with short hair and tennis shoes. At a time of developing Stalinist conformity, it was almost shocking.

Lyuba and Lev moved in with Aunt Olya at 23 Gogolevsky bulvar, and a year later their son, Andrei, was born. The population of the apartment even included Lev's old nanny, Fanny Stangel, who still spoke only German. Lev himself, however, was hardly ever there. He was supposedly touring Central Asia, composing songs for the Red Army, to whose propaganda department he was now attached.

Lev's apparent freedom to roam seems extraordinary at such a time of bureaucratic controls. In 1930, the year of his marriage, he travelled down the Caucasus, through South Ossetia and along the Black Sea coast. He was fascinated by the polyphonic singing he had heard on the way, but his real reason for vowing to return was a growing obsession with the mountains themselves. 'I was addicted for ever,' he wrote later. He argued that this love of rock climbing was not to conquer peaks, but to explore his own limits of endurance, to train his will and to survive everything that nature put in his path.

As the tensions of the Stalinist regime began to build in the 1930s, the dangers would not come on a cliff-face. Nobody would be safe, even in their own apartment. Fear took on a different dimension as people lay in bed before dawn, awakened by the footsteps of an arrest squad rushing up the communal staircase. They relaxed only after they heard the hammering on somebody else's door.

14. The Totalitarian Years

On 30 January 1933, after a day of confusion and uncertainty, the evening paper in Berlin announced: 'Hitler Reichschancellor'. A few hours later, massed ranks of SA Brown Shirts marched in a victory parade through the floodlit Brandenburg Gate. Their supporters on both sides of the Pariser Platz cheered and chanted, their arms erect in the Nazi salute.

From the windows of the Adlon Hotel, the rich looked on as if from theatre boxes, still unable to take such vulgar street drama seriously. But even those who could imagine what it signified experienced a sense of angry disbelief. There were many who loathed the Nazis in Berlin, a city which had always taken pride in its irreverent jokes. The Nazi vote, to the frustration of Goebbels, who had been put in charge of the party in the capital, had always been lower than anywhere else. But the parade that evening was a warning that electoral percentages were about to become as irrelevant as the rule of law.

Those who believed that such a grotesque political movement could not last long were rapidly disabused. Carnival in Berlin, a more nervous one than in previous years, was suddenly pushed aside by the Reichstag fire on 28 February. The Nazis had called the Reichstag a 'hot air factory', but Hitler, seizing the opportunity, promoted it to the symbol of German civilization. Well before dawn, the first Nazi snatch squads were on their way to arrest Communists and Socialists alike. Within hours, emergency legislation gave Hitler total power.

Even after the suspension of all civil liberties, many Berlin Jews still joked that they had passed through the Red Sea and

that they would 'pass through the brown shit'. Others had a
clearer idea of what was at stake. Left-wingers and Jews in the
theatre and cinema would never be allowed to work again.
Ernst Toller and Max Reinhardt soon left for the United
States. Altogether that year, 40,000 Jews left Germany, including twenty Nobel laureates, Einstein among them. Others in
artistic and scientific circles waited much longer, in many cases
until 1938, to see whether their world would return to its
senses. Conrad Veidt, who in 1931 had starred with Olga
Chekhova in *Die Nacht der Entscheidung* (*The Night of Decision*),
left because his wife was Jewish. Yet he later became famous
in the English-speaking world for his role as Major Strasser 'of
the Third Reich' in *Casablanca*.

The very fact of staying enforced a large degree of collaboration on actors who continued to work. Some of the theatrical
anecdotes which tried to mitigate their complicity with the
regime were less than convincing. Olga Chekhova recounted
the following story. She and a friend, the elderly comic actress
Adele Sandrock, who called her 'Mouse' (presumably because
she was so unmouselike), were apparently invited to the propaganda ministry, known to Berliners as the Promi. 'Adele had
some fluffy garment wrapped around her and had a huge
embroidered handbag. Hitler appeared and started one of his
monologues as always. He said that he knew the Burgtheater,
where Adele was playing, and he had admired their previous
plays, but he had to point out that in a recent performance
Jewish actors had been enthusiastically applauded. Adele interrupted him. "Herr Reichschancellor," she said. "Please drop
this subject. I don't want to hear about it. But between you
and me, I must admit that my best lovers were Jewish." Hitler
was stunned into silence. Adele got up from her chair, turned
to Olga Konstantinovna. "Mouse, can you take me home,
please?"

'"Of course, dear Adele," she said, and bade Hitler and Goebbels farewell: *"Alles Gute, meine Herren."*'

This highly dubious vignette raises a question about Olga Chekhova's first meeting with Hitler. Her version of events depended upon her audience. In her two post-war volumes of memoirs, she of course played down her contacts as much as possible. She was also a good deal less than frank in her written report for Abakumov, the chief of SMERSh, in Moscow in May 1945. Yet she did reveal in her first SMERSh interview in Berlin on 29 April, while the fighting still raged in the city, that she had been presented to Hitler very soon after the Nazi takeover:

Q [COLONEL SHKURIN]: Did you happen to meet leaders of the German fascist state?

A [OLGA CHEKHOVA]: When Hitler came to power in 1933 I was invited to a reception given by Propaganda Minister Goebbels where Hitler was also present. I and other actors were introduced to Hitler. He expressed his pleasure at meeting me. Also he expressed his interest in Russian art and in my aunt, Olga Leonardovna Chekhova.

It is a great pity that she did not record in more detail Hitler's opinions on Russian art. Would he, like Lenin, have enjoyed the plays of Chekhov, while wanting to exterminate the human material in which they were set? Or was he, the arriviste dictator, simply fawning upon a star he had worshipped in his years as an outcast?

Both Hitler and Goebbels were obsessed with the cinema. Goebbels is estimated to have seen more than 1,100 films in the dozen years of the Nazi regime. On Hitler's fiftieth birthday, Goebbels presented him with a collection of 120 movies for the screening room in the Führer's Alpine retreat, the Berghof.

Albert Speer later recounted how Hitler used to keep them up into the early hours of the morning, lecturing them on what they had just seen as if he were a frustrated movie critic.

Hitler was also fascinated by the Swedish actress Zarah Leander, who was frequently compared to Olga Chekhova. Leander was famous for her singing in a low, husky voice. Hitler used to coax his adored dog, Blondi, to sing when he wanted to impress his inner circle of secretaries and officers at the Berghof. Then, when she began to give voice, he would say: 'Sing lower, Blondi, sing like Zarah Leander!' and she would howl like a wolf. It has recently emerged that Zarah Leander was probably a much more active agent for Soviet intelligence than Olga Chekhova. Leander, who was given the NKVD codename of 'Rose-Marie', had the advantage of being able to travel back to Sweden, where she could make contact unseen with her controller, Zoya Rybkina, the deputy *rezident* in Stockholm. Rybkina would not have been informed of Olga Chekhova at that time, but Beria made Rybkina Olga Chekhova's controller in extraordinary circumstances in 1953, as will be seen later.

For Hitler and Goebbels, the movies were a make-believe world of intoxicating power. Nazism, like Communism, had copied much from the Church, but it owed just as big a debt to the artifical glamour and emotions of the *Kino*. It is highly significant that the Nazis saw nothing strange in the idea of politics imitating popular art. It was part of their breathtaking irresponsibility. Of course, Hitler and Goebbels also saw the cinema as a powerful weapon of propaganda and social engineering. The Nazification of the industry was vital for their purposes and UFA returned to the role originally planned for its prototype in 1917.

Yet this was not an entirely dramatic change of course.

During the two years before Hitler's assumption of power, the UFA studios, financed by right-wing money, had produced a series of strongly patriotic historical movies, such as *Der Choral von Leuthen*, another Frederick the Great film in which Olga Chekhova starred, *Yorck*, the hero of the Prussian volte-face against Napoleon, and *Der schwarze Husar* (*The Black Hussar*). Another film, the story of a heroic struggle by a German U-Boat crew against a British destroyer during the First World War, happened to be launched on the day after the Nazi assumption of power.

In the beginning, the new rulers of Germany also needed glamour, especially at their government receptions. Most of the heavily built Nazi wives constituted both an aesthetic and a social embarrassment. Some of the leaders themselves were little better. Himmler, according to Olga Chekhova, used to shuffle his feet. He was both gauche and uneasy in female company. The presence of movie stars, especially one like Olga Chekhova, famous for her roles as a baroness, was important for the *nouveaux puissants*. It was slightly reminiscent of Napoleon's hope that the young émigré nobles whom he had allowed to return would raise the tone of his court. But the cosmopolitan sophistication of stars like Olga Chekhova was also needed to make the regime more acceptable internationally.

Olga's mother, Baba Knipper, was indignant when an early-morning call summoned her daughter to an early-evening reception given by Goebbels. 'What sort of manners is it to invite a lady by telephone in the morning to command her to come to something in the afternoon?' she demanded. Olga Chekhova, a true professional, was far more concerned with the effect on the day's filming, which did not finish until seven. Her director, however, told her that she must go. Nobody at Babelsberg could afford to thwart the Reichsminister for Propaganda and People's Enlightenment. As Olga left the studio, she found a 'little man' from the propaganda ministry waiting to drive her in a sports car to the reception in the Wilhelm Strasse. On the way, she insisted that he stop so that she could buy a rose to smarten up her dress.

Magda Goebbels, the only *grande dame* the Nazi regime possessed, reproved her gently. 'So late, Frau Chekhova.'

'I came here straight from work, Frau Goebbels,' she replied, 'and I only received the invitation by telephone this morning.'

Hitler on this occasion was talking about what he expected from the arts, which led him on to the subject of his own painting as a young man. He spoke to Olga Chekhova about her movie *Burning Frontiers*, released in 1926. 'Hitler flooded me with compliments,' she recounted, and she remarked on his 'Austrian courtesy'. In her view Hitler made an effort to be charming, while Dr Goebbels succeeded by dint of tremendous application, 'a polished intellect' and a sun-ray lamp. According to one of Hitler's secretaries, her counterparts at the propaganda ministry used to rush to the window to watch him leave the building. 'Oh,' they gushed to her amazement, 'if you only knew what eyes Goebbels has, and what an enchanting smile!'

Goebbels often described Olga Chekhova in his diaries as '*eine charmante Frau*', but how far he attempted to exercise his own charm with her is not known. The Reichsminister for Propaganda was so famous for his casting-couch tactics that starlets were known as '*Goebbels-Gespielin*' or 'Goebbels playthings'. Berliners used to joke that he did not sleep in his own bed, but in his own big mouth, because the slang word for mouth – '*Klappe*' – also meant a clapperboard in the movies.

The diminutive and club-footed 'Goat of Babelsberg' was not, however, all-conquering. His pouncing was seen as an unpleasant rite of passage to be brushed off by those who had the courage. The actress Irene von Meyendorff said of him:

'*Ach, der mit seinem Regenwurm!*' ('Oh, him with his little worm!')

Goebbels probably did not really love women. He just needed to conquer them because he had a severe inferiority complex due to his physical limitations. One of the intriguing paradoxes is that Goebbels preferred exotic-looking women and was not attracted by the stereotypes of blonde Aryan beauty which he lauded in his propaganda films. Nevertheless, all that can be said in his favour is that his approach was less brutal than Beria's technique of kidnap, rape and then Gulag for those who resisted.

The Goat of Babelsberg's greatest mistake was to fall dramatically in love with a young Czech actress called Lida Baarova. He met her just before the 1936 Berlin Olympics on the set of the aptly named movie *Stunde der Versuchung* (*Hour of Temptation*). Lida Baarova, who was slim and extraordinarily beautiful, with wonderful eyes, lived with her co-star, Gustav Fröhlich. They shared a house close to the Goebbels villa on the Schwanenwerder peninsula next to Wannsee. Fröhlich is said to have surprised the secret lovers in the back of a car. According to some versions, Fröhlich punched the Reichsminister for Propaganda, but he is more likely to have taken it out on Lida Baarova.

The rumours in movie and Nazi circles intensified over the next eighteen months. Goebbels tried to cover his tracks in the evening. On several occasions, he invited himself to Olga Chekhova's apartment to provide himself with an alibi. Not surprisingly, he was unable to keep the affair secret. When confronted by his outraged wife, Magda, he told her that he wanted a divorce. This was unwise. Magda was a formidable opponent. She worshipped Hitler, and he in return admired her enormously for her *damenhaft*, or 'ladylike' qualities, which were so rare among the wives of the Nazi élite.

Hitler was furious when Magda Goebbels told him what

was happening. He had no idea, because nobody around him had dared to repeat the stories. Goebbels was the great propagator of Nazi family values. His ministry had even issued an immodest amount of newsreel footage about the perfection of the large Goebbels family, with a row of shining, well-drilled children, almost as if they constituted the *ersatz* royal family of the National Socialist state. And now Goebbels wanted to divorce Magda and marry a non-German – in fact a Slav. Hitler clearly thought that his most trusted deputy had taken leave of his senses. Goebbels was told in very harsh terms that he must return to his wife immediately. Lida Baarova was never to be seen in Berlin again. Her last movie for UFA was *Preussische Liebegeschichte* (*Prussian Love Story*) in 1938. She returned to Prague that autumn, just as a far more tragic event befell her country as a result of the Munich agreement.

A frenzy of gossip had spread from Babelsberg back to the capital. Berliners of all political persuasions were fascinated by the tale of the Reichsminister's thwarted love affair. Goebbels, who had been one of Hitler's closest friends, now found himself distanced from his beloved leader. The two of them only really became close again during the final days in Berlin in April 1945, when Goebbels proved himself to be the sole leading Nazi prepared to die with his Führer. Not only that, he and Magda were ready to kill all of their six idealized children to save them from the horrors of a non-Nazi world. Goebbels never saw Lida Baarova again, but he had kept a photograph of her hidden in his desk until just before his decision to destroy the whole family. It was one of the last things he burned at Schwanenwerder as the Red Army approached the outskirts of Berlin.

A curious part of the relationship between politics and culture is the way that artists and writers generally achieve a far greater significance in a dictatorship than in a democracy. They are either demonized as traitors – Mandelstam remarked that poetry was nowhere so highly valued as in Russia, where people were shot for it – or, if compliant, seen as a status symbol for the regime, bolstering the vanity of the tyrant. Stalin, for example, spent almost as much effort in persuading the writer Maxim Gorky to return to the Soviet Union from his exile in Italy as he had in forcing Trotsky to leave.

Gorky and Lenin had been very close before the revolution, but Lenin had forced his increasingly outspoken friend to leave the country. 'If you won't go, then we'll have to send you,' Lenin had told him in October 1920. Gorky had finally left a year later. Although strongly on the side of the revolution, he had been a fearless critic of the Bolshevik suppression of other parties. His great achievement was to save the intelligentsia of Petrograd from starvation or arrest by the Cheka. Gorky's pronouncements from abroad on Bolshevik tyranny were one of the most painful thorns in the side of the regime. Yet when wooed by Stalin, who begged him to put his great art at the service of the Russian people, Gorky found it hard to refuse. He returned for the first time in 1928, not realizing that the OGPU was infiltrating and bribing his entourage. Yagoda, the terrifying chief of the OGPU, had been ordered by Stalin to stay close to Gorky.

In 1932, Stalin ordered a massive celebration to honour Gorky's forty years as a writer. Countless streets, factories and collective farms were named after him; even the city and region of Nizhny Novgorod. The main park in Moscow became Gorky Park, and the Moscow Art Theatre had his name attached, despite a reminder to Stalin that Chekhov was the playwright most associated with it. 'That doesn't matter,' Stalin retorted. 'Gorky is a vain man. We must bind him with cables to the party.'

Gorky seems to have mislaid all the intellectual honesty he had shown in his earlier years. Above all, he failed to perceive a truth which the optimistic Stanislavsky had taken a decade to recognize. 'Revolution,' wrote Stanislavsky, 'violates art, stuffing it with sharpness of form and content', an observation as true of the National Socialist revolution as it was of the Communist. Stalin's cruellest humiliation for Gorky in that year of his celebration was to make him approve a far more intensive stage in this process.

On 26 October 1932, a party was organized in the Moscow mansion on the Boulevard Ring which Stalin had presented to him. The gathering was a curious mixture of Kremlin leaders and around fifty members of the Soviet literary élite. Politically unreliable writers and poets, such as Osip Mandelstam, Anna Akhmatova, Mikhail Bulgakov, Boris Pasternak and Isaac Babel had been deliberately excluded. Food and drink were served on tables covered in white tablecloths and the chandeliers were dazzlingly bright. After a variety of speeches, Comrade Stalin himself spoke. He expounded the doctrine of what was to be called Socialist Realism and announced that writers should be 'engineers of the human soul', and added that the production of souls was more important than the production of tanks. Socialist Realism should depict 'the heroic present in brighter tones and speak of it in a more elevated and dignified manner'. In other words, it meant that all artists and writers were to be conscripted into the service of Stalinist propaganda. Even Goebbels himself would not have dared go so far. Gorky said nothing.

Musicians at this stage were under less pressure to conform than writers, yet Lev Knipper, who ten years before had taken such pride in controversial experimentation, was now receiving a great deal of approval.

He was obviously treated more seriously by the OGPU. Lieutenant Colonel of State Security Maklyarsky had taken over as his controller from Major Ilin. Other officers were also involved in his work, including Lieutenant Colonel of State Security Marsia. With such backing, Lev enjoyed a great deal of travel at this time in his guise as musical adviser to the political directorate of the Red Army. In 1932 he had been 'unexpectedly asked to join a team of actors and go with them as an amateur instructor through Siberia and down the Amur to Sakhalin and back to Vladivostok'.

He certainly made use of the experience. The following year, his Third Symphony, known as 'The Far Eastern Symphony', was performed for the first time in the Central House of the Red Army and highly praised. These could be dangerous times for a composer. In 1934, Stalin famously walked out of the first performance of Shostakovich's opera *Lady Macbeth of Mtsensk*. This triggered an immediate attack by *Pravda* under the heading 'Nonsense instead of Music'. Lev, on the other hand, was taking no chances with the avant-garde. In 1934, he worked on his Fourth Symphony, a work that was politically irreproachable. The original idea had been a set of four symphonic marches set in the civil war, but the final version took a more narrative form in honour of a Komsomol member who was a hero of the time. Some twenty years later, it was turned into an opera called *The Komsomol Soldier*.

Whatever Lev's work for the OGPU at this stage, it is striking how hard the former White Guard who had fought on the other side was trying to redeem his past. It is impossible to say whether this was out of a new attempt to convince himself of the rightness of the Soviet regime or because he sensed the looming Terror. He was clearly trying to persuade himself that somehow he had been reborn. 'I am thinking about you, "Aunt who's given birth to her nephew",' he suddenly wrote to Aunt Olya. 'I think back to the years of my "birth" – 1919–1922.'

The great success of his Fourth Symphony in the Soviet Union was assured by a musical theme which later became known as the song 'Polyushko polye' – roughly translated as 'My Field, My Sweet Field'. Even its usually less than modest composer was astonished by the effect it had. 'I didn't realize then that I had discovered a pearl,' he wrote later. While working on the symphony, he had asked the poet Viktor Gusev to write a song to accompany this particular tune. In a very short time it was being sung all over the Soviet Union.

Lev was amused and complimented to hear that everyone imagined it to be a traditional folk song. But the scale of his ambition was revealed a few years later, when his young cousin Vova, the son of the opera singer Vladimir Knipper, asked why he did not write any more songs. 'Songs don't live long,' Lev answered, 'and I want to write things which last for ever.'

Lev was away from Moscow a great deal in the early 1930s. He travelled in Buryat Mongolia and with Gusev on a ship called the *Paris Commune*. He spent time afloat with the navy, running musical master classes on warships and even torpedo boats. But whenever he could, he returned to the Caucasus for rock climbing. He composed a symphonic poem after looking out from the Caucasian mountains, thinking of the civil war.

Sometimes his wife, Lyuba, and their little son, Andrei, accompanied him. But Andrei's happiest memories of childhood came from living in Aunt Olya's apartment at 23 Gogolevsky bulvar. The little boy loved the improvised parties when people dropped by. But this was not to last once the cycle of arrests and forced denunciations began.

★

In the summer of 1936, the rising of Nationalist generals in Spain led by General Franco began the Spanish Civil War. Stalin was loath to become involved, even though a Popular Front government was being attacked. Trostky condemned his inaction from abroad and a furious Stalin was forced to react. News of International Brigade volunteers encouraged Vadim Shverubovich, Lev's friend from the 'years of his birth', to put his name forward. Vadim, Kachalov's son, could not resist a war, but since he had been on the wrong side in the last one it was not entirely surprising that the OGPU should treat his application with deep suspicion. He belatedly understood that the Soviet definition of a 'volunteer' was not the same as in other countries. The only Soviet citizens being sent to Spain were designated Red Army officers and members of the OGPU with the task of eliminating Trotskyists abroad.

Another of Lev's adventure-loving friends did, however, go to Spain. Paul Armand, a colourful Lithuanian who had saved himself from starving in Paris by becoming a pickpocket, was sent as part of the small Soviet tank force. Their T-26 tanks helped smash the Nationalist attempts to encircle Madrid in the autumn of that year. For conspicuous if not foolhardy bravery, he received the gold star of Hero of the Soviet Union. But like other veterans of the war, Armand was to suffer on his return to Russia. Influenced by Stalin, the OGPU had started to suspect almost anyone, including their own colleagues in the Inostrannyi Otdel, or Foreign Intelligence Department, of being tainted with treason simply for having had contact with foreigners.

In that autumn of 1936, Olga Chekhova, to the surprise of all her family, concluded her own foreign alliance. At this time, a year after she had been appointed *Staatsschauspielerin*, or 'Actress of the State', by the Nazi regime, she had just finished filming Willi Forst's *Burgtheater*. 'Our Olga has made up her mind to get married by Christmas,' her sister, Ada, wrote to Aunt Olya. 'I still can't quite get used to it in my mind, but it's more than likely to happen. After two "mad" weeks in Berlin, Olga took off for Brussels. The "fiancé" is Belgian, almost a millionaire, forty-one years old, very good-looking. Maybe it will all turn out well this time. He produces a good, very special, impression, has a huge place in Brussels, and no end of money.'

Olga Chekhova's wedding to her Belgian businessman, Marcel Robyns, took place at the registry office in Berlin-Charlottenburg on 19 December 1936. Olga wore a fur coat and her silver-haired bridegroom wore a black silk top hat. The reception took place at the Hotel Bristol. Olga Chekhova may have been marrying a foreigner, but she had been reassured on one point. On the day before the wedding, Hitler had invited her to a small breakfast reception in the Reichschancellery. During their conversation, he gave her permission to retain her German nationality. This may well have been at Goebbels's instigation. He had made plain his determination to help the month before in his diary. 'I will do it gladly,' he wrote. 'She is a charming woman.'

Olga's sister, Ada, went to Brussels to stay with the newly married couple a month later, in January 1937. Reading between the lines of Ada's letter to Aunt Olya in Moscow, all was not well with the marriage from the start. One suspects that Marcel Robyns had simply wanted to acquire a trophy wife, while Olga had sought security away from the hectic world of Babelsberg. All she found was a sense of claustrophobia. From being the central figure in the Knipper matriarchy in Berlin, she suddenly found herself expected to play a very subsidiary role entertaining his boring business associates.

The apartment on the Avenue des Nations in Brussels was

very modern in the Art Deco style. Even the dining plates were made out of black glass. Yet Olga lacked her 'own little corner, where one could sit cosily'. The couple had four servants and, in true Belgian style, the food was munificent. 'There are always people in the house – all of them businessmen. Conversations are in French, German, English, Dutch, Flemish, and Russian.' Ada now had very mixed feelings about her new brother-in-law. 'He is a very good and decent man, looks extremely well, very pampered, but he is a hard, dry businessman. One feels quite uneasy in his company, and somehow it's not comfortable here in spite of all the external beauty. Olga cheered up when I arrived. She wants to go to Berlin with me for a couple of weeks – she is better off there.'

Marcel Robyns came as often as he could to Berlin to bask in the reflected glory of his wife, especially during the great success of her role in the play *Der Blaufuchs* (*The Blue Fox*). Olga's friends dubbed him 'Herr Tschechowa' behind his back. She and her family began to be increasingly irritated by his presence. He then brought his own family to stay at Olga's apartment at 74 Kaiserdamm.

'We have had guests staying for three weeks,' Ada wrote to Aunt Olya. 'Olga's husband, his mother, and his daughter with a governess. We had to employ a cook, and I slept in a corner in Mother's room, Olga was feeling nervous and always escaped from the house, as every evening she is performing, with a stunning success, in *Der Blaufuchs*. The theatre is always full, Olga is spoken about as a remarkable actress. And our Belgians have turned the whole household upside down. To make things worse, Maman [Robyns] does not speak a word of German, and Marcel is afraid to go out on his own. It's a mystery to me why Olga married him, as she has to pay for everything with her own money.'

Another thought crossed Ada's mind. 'I've been thinking that maybe you don't really want to receive letters from us any more,' she wrote in the same letter. The show trials in the Soviet Union and the atmosphere of Stalinist xenophobia had been reported in the German press. It would not be long before the two sides of the Knipper family, the German and the Russian, would be split by greater events.

15. The Great Terror

It may seem strange that the Knipper family correspondence between Nazi Germany and the Soviet Union should have been able to continue until the end of 1937. But there can be little doubt that the NKVD was far more thorough in its censorship of letters and the examination of parcels than the remarkably idle Gestapo.

Olga Chekhova had clearly enjoyed playing 'the American uncle' with her presents from abroad in the early 1930s. She had sent her young cousin Vova (the son of her Uncle Vladimir) a series of gifts: a German alphabet when he was a baby, then a sweater, then a suit. Finally, she sent him a gnome with eyes which lit up with a crackle when you pressed a button. She also sent Lev's son, Andrei, a sailor suit, as if the Tsarist fashion for dressing children remained *de rigueur* in the Soviet Union.

Vova asked his father who had sent him the gnome. 'Papa flew into a fury and talked loudly for a long time, saying that they were going mad in Germany.' He showed Vova a photograph of a beautiful woman wearing a white summer dress and told him that she was his cousin and an actress in the movies. Vova's father then hid the gnome and the photograph of Olga Chekhova in the bottom drawer of his desk and ordered Vova not to say anything to anybody about the present or about the members of the family in Germany. The Knippers in Moscow had been getting increasingly nervous since 1934. They were not only of German origin, they were also members of the closely watched artistic community.

★

The dragooning of artists for political purposes in the Soviet Union involved measures against any recalcitrants. Action against 'counter-revolutionary writers' who rejected Socialist Realism began comparatively gently, then intensified along with the Great Terror of 1937 and 1938.

During the night of 16 May 1934, soon after the poet Anna Akhmatova reached the apartment of Osip and Nadezhda Mandelstam, three OGPU operatives burst in. (The OGPU became the NKVD two months later.) They examined every scrap of paper and took every book to pieces. The object of their search was a copy of a poem about Stalin which Mandelstam had recited to friends. One of them must have been an informer. The OGPU officers never found the poem, but Mandelstam was forced to write it out for them at the Lubyanka, with the introductory confession: 'I am the author of the following poem of a counter-revolutionary nature.' Its most dangerous line referred to Stalin's 'large laughing cockroach eyes'.

At first Mandelstam was sent into internal exile. Perhaps Stalin did not want to attract too much controversy. But a second arrest and condemnation to the labour camps left him, a sick man, with no hope of survival. He died on 27 December 1938 in a transit camp outside Vladivostok. He was buried in a mass grave for Gulag prisoners. In a final, unintentional insult, the NKVD even spelt the writer's name wrong on the death certificate.

The event which provided the rationale for Stalin's purges took place on 1 December 1934, when Sergei Kirov, the chief of the Communist Party in Leningrad, was assassinated. This was Stalin's equivalent of the Reichstag fire. All civil liberties, notional though they had been already, were suspended. The NKVD started to work night and day as the witch-hunt against Trotskyist saboteurs widened to include almost anyone with

1. Victory celebrations in Red Square, 9 May 1945.

2. The searchlights and fireworks of victory night, 9 May 1945.

3. Anton Chekhov reading *The Seagull* to the Moscow Art Theatre, 1898: (rear left) Nemirovich-Danchenko; (central group) Olga Knipper-Chekhova (Aunt Olya), Stanislavsky, Chekhov and Lilina (Stanislavsky's wife); (far right) Meyerhold.

4. Stanislavsky, Gorky and Lilina, Yalta, 1900.

5. Anton Chekhov and Olga Knipper-Chekhova.

6. Konstantin and Lulu Knipper in the Caucasus soon after their marriage.

7. The Knipper children in 1904: Lev, Ada and Olga (right).

8. A rather larger Lulu Knipper, with Olga (behind), Ada and Lev on Konstantin's lap.

9. *The Cherry Orchard*, with Vasily Kachalov as Trofimov and Olga Knipper-Chekhova as Ranyevskaya.

10. Konstantin Knipper in front, with Aunt Olya holding her beloved nephew Lev, young Olga (with Ada just behind) and Kachalov.

11. Lubyanka Square in Moscow before the First World War.

12. The future Olga
Chekhova with a dog,
c. 1913.

13. Lev Knipper in cadet
uniform, 1912.

14. Cousins and friends in 1914:
(back row) Misha Chekhov,
unidentified, Volodya Chekhov;
(front) Stanislavsky's son Igor, Ada
and Olga.

15. Members of the bourgeoisie trying to sell their possessions to survive, 1918.

16. Red troops on an armoured train in the civil war.

17. Olga Chekhova assaulted by a Red Guard in the controversial silent movie *Der Todesreigen* (*Dance of Death*, 1922).

18. Olga with Oskar Homulka (right) in *Brennende Grenze* (*Burning Frontiers*, 1926), the film in which Hitler so admired her.

19. Olga, the rising star in Germany, with her Talbot convertible and chauffeur.

20. Olga, the star of the first *Moulin Rouge* (1928).

21. Olga Chekhova directing her ex-husband Misha Chekhov in *Der Narr seiner Liebe* (*The Fool of Love*, 1930).

22. Left: in *Die Nacht der Entscheidung* (*The Night of Decision*, 1931) with Conrad Veidt, later famous as Major Strasser in *Casablanca*.

23. Olga in *Liebelei* (1931) by Max Ophüls.

24. Olga in *Der Favorit der Kaiserin* (*The Empress's Favourite*, 1936) with Ada, her daughter by Misha Chekhov (right), and Adele Sandrock (left).

25. Top left: Lev Knipper, Lyuba and their son Andrei, 1931.

26. Top right: Lev Knipper in Red Army uniform, 1936.

27. Left: Lev Knipper, composer and NKVD agent, 1938.

28. Olga Chekhova's wedding to Marcel Robyns, Berlin, December 1936. Her sister Ada (left), her new mother-in-law and her daughter, Ada (front right).

29. Olga celebrates New Year 1938 surrounded by friends from the Babelsberg film studios.

30. Olga and Willi Forst in *Bel Ami* (1939).

31. Olga Chekhova
with Hitler.

32. Olga's lover Jep, the Luftwaffe fighter
pilot in the Battle of Britain.

33. Ribbentrop's reception, May 1939: (front row) Göring, Annelise
von Ribbentrop, Hitler and Olga Chekhova. Field Marshal Keitel
is behind Hitler.

34. Olga with Wehrmacht troops in Paris, October 1940.

35. Olga visits a Luftwaffe fighter wing in September 1940, during the Battle of Britain.

36. Mariya Garikovna, Lev's fellow NKVD agent and second wife.

37. Lev and his fellow composer Prokofiev, 1941.

38. Red Army troops march past Stalin in Red Square on their way to fight the Wehrmacht at the gates of Moscow, 7 November 1941.

39. Lev in Teheran in the grounds of the Soviet embassy, 1942.

40. Olga with Rudolf Prack in *Der ewige Klang* (*The Eternal Tune*, 1944), one of the very last films produced by the Nazi film industry.

41. Abakumov, the chief of SMERSh, receives the Order of Kutuzov 1st Class on 21 April 1945, just before he has Olga flown back to Moscow from Berlin.

42. Lev and Aunt Olya soon after the war.

43. Lev climbing again in the Caucasus after the war.

44. Olga Chekhova, along with Konrad Lorenz, receives the Cross of the Order of Merit in 1972.

foreign contacts. Soviet authorities later admitted that between 1935 and 1940, 19 million people were arrested, of whom over 7 million died, either in the Gulag or by execution.

In Moscow, the executions took place in specially constructed cellars with sloping concrete floors which could be hosed down. Bodies were burned in the ovens of the Donskoi monastery in central Moscow and ash covered the whole area as if from a reactivating volcano. Thousands of others were driven out in covered trucks to Butovo, where KGB officers later built their dachas. 'The execution squads worked in a terrible hurry, day and night, the shots drowned out by the deafening noise of the running engines. People were lined up above a previously dug trench and shot . . . They filled in the pit, levelled off the earth and prepared another trench.' In a typical touch of the Soviet 'security organs', orchards were planted over the graves to hide their crimes, and so that the citizens of Moscow could benefit in ignorance from these enemies of the people.

The main frenzy of denunciations, false accusations and forced confessions of the Great Terror was known in Russia as the 'Yezhovshchina', after the diminutive NKVD chief Nikolai Yezhov. Stalin had put this wildly unstable character in charge of what became known as the 'mincing machine'. He was given every encouragement, only to be punished later for all the 'excesses'. Stalin brought in his fellow Georgian Lavrenty Beria as Yezhov's deputy in July 1938, then crushed Yezhov at the end of the year.

An imperceptible hint of the horrors to come from Nazi Germany reached Aunt Masha in Yalta in the summer of 1935. A postcard arrived from Berlin showing Olga Chekhova in one of her roles. On the other side, Olga's sister, Ada, asked Masha to send a 'certain document' as soon as possible.

The document in question, a deposition finally signed in
Yalta on 14 August 1935 by Aunt Masha and her brother
Mikhail Chekhov, testified that the Chekhov family was
entirely of Russian Orthodox descent. This was because Olga
Chekhova's daughter, Ada, was at risk. Misha's mother, Natalya
Golden, had been Jewish. Olga Chekhova had decided to act
quickly, having perhaps heard at some propaganda ministry
reception of the forthcoming Nuremberg Laws, which were
announced at the Nazi Party rally in September.

Aunt Masha and her brother were prepared to perjure
themselves in a good cause. 'There were not any persons of
non-Christian faith in our family, either on our father's or
our mother's side,' they wrote. 'Our late brother Alexander
Pavlovich Chekhov was married to a resident of Moscow,
Natalya Alexandrovna Galdina, Russian and Orthodox Chris-
tian.' Misha's mother, with her name changed from Golden
to Galdina, became a Gentile posthumously. The registration
fee was two roubles.

Apart from a small group in the Kremlin, hardly anybody
in the Soviet Union knew of Hitler's racist theories. 'Fascism'
was never explained in anything other than the most misleading generalities. It was, according to Stalinist definition, the
most extreme form of capitalism and thus the Antichrist to
Communism. Yet Stalinism was to produce its own version
of xenophobia. Foreign Communists sheltering within the
Soviet Union, especially Germans, Poles and Yugoslavs, were
at great risk. Meanwhile, Soviet citizens of German origin,
like the Knippers, risked becoming the Jews of Stalinist totali-
tarianism. Lev Knipper was later to be accorded a special role
in the filtration process.

During the Great Terror, Lev, like hundreds of thousands of
Soviet citizens, was clearly going through a personal and

political crisis. He was trying desperately to convince himself of the rightness of the Stalinist purges, even when surrounded by the madness of arrests and denunciations all around him. We have no proof that he was directly involved in such NKVD work himself, yet he knew many of those who were arrested, especially in the purges in the Crimea, where many of Aunt Olya's friends disappeared.

The first hint within the family of Lev's political harshness had emerged suddenly during a New Year party, almost certainly for 1937, at 23 Gogolevsky bulvar. Aunt Olya asked young Vova Knipper to call everyone to the table. '*Gospoda!*' he called out, meaning ladies and gentlemen. Lev interrupted him. 'Volodya, ladies and gentlemen are long gone to the bottom of the Black Sea and fish are feeding on them.' Those present were clearly shocked at this remark coming from a former White Guard who had himself escaped across the Black Sea.

'Really?' said Aunt Olya, clearly not agreeing with Lev. '*Gospoda*, will you please come to the table?'

In early April 1937, not long after the second wave of show trials, Lev wrote a striking letter to Aunt Olya. 'My life has become a lot more complicated, confused, and harder than it was before, when I still had many illusions of youth, self-importance, young unspent strength and boiling energy which covered up for everything else. And now the time has come to pay the bills. And it's turned out that I've accumulated next to no interest on my capital, and that I will have to pay from the reserve.

'When I was twenty-three, a new life began for me, thanks to you . . . I was somehow careless about everything – like a bird which knows nothing of tomorrow, like a creature who, it seemed to me, was "lucky" in its life. And really, I'd soared over dozens of my colleagues, like a rocket. I won't say it was undeserved. My talent isn't a minor one, I possess a huge supply of energy, and my will for life is also not small . . . Selfishness and a somewhat exaggerated self-assurance are the reasons for my loneliness. And now, thirty-nine years old, I am facing myself, absolutely alone in all senses. And this is the most terrible of all. With all the force of my brain, I desire to be a *true* Bolshevik, and for this I lack knowledge. This has impeded my development as a composer in the last three to four years . . . Nothing can ever remove my feeling of guilt towards the party and the Soviet regime about the years of the civil war. Because every time someone mentions, in any connection, "White Guardist" in my presence, it's like a knife in my flesh, and I always think they've said it about me. This is the hardest trauma in my life, and there're only two ways to cure it – either the party would accept me in its ranks, or death will get me. I am not afraid of it, and I've thought of it frequently in the last five to six years.'

We do not have Olga Knipper-Chekhova's reply to her nephew, but she was clearly quite angry, especially about one part of the letter, when Lev wrote: 'What had I got from life before the age of twenty-four? Nothing. Or rather, negative values only. I blame no one for that.' Considering everything that she had done for the sick child and all the encouragement she had given him, growing up in a highly musical family, she found his remarks about 'negative values' ungrateful to say the least. Above all, she must have hit the mark by suggesting that he was desperately trying to persuade himself of these doctrines rather than believing in them naturally.

His reply can hardly have soothed her feelings. 'You see, my dearest Aunt Olya, politics is one of the reasons which make the two of us unable to talk to each other from soul to soul. And the reason for this is that for me politics is something deeply personal, lyrical, exciting. I am fighting for the Soviet regime (and therefore I love it, and mistakes are painful for me).' The 'mistakes' he referred to were presumably the millions of false accusations of the Great Terror. But Lev was unrepentant. 'For me, my personal life, my creative work, absolutely everything is intertwined with the issues of the party life. You don't want to believe in this, you think that I want to "be this way", rather than I already am this way.'

He went on to reject 'absolute' human values, dismissing them as 'intelligentsia ethics'. Lev had imbibed the essential ruthlessness of Leninism. 'More than anything else, I can't stand people who use "intelligentsia principles" and "humanity" to justify a general, deeply anti-Soviet behaviour.

'I need to learn what sort of a person one has to be to become, in this decisive moment of the fight, part of the millions giving all of themselves (not from the brain, but from the heart) to the future of humankind.

'By the way,' he added at the end, 'all that I've written above about "negative values" is not related to you at all. On the contrary, I consider you one of the most positive factors, and this makes me love and respect you even more. However, your attitude towards people around you (though not towards yourself) sometimes makes you draw very erroneous conclusions, and this makes me angry, when you, clever woman, want to overlook so many things. By the way, could you tell Masha that Rekst has been fired, and his case has been handed over to the investigative organs. I think he is in trouble. I said so to Masha a month ago.' It is very hard to know how far Lev wrote these letters conscious of the NKVD censor, who would read them, and yet if he had, he surely would have seen that the very nature of his argument with Aunt Olya could put her at risk. Unless, of course, Lev had so immersed himself in Stalinist brutality that even the 'aunt who gave birth to her nephew' might have to be seen as an incidental casualty in the great struggle.

Lev's first cousin Vova Knipper had a friend who was a barber in the proezd Serova near the Lubyanka. Most of his clients were NKVD officers. When the barber's shop opened at eight in the morning, NKVD interrogators, in a nervous state with heavy stubble, turned up in either military uniform or civilian clothes. They wanted a shave and a face massage to freshen up after a hard night's work beating confessions out of their prisoners. They asked for bloodstains to be daubed from their tunics and trousers with eau-de-Cologne. Some were so exhausted that they would fall asleep in the chair, and the barber found it hard to wake them up afterwards. But those who stayed awake talked compulsively about their work. The hairdresser warned Vova about the need to keep his mouth shut at all times. 'We're all in a trap,' he warned.

Aunt Olya herself was only too well aware of the dangers of the age. She and Kachalov went with a touring group of the Moscow Art Theatre to Paris in August 1937. The great international exhibition there was turned into a symbolic struggle between Fascism and Communism as the Spanish Civil War still raged. Nazi Germany and Soviet Russia competed to provide the most impressive pavilion. Picasso finished his painting of *Guernica* to conjure up the Luftwaffe's barbarity of aerial warfare for the pavilion of the Spanish Republic. Even the visit of the Art Theatre formed part of the propaganda war. Attacks in Paris on the show trials in Moscow had encouraged the Soviet authorities to send the Art Theatre there to give an impression of political freedom. Yet the members of the theatre were closely watched by NKVD agents, whom they dubbed 'archangels'.

A Russian émigré in Paris called Leo Rabeneck, who had

helped Olga Knipper-Chekhova in 1904 as Anton Chekhov was dying at Badenweiler, spotted her one evening. She was sitting at a table in a restaurant with two men. As soon as she recognized him, she looked down at her plate. Rabeneck realized that something was wrong and kept his distance. The next morning he ran into Kachalov on the Champs-Elysées and told him what had happened. 'She was sitting with two archangels,' Kachalov replied. 'How could she speak to you? They watch us here. They don't allow us to fraternize with émigrés.'

What is much more surprising is that Aunt Olya was apparently allowed to stop off with her namesake niece in Berlin on the way back to Moscow. According to Vova Knipper, Aunt Olya claimed later that Olga, to her horror, threw a party to which Nazi leaders came. But this sounds more like family folklore. Both women would surely have been much more circumspect at such a time.

Olga Chekhova claimed after the war that she was hardly a favourite with the Nazi regime, because she was never invited to the small, intimate parties of only twenty or thirty people. This was partly true, but also disingenuous. On a number of occasions, she seems to have dropped in to see Goebbels to talk of her 'worries and joys' or 'professional concerns', as the Reichsminister recorded in his diary, repetitiously adding that she was '*eine charmante Frau*'.

Yet the fact remained that Nazi leaders did not entertain in the same way as the theatrical community. Olga Chekhova was naturally not a habituée of the Reichschancellery or the Berghof above Berchtesgaden, because she never belonged to the exclusively Nazi inner circle of the leadership. But it was hardly surprising that the Soviet embassy saw her as the 'prima donna of the Nazi film industry', because she was invited to the major receptions which received great publicity.

'From 1936 I had a lot of invitations,' she later acknowledged, 'because from that year on I had a great success on the stage and all the foreigners who came to visit Berlin were brought to see my performances as if it were a zoo.' Yet Olga also sought peace and quiet away from her smart apartment at 74 Kaiserdamm, which no doubt reminded her too much of her second failed marriage.

Marcel Robyns does not appear to have accompanied her to any of the Berlin parties after 1937, mainly because an exasperated Olga had packed him off back to Brussels. By September 1938, she had decided to divorce him. 'Well, that's life!' Goebbels noted in his diary. The marriage had lasted just over two years and then only in name. Olga, realizing she had made a major mistake, sought consolation in the arms of a younger and far more amusing man, the actor Carl Raddatz, with whom she had filmed *Befreite Hände*. Fair-haired, with unconventional good looks, the pipe-smoking Raddatz was a frequent visitor to the Knipper family dacha out at Gross Glienecke. This simple, single-storey wooden house west of Berlin was some way across the Havel from the Goebbels villa at Schwanenwerder. It offered great peace and Olga used the apartment on the Kaiserdamm less and less. The other big advantage of the dacha was that it was an easy drive from Babelsberg.

In May 1939, Olga Chekhova saw a lot of Goebbels. On 4 May, he came to see her at the theatre in *Aimée*. 'The piece was not up to much,' he wrote in his diary, 'but la Tschechowa played wonderfully. So full of charm and grace.' He went round afterwards, laughed and chatted with her and Raddatz for a long time and went to bed late. It must have been a great success, because Olga invited him to Sunday lunch at Gross Glienecke ten days later. It was 'a beautiful, sunny May Sunday', and the Reichsminister drove with pleasure through 'awakening Nature' on the way there. He recorded that he had 'laughed and chatted all afternoon', adding, 'That does so much good after so much work.'

Also that May, Joachim von Ribbentrop gave a lavish garden reception for the diplomatic corps. Olga was seated in the front row next to Hitler. The photograph was widely published, and rumours of it spread back to Moscow, to the great unease of the Knippers still there.

According to Olga, she danced that evening with Count Ciano, Mussolini's son-in-law and foreign minister, and he asked her to play Anna Karenina in Italy. She claimed that, as she left, she heard Goebbels saying to his wife that she and Contessa Attolico, the wife of the Italian ambassador, should keep the Italians in the little saloon, as they are 'poking their noses everywhere'.

The following month, the Nazis held eight days of celebrations in honour of the Yugoslav regent, Prince Paul, whom they were trying hard to woo. Hitler began with a banquet at the Reichschancellery and five hours of Wagner's *Meistersinger*. Goebbels gave a party at his country house forty miles north of Berlin. Ribbentrop then gave one at Potsdam. But the most extravagant of all parties was of course given by Göring, who organized a huge candlelit reception in Schloss Charlottenburg with everyone in the period dress of Frederick the Great. Costumes were not hard to obtain, since the king was the favourite subject of Nazi movies. 'After supper I sat in the garden with the royal couple,' Olga recorded later, 'and we spoke about my films and my guest appearances.' She claimed that her presence had been specially requested because they had seen her films and the regent's wife, Princess Olga, who was half-Russian, wanted to meet her.

There has been a certain temptation in the former Soviet Union to overstate the role of Olga Chekhova at this time.

Some sources claim that she stayed in touch with Moscow through 'our people in Scandinavia', but this is most unlikely. Others say that she lost touch with Moscow from 1937 as a result of the purges of the Foreign Intelligence Department of the NKVD, yet she was not a regular agent, like Zarah Leander. Almost certainly, contact through Lev became far too dangerous at this time.

Her role, if called upon, was to establish contact with German generals and officials who were against the idea of a war with Russia. This was indeed a high priority for Stalin at the time. He knew that, after his purge of the Red Army, he must buy time before taking on the Wehrmacht. British weakness over Czechoslovakia convinced him that he could not possibly rely on the Western democracies. With true Stalinist paranoia mixed with outrageous falsehood, the Kremlin convinced itself that this appeasement was part of a British and French secret plan to encourage Hitler to attack the Soviet Union.

After the conclusion of the Ribbentrop–Molotov pact in August 1939, the Kremlin decided to show the German military attaché their arms factories in the Urals to convince him that the Wehrmacht would have to fight a long, hard war if it did attack. And after the German invasion of Poland in September 1939, when the Red Army occupied the eastern part of the country, Beria ordered that Prince Janusz Radziwill should be brought straight to the Lubyanka. Beria interviewed him in person and, when Radziwill agreed to work for him, he said to him: 'Prince, people like you will always be needed in this unstable world.' Radziwill was sent back to his estates in Poland with full honours. He was to go to Germany to contact his great shooting companion Hermann Göring, to persuade him against the idea of invading the Soviet Union.

★

Lev Knipper's love for the mountains of the Caucasus had drawn him into a relationship that could have been even more dangerous. At the end of the 1930s, he had begun on an increasingly frequent basis to leave Lyuba and Andrei in Moscow with Aunt Olya in order to spend more time with Marina Garikovna Melikova, a striking young woman, half-Armenian, half-Ukrainian. Her father, Garik Melikov, had been a senior Tsarist prosecutor in Tiflis whom Beria had pardoned after the revolution in return for his cooperation.

Beria, before he took over the NKVD, had started to create his own network of spies and informers. Mariya Garikovna (as she was always known) became one of his unofficial agents, either through gratitude or obligation. To a certain degree she also became Beria's protégée. She was a tall, loose-limbed woman of great intelligence, dark good looks and an astonishing elegance for Soviet Russia.

In 1932, at the age of twenty-two, she had come to Moscow, where she was given a clerical job with the OGPU. She then attracted the attention of an outstanding foreign service officer, General Nikolai Baldanov, a Buryat from the borders of Siberia and Outer Mongolia. They soon began to live together and she travelled with him on his missions abroad to Paris and even to China.

Mariya Garikovna was related through her Ukrainian mother to a prominent White émigré, Prince Kochubei, then living in Brussels. As a result, she was associated with Soviet operations against émigrés in the mid-1930s, and proved herself to be a most effective agent. But, in 1937, Baldanov was arrested and executed, another victim of service abroad at a time of paranoid xenophobia. Mariya Garikovna was perhaps fortunate to escape with nothing worse than the confiscation of Baldanov's apartment and belongings. But with the progressive downfall of Yezhov in the second half of 1938, Beria was able to reinstate her.

To have foreign connections as a citizen of the Soviet Union was tantamount during the 'Yezhovschina' to 'organized treachery in our rear'. Lev's great friend Paul Armand, despite his gold star of Hero of the Soviet Union, was arrested not long after his return to Russia, like many veterans of the Spanish Civil War. Armand, however, was unusually fortunate. He was suddenly released, which may well have been Lev's doing. In any case, Lev's son, Andrei, remembers Paul Armand turning up at Aunt Olya's apartment. 'Lyovka, you son of a bitch!' he yelled. 'Why aren't you in jail? All the honest people are.'

Soon after the German invasion of Poland in September 1939, Lev was recalled to active duty by the NKVD. He was sent to the south-eastern parts of Poland, now renamed 'the Western Ukraine' by its new Soviet occupiers. Lev Knipper, according to the son of his subsequent controller, 'became the key figure in unmasking German espionage in these most risky operations', for which he was issued with a Walther pistol. He was also responsible for the Bukovina and the region of Bessarabia seized from Romania.

Lev had gone with a group of Red Army dancers as a cover, but his real mission was to interrogate and filter Germans picked up by the NKVD under General Serov, who was carrying out mass deportations and executions of Poles. Lev was apparently responsible for identifying an Abwehr agent with the codename of Alma. The weasel-faced Serov intended to enjoy life during his appalling repression of the Poles. He apparently acquired, whether by force or not, the famous Polish singer Bandrowska-Turskaya as a mistress.

Although Stalin did not want to upset his new allies, Soviet intelligence was certain that the Germans had infiltrated many agents in the region to spy out the land. The Stalinist regime was already trapped in the curious imagination-lock of knowing that Hitler intended to attack the Soviet Union after the defeat of France, yet refusing to believe it.

16. Enemy Aliens

As the fragile peace in Europe came to a close, the most important of Olga Chekhova's pre-war movies, *Bel Ami*, was released. A sophisticated, slightly decadent film based on a Maupassant story, it belonged more to the Weimar era than to the uncompromising age of National Socialism. Once war was declared, however, Babelsberg was mobilized. Movies became more nationalistic and stars were expected to volunteer for their own form of duty – helping to publicize the war effort and entertaining the troops. In a phrase that only a Nazi bureaucrat could have invented, the programme was known as 'Edification and Cheerfulness in Hard Times'.

In September 1940, during the Battle of Britain, Olga Chekhova visited a Luftwaffe fighter wing based near the Château de Beauregard in Normandy. There was a parade in her honour with a band, she signed autographs for the men and she was photographed by the yellow nose spinners of Messerschmitt 109 fighter aircraft. In Paris in October, where she was playing at the Théatre des Champs-Elysées, she was shown surrounded by soldiers on the front cover of *Das Illustrierte Blatt*. She also visited German forces in Brussels and Lille.

It was in Lille, in a restaurant where she had been invited for a drink by the boring town commandant, that she met the new love of her life. This young Luftwaffe captain was, according to her, 'tall and sure of himself, but without a trace of arrogance'. She was fascinated by his eyes as he gazed at her from the door and then laughed. He walked up to her and said: 'I knew that I would meet you.' They began to talk like old friends. He turned out to be called Jep and was a squadron commander in General Adolf Galland's fighter group.

After her dismal marriage to Marcel Robyns, Olga Chekhova, now forty-three, had acquired a taste for much younger and livelier men. Carl Raddatz had been fifteen years younger than her and there was a similar age gap with Jep. But for Olga, her meeting with Jep was clearly a question of fate. However, while her affair with Raddatz had been easy to maintain, with her waterside dacha at Gross Glienecke so close to the Raddatz house, Jep's posting to northern France meant that the lovers had to rely mainly on letters and the occasional telephone call. He wrote to her about aerial dog-fights over the Channel and southern England, while she entertained him with studio gossip.

Olga was preparing a new film, *Der Fuchs von Glenarvon*, a piece of anti-British propaganda set in Ireland. She played Gloria Grandison, an Irish patriot staunchly supporting freedom fighters at a time when the Wehrmacht was shooting them on the spot, along with hostages, in occupied Europe. It was to be followed a year later by *Menschen im Sturm*, which supposedly justified the German invasion of Yugoslavia on the grounds of a persecuted family of German origin. The fact that there was no German minority in the country to speak of did not of course get in the way of a good nationalistic melodrama. It ended with Olga Chekhova being shot by Yugoslav soldiers during an escape in a horse-drawn carriage towards the German frontier. She dies a martyr, with her last words: '*Wir fahren in die Heimat*' − 'We are going home.' But how Olga Chekhova would have defined her own homeland at this time is not easy to tell.

On 13 November 1940, soon after a grey, wet dawn, a train with two luxurious saloon carriages reached Berlin. It pulled into the Anhalter Bahnhof just a few hundred yards south of the Reichschancellery. As well as a guard of honour from the *SS Leibstandarte Adolf Hitler*, Joachim von Ribbentrop and General Wilhelm Keitel stood by the red carpet. The station itself was decorated with flags – the Nazi red banner and swastika paired incongruously with the yellow hammer and sickle on the Soviet red flag.

The band struck up as the Soviet foreign minister, Vyacheslav Molotov, stepped down from the carriage on to the platform. Ribbentrop and Keitel gave the Nazi salute. Molotov's interpreter, Valentin Berezhkov, thought that this must be the first time the Internationale had been played in Berlin since Hitler crushed the German Communists seven and a half years before. 'For singing that song of the proletariat, people had been thrown into death camps by the Gestapo, and now here in the Anhalter Bahnhof, German generals and high-ranking officials of the Nazi Reich had to stand to attention while the Communist anthem was played.'

A motorcade of huge, six-wheeled black Mercedes with SS motorcycle outriders swept them northwards to Schloss Bellevue, where they were staying. Berezhkov claims to have seen workers secretly waving red handkerchiefs from the windows of a nearby factory, but this is more likely to have been the product of an optimistic imagination.

After a sumptuous breakfast, they were driven back across the centre of Berlin to the Reichschancellery. Berezhkov describes how Molotov and his party were taken through 'tall bronze-clad doors' and 'an enfilade of dimly lit rooms and windowless hallways' lined by sentries who clicked their heels and raised their arms in the Nazi salute. The entry to Hitler's huge study 'was invested with the theatricality that only the Nazis were capable of. Two tall blond SS men in black, tightly belted uniforms clicked their heels and threw open the tall, almost ceiling-high doors with a single, well-practised gesture.' Hitler, wearing his usual mouse-grey tunic, with Iron Cross, was dwarfed by the huge size of his own room.

German intelligence appears to have been unaware of the real identity of Molotov's two most important companions. His deputy, Vladimir Dekanozov, a diminutive, balding Georgian associate of Beria, was the first head of the NKVD's Foreign Intelligence Department to be posted as an ambassador abroad. His appointment to the Berlin embassy was announced during the visit. But Dekanozov, despite all his experience, was to follow Stalin's wilful blindness about the growing threat from Germany. Over the coming months, he convinced himself, like Stalin, that every warning of Operation Barbarossa was a provocation from British intelligence. It was all part of a plot by Churchill to trick the Soviet Union into war with Germany.

Molotov's other chief companion, Vsevolod Nikolayevich Merkulov, was even less of a diplomat. It emerged many years later that he was responsible, on Beria's orders, for the massacre of Polish officers in the Katyn forest. This visit was Merkulov's very convenient cover 'to assess personally the operational situation in Germany'. The purges had caused chaos in the Foreign Intelligence Department, and, to make things worse, Stalin had imposed restrictions on spying in Germany to avoid antagonizing Hitler any further. The only worthwhile agent networks were linked to Soviet military intelligence, the GRU. Just about the only agent the NKVD had on its files in Berlin was Olga Chekhova, even though she was just a 'sleeper'. The purge of foreign intelligence officers during the Great Terror had proved disastrous.

That day's meeting with Hitler was extremely frustrating, if not alarming, for the Soviet delegation. Hitler wanted to talk about his imminent victory over Britain and his plans for the dismemberment of its empire. The implication was that he was prepared to share the spoils with the Soviet Union. Despite Molotov returning again and again to the main Soviet concern, the increase of German troops in Finland and Romania, Hitler refused to provide satisfactory answers. He even tried to claim that his forces in Finland were on their way to Norway, which seemed rather a roundabout route. While Hitler talked, Ribbentrop sat with his arms folded, staring at him. The Nazi foreign minister was nothing but a vain and empty poseur. 'Occasionally,' noted Berezhkov, 'he would put both his hands on the table and tap it lightly with his fingers, and, after looking round the table at each of those present in a manner that gave none of his thoughts away, would resume his former position.'

That evening, Molotov held a reception for his Nazi hosts at the massive Soviet embassy on Unter den Linden. In the marble hall, a buffet for 500 people had been prepared on tables covered in white cloths, with displays of carnations and antique silver confiscated after the revolution. Hitler did not attend, leaving this duty to other Nazi leaders, including Ribbentrop, Rudolf Hess and Reichsmarshal Göring, who appeared in the sky-blue and silver uniform which he had designed himself. The Soviet officials were fascinated by his huge rings, and the stories they had heard of him dressing in a Roman toga and sandals studded with diamonds when relaxing at home.

Photographers and newsreel cameras recorded the arrival of the guests and their reception by Molotov. At some stage, Olga Chekhova was drawn aside, perhaps by a junior member of the embassy staff, to be introduced to Merkulov. This was not dangerous, even if a Gestapo agent had been watching. In German eyes, it would have been perfectly normal for a Russian to want to meet a member of the Chekhov family.

And it presumably became much easier for them to talk undisturbed, since just after glasses were raised for the first toast, air-raid sirens warned of another bombing raid by the Royal Air Force.

According to Berezhkov, the Nazi leaders made straight for the door to be driven to their air-raid shelters round the corner in the Wilhelm Strasse. The Soviet embassy had its own torture chamber for interrogating suspect members of the staff and the Soviet community in Berlin, yet it lacked an air-raid shelter, even though Britain and Germany had been at war for over a year. It was almost as if Stalinist conspiracy theories did not allow them to believe that the perfidious British were dropping real bombs.

Although the idea 'was not to use [Olga Chekhova] as a rank and file informer', she certainly appeared to be in a good position to assist the two main priorities for Soviet intelligence. The first was Stalin's insistence that they must discover 'Hitler's source of strength' within his own country. How had he managed to achieve such a following and such power? The other, as already mentioned, was to identify influential people in Germany who opposed the idea of an attack on the Soviet Union. Certain members of the old school, such as the German ambassador in Moscow, Count von der Schulenberg, strongly believed in Bismarck's dictum that Germany should never attack Russia. It was hoped that Olga Chekhova, like Prince Janusz Radziwill, could help in this way. What they could have achieved in practical terms is hard to imagine, and in any case Soviet intelligence had almost certainly over-estimated the effectiveness of Olga Chekhova's contacts, probably as a result of seeing the photograph of her seated next to Hitler. Rumours had circulated in limited circles in Moscow that she virtually acted as Hitler's hostess on occasion.

For Olga Chekhova at least, the meeting with Merkulov

offered reassurance that her family was safe in the Soviet Union. It is said that Merkulov almost certainly brought a message from Lev to reassure her that her family was protected.

Olga Chekhova returned to France the following month to see Jep again. In Paris on 23 December, she received a large Christmas parcel from Hitler, passed on to her via the German embassy there. It contained a card showing the Führer's portrait and signed by him with a dedication, together with cakes, chocolate, nuts and gingerbread, as if she were a soldier at the front. As she was about to return to Germany and hoped to smuggle large supplies of expensive scent and other presents back, she threw out all the little delicacies and refilled the package with her forbidden luxuries. At the frontier, the customs officer and frontier guard insisted on searching the large, heavy package. But when they came across Hitler's Christmas card, with the handwritten dedication, 'Frau Olga Tschechowa in sincere admiration and veneration, Adolf Hitler', they leaped to attention with their right arms thrust out in the Nazi salute and cried, '*Heil Hitler!*'

For the Knippers left in Moscow, this was a time of great anxiety. If war broke out with Germany while the other half of the family in Berlin was associating with the Nazi élite, they would be in a very dangerous position. By the time the rumours of Olga in Berlin reached her Uncle Vladimir, the story went that Hitler had actually introduced her to Molotov as his hostess. Soon after, a small truck with an antenna revolving on top was spotted driving slowly along Gogolevsky bulvar. The Knippers immediately thought that it was spying on them.

'We've got to look after ourselves,' Vladimir Knipper explained, more to himself than to his son, Vova. 'They were sweet girls [Olga and Ada], but we had to stop corresponding. It's crazy, but that's what one has to do nowadays.'

Only Lev seemed unaffected by these fears. If anything, he seems to have rediscovered his confidence on his return from the mission in Poland in the spring of 1941. Much of this may of course have been due to his relationship with Mariya Garikovna, whose extrovert nature complemented his character and if anything encouraged him to relax.

Sources disagree on when they met. Some people do not think that their relationship began until 1941. Former Lieutenant Colonel of State Security Shchors, who was later the liaison officer between Lev and General Kobulov, even believes that Mariya Garikovna was selected as Lev's fellow agent and that they were ordered to marry. This was apparently a common practice at the time and few objected. 'Well,' said Shchors, 'I have heard about a man who, on a similar occasion, demanded a medical certificate proving that his bride was a virgin. But usually everything was all right.' Shchors himself never set eyes on his wife before she turned up at his apartment with a new passport in the name of Natalya Shchors. Now they have been together for sixty years. So he does not imagine that Lev would have objected.

Vova Knipper, then just about to finish high school, remembered the telephone ringing in their apartment. He answered it and recognized Lev's voice.

'Who's that? Is that young Knipper? Is your father at home?'

Half an hour later Lev appeared. Vova admired his much older first cousin enormously. 'I tried to learn to walk like he did with springy steps like tennis masters should,' he wrote later. 'He had played for the main Red Army team and was champion in the Crimea, but Lyova's chief passion was for mountains. At this time he was an instructor for the Red Army in mountain warfare.'

Vova was at a very impressionable age, as he admitted. He had naïvely refused to believe that prostitutes existed under Soviet society, so schoolfriends dragged him off to watch them hanging around the square in front of the Bolshoi Theatre, just a few hundred yards from the Kremlin. But he was not blinded by his hero-worship for Lev. He sensed that there was something deeply unsettling about him.

17. MOSCOW 1941

An unexpected declaration of war is bound to produce a sense
of shock, yet no country was as psychologically unprepared as
the Soviet Union on 22 June 1941. Stalin, the great trickster,
had refused to believe warnings of Hitler's betrayal.

Ordinary Russians, persuaded by countless newsreels and
radio programmes about their country's industrial and military
might, never believed that the Germans would dare attack.
But once the truth sank in, the Russian people reacted far
more rapidly than their leaders. There were queues of volunteers within hours of Molotov's wooden announcement on
Radio Moscow. Stalin was too traumatized to speak.

Some of the improvisation might have appeared ridiculous
to a professional eye, but there can never be any doubt about
the determination to defend the Motherland. Even the Moscow Art Theatre put itself on a war footing. Classes in civilian
anti-aircraft defence were held in the theatre's 'red corner',
the obligatory Communist shrine with a bust of Lenin. Olga
Knipper-Chekhova, at the age of seventy-two, lectured new-
comers on how to deal with incendiary bombs: 'One has to
take it by the fins,' she told them, 'and throw it out of the
window into the sand [piled outside]. It is very simple.'

Popular belief in the might of the Soviet state was soon
shaken when it became clear that the Germans had not been
thrown back at the frontier. The Wehrmacht was advancing
with great speed. One army group was heading for Leningrad,
another was pushing through Belorussia on the road to Moscow and a third was driving into the Ukraine. 'This,' wrote

Lev, 'was when we really started to learn the geography of our country from the names of villages and towns which we had hardly known before and which were like burning scars on the body of the Motherland.'

When war broke out, Lev had been in the central Caucasus, training Red Army soldiers in mountain warfare at a camp named 'Rot Front', in honour of German Communists. They had been scaling a peak, and on returning to their camp on 23 June, the day after the invasion, they had expected their comrades there to come out to welcome them. But the faces of those they encountered gave the first intimation of the disaster which had befallen the country. 'Don't be surprised if you find out I am at the front,' Lev immediately wrote to Aunt Olya. 'This is my greatest desire.' But Lev, to his evident frustration, was ordered to stay there and continue training his men.

In July 1941, a few weeks after the invasion, Magda Goebbels rang Olga Chekhova to invite her to a Sunday lunch out at Schwanenwerder. A ministry car would be sent to fetch her. There were about thirty-five people at the lunch, a mixture of actors, diplomats and officials from the propaganda ministry.

Goebbels was exultant at the rapidity of the Wehrmacht advance. He was convinced that the capture of Moscow was a foregone conclusion. Goebbels turned to Olga Chekhova and, according to her account, the following conversation took place.

'We've got a Russian expert here, Frau Chekhova. Don't you think, Madam, that this war will be finished before winter comes and that we will celebrate Christmas in Moscow?'

'No,' she claims to have replied.

'Why not?' Goebbels demanded.

'Napoleon saw what the space of Russia was like.'

'There's a huge difference between us and the French,' Goebbels smiled. 'We've come to Russia as liberators. The Bolshevik clique is going to be overthrown by the new revolution.'

'In the face of new danger, Russians will show solidarity as they have never done so before.'

Goebbels leaned forward slightly and said coldly: 'I wonder, Madam. Does this mean that you do not believe in German military power? You are predicting a Russian victory.'

'I am not predicting anything, Herr Minister. You just asked me whether our soldiers will be in Moscow by Christmas and I just expressed my opinion, which may prove right or wrong.'

Goebbels, she wrote later, gave her a long suspicious stare. There is no mention of this exchange in the Goebbels diaries, and it has proved impossible to verify. It may well have been what she would like to have said.

It looked as if Goebbels would be proved right. Smolensk had fallen, and Field Marshal von Bock's Army Group Centre, with 1.5 million men, appeared unstoppable. On 22 July, Moscow was bombed for the first time. The Luftwaffe followed up the attack on the two following nights. The windows of apartments, including those of 23 Gogolevsky bulvar, were blasted in and dogs went wild in terror, but there was comparatively little structural damage.

Food was already in short supply. Vladimir Knipper as an opera singer received a free lunch of soup and potatoes each day at the Central House of Workers in the Arts. His son, Vova, depended more and more on the contents of the little billycan in which his father brought the meal to share with him. Vova's ration was only 400 grams of bread, and yet he had been drafted already into digging anti-tank ditches outside Moscow. Their dog was the first to succumb to the combination of stress from the air raids and starvation. Vladimir Knipper was also having to borrow money from Aunt Olya, who continued to act with uncomplaining generosity as the family banker. In the middle of that terrible summer for the Soviet Union, Aunt Olya and her great friend Sofya Ivanovna Baklanova came to say goodbye to Vladimir Knipper and his son, Vova. A group of actors from the Moscow Art Theatre was being evacuated from the capital to the Caucasus. Conversation was halting. Aunt Olya suggested that he and Vova should come with them, but Vladimir, apparently sad and nervous, said that he could not leave his books and piano.

Aunt Olya wrote once a week back to Moscow. On 15 August, she described how they were living in a train parked beside a huge pear orchard, with the snow-capped peaks of the Caucasus range in the distance. She could think only of home. A week later, she asked Vladimir to check on other members of the family to see how they were.

In September, she told Vladimir that two of the leading members of the Moscow Art Theatre group, Tarasova and Moskvin, were trying to leave for Moscow. She was clearly upset and jealous. 'They have been asked by the theatre to come back and we are just "Firsovs".' Firsov was the old servant forgotten and abandoned at the end of *The Cherry Orchard*.

The only consolation for her was a visit from Lev, who had come up from his mountain-warfare training camp. But her great friend Sofya was clearly uneasy about Aunt Olya's surrogate son. 'We are at a complete loss as to what we should do,' she wrote to Vladimir Knipper. 'Many Moscow Art Theatre people are already going back. Lyova is going back to the mountains. Lyova is still the same. There is a lot in him that isn't clear to me. Olga Leonardovna doesn't know anything about Andryusha and we are worried.'

They were right to be concerned about Lev's young son, Andrei. He and his mother, Lyuba, were almost starving in Tashkent and Lev did not reply to their pleas for help. When Vova Knipper asked him a month later for news of Andrei, Lev was clearly embarrassed. He tried to pretend that the situation with Mariya Garikovna made it very hard for him to stay in touch with Lyuba.

Personal suffering attracted little attention at this moment of supreme danger for the Motherland. Operation Typhoon, the German assault on Moscow, was launched on 30 September 1941. Guderian's tanks dashed forward on the southern flank and entered the centre of Orel, overtaking streetcars whose occupants had no idea that the enemy was upon them.

On 5 October, a Soviet reconnaissance aircraft spotted a twelve-mile-long column of German armour on the Yukhnov road, no more than eighty miles from Moscow. The news caused such disbelief in the Kremlin that Beria wanted to arrest the air force officer concerned for 'provocation'. Two more aircraft were sent up and their pilots confirmed the news. There was panic in the Kremlin. Stalin gave the order to the commander of the Moscow military district to mobilize everything he had. He did not know that Hitler had already claimed that the victory was won and had sworn a Carthaginian fate for Moscow. The city was to be razed to the ground and the site flooded to create a huge lake.

Field Marshal von Bock's panzer forces achieved a stunning double encirclement at Bryansk and another round Vyazma. They destroyed 1,242 Soviet tanks and cut off 665,000 Soviet soldiers. These captured Red Army men were destined for terrible suffering, in most cases death through starvation and disease, in German prisoner of war camps. One of them was Kachalov's son, Vadim Shverubovich, the White Guard who had become Lev's companion in exile. The forty-year-old Vadim, having been prevented from volunteering for the Spanish Civil War, was now one of 4 million people to come forward to join the *opolchentsy* home guard. These scandalously ill-armed forces were thrown into utterly hopeless attacks against Wehrmacht and SS divisions and suffered terrifying casualties. Many of the men were still in civilian clothes and risked being shot out of hand as partisans.

Vadim and his comrades had exhausted themselves trying to find a way out of the German encirclement. They woke up one morning, stiff from an early frost and snowfall, to find German soldiers standing over them. They were marched to a camp near Yukhnov and began to experience the horrors of capture on the eastern front. They received no shelter, little drinking water and hardly any food. From time to time food was thrown over the fence, and the guards laughed to watch them fight each other in their desperation to grab morsels from the mud. With no huts, tents or latrines, the conditions were unspeakably squalid. Soon real winter arrived, and 'they were left to die in the snow'.

One morning, Vadim Shverubovich woke up to find himself surrounded almost entirely by corpses. He realized that he too was going to die if he continued to lie there. Some instinct of self-respect made him decide to shave. In his pouch he had, like most Red Army soldiers, a small piece of broken mirror and a rusty razor. He had no soap, of course, so he used spittle. A German officer observed this curious act amid such appalling surroundings. He called out as a joke: 'Cream, powder, mass-age?' Shverubovich looked up at him. The German officer ordered him to stand to attention. Shverubovich did as he was told.

'Do you speak German?' the officer asked.

'Yes, I do.' His German was in fact excellent.

'Do you want to work?'

'Yes.'

'Translate for the others. I want to know who else can work.'

Shverubovich translated and several men hauled themselves to their feet.

'If you want us to work,' Shverubovich said, 'you should first feed us.' They were given some soup. Almost immediately Shverubovich felt his strength returning.

Vadim's father, Kachalov, who was with Aunt Olya in the Caucasus, received with great self-control the news that Vadim was missing. Aunt Olya could imagine only too well what he must be suffering. She knew what it would have meant to her if Lev had been posted missing.

On 14 October, the *SS Das Reich* and the 10th Panzer Division reached the Napoleonic battlefield of Borodino. Memories of 1812 and Napoleon's entry into Moscow were rife, but many drew the wrong conclusions. On the same day, the 1st Panzer Division seized the town of Kalinin, with its bridge over the Volga, and severed the Moscow–Leningrad railway line.

On the evening of 15 October, foreign embassies and government departments were told to prepare to leave the city. Orders were issued for the evacuation to Kuibyshev, 500 miles to the east. Even Lenin's mummified corpse was removed secretly from the mausoleum on Red Square and sent east in a refrigerated railway car. Government files were destroyed in huge bonfires in the courtyards of ministries. There was a smell of burnt paper as charred fragments floated over the centre of the city, rather as the human ashes from the Donskoi monastery had done during the purges four years earlier. 'We were walking on black snow,' Vova Knipper wrote later.

There was indeed an echo of the purges, as the execution squads in the Lubyanka and other NKVD prisons worked overtime shooting prisoners to prevent them falling into the hands of the Germans.

Around the city, steel hedgehogs were set up to block roads against enemy armour, and tens of thousands of ill-equipped civilians were marched out to dig more anti-tank ditches. Word spread that Moscow was about to be abandoned to the enemy and large parts of the population became panic-stricken. Families stormed the city's eastern railway stations, especially the Kazansky station, desperate for a place on what they thought might be the last train out before the Germans encircled the city. People had barely left their apartments before neighbours and block supervisors began looting them.

Even government officials who were supposed to stay behind deserted their posts to escape the city. On 16 October, Aleksei Kosygin, the deputy chairman of Sovnarkom, the Council of People's Commissars, entered its headquarters to find the place abandoned. A few sheets of paper were blowing around in the draught, and once or twice a telephone rang, but the person at the other end rang off as soon as he answered it. Eventually one caller asked quite brazenly whether Moscow would be surrendered.

Stores of alcohol as well as food shops were stormed and there was much drunkenness on the streets. Wild rumours described the drop of German paratroopers on Red Square. Natalya Gesse, a friend of the physicist Andrei Sakharov, was nearly lynched as she hobbled along on crutches after an operation. People were convinced that she had broken her legs when coming down by parachute. Other panic-mongers claimed to know on the best authority that Stalin had been arrested in a Kremlin coup. A rumour, which in this case proved accurate, ran round the city that huge demolition charges were being laid in the Metro 'for well-known reasons'. Most people still feared to voice openly the idea of Moscow falling to the enemy. The crime of defeatism was dealt with by firing squad. Yet the panic in the Moscow Conservatoire had been such that Vova's father had seen fellow teachers openly burning their Communist Party cards, an act which could carry the death penalty.

On 19 November, Beria sent in several regiments of NKVD troops to restore order through summary executions. Anyone suspected of desertion, looting or even drunkenness after the storming of alcohol outlets was seized and put up against a wall without the slightest pretence of an investigation.

In this atmosphere of collapse and despair, the seventeen-year-old Vova found that his girlfriend, Margo, had fallen for a lieutenant colonel of NKVD troops with a bull-like neck who was old enough to be her father. Vova, on entering her apartment, discovered her sitting on his lap. She slipped off when Vova burst in and hurriedly said that they had just returned. 'Nikolai is hunting for deserters,' she added, as if that was an explanation for her conduct. As Vova stormed out, he passed Margo's mother in the corridor. She turned her head away in embarrassment. Vova left the building in tears. Margo's attachment to such a man at such a moment was part of the desperate *sauve-qui-peut* atmosphere.

Vova must have been frightened, bearing a German name at this moment of pitiless struggle. Daily bulletins from Informburo were attached to trees and walls. On one of them he was shaken to see an excerpt from a letter taken off the body of a German soldier called Hans Knipper. And a school-friend of his, a Volga German about to be transported to Siberia, came to see them in despair. Vova's father, Vladimir, advised him to volunteer for the army to save himself from an exile of forced labour which would be as bad as the Gulag, but Vova's friend replied that the description 'German' was stamped on his papers and they would not accept him in the army. Those of German origin were implicitly categorized as potential enemies of the state. The NKVD had not wasted time assembling records on every Soviet citizen of German descent, some 1.5 million people. Local NKVD departments 'from Leningrad to the Far East' began a programme of arrests immediately after the Wehrmacht invasion. Yet no member of the Knipper family was touched.

Other Germans in Moscow were also in a strange position, but for different reasons. In the same building as the Knippers lived the family of Friedrich Wolf, the famous German Communist playwright, who had left Germany as soon as Hitler came to power in 1933. They were part of the so-called 'Moscow emigration' of foreign Communists seeking sanctuary and would have faced instant execution at Nazi hands if the city fell. Vova used to act as a roof-top fire-watcher, ready to deal with incendiary bombs, along with Wolf's two sons, Markus and Koni. Markus later became the chief of East German intelligence and the original of Karla in John Le Carré's novels, and his younger brother, Koni, became a film-maker, writer and the president of East Germany's academy of arts. During air raids, Vladimir Knipper and Friedrich Wolf sat in the cellar, chatting together in German. 'People sitting round us,' wrote Vova, 'turned to look at the two of them with anger and fear. There they were in the centre of Moscow arguing about something in the enemy's language.'

To Vladimir and Vova's surprise, Lev suddenly turned up at their apartment just after they had received an anxious letter from Aunt Olya asking for news of him. Despite the desperate situation, Lev still had 'an energetic sporty gait, his left eyebrow was always raised'. He was accompanied by his new wife,

Mariya Garikovna, whom Vova remembered as 'a very beautiful Armenian woman with long strong legs'. Lev talked to
Vladimir and Vova about the threat to Moscow and offered
to organize their evacuation. He asked Vova to come into the
adjoining room with him, which was Vova's bedroom. Lev
looked at the photo of his girlfriend, Margo, and guessed that
she was the reason why Vova did not want to leave Moscow.
'Well, you should remember,' Lev told him, 'that you're a
Knipper and you'll have lots of such girls.' The seventeen-
year-old Vova did not know how to reply. 'I was in awe of
Lyova,' he wrote later. 'He lived a strange, different life. He
disappeared from Moscow when everyone else was still there
and then reappeared on the coldest of winter days with the
deepest of suntans. He often smiled, showing his strong teeth,
slightly yellowed by tobacco. At that time in the war I did not
like him very much.'

His father, on the other hand, was touched by Lev's visit.
His nephew had brought them some real coffee, which was
unobtainable in Moscow, and Vova began to grind it. 'Ah,'
sighed Vladimir, 'the air smells of peacetime.'

Vladimir, with his bad legs and a horror of abandoning his
books, declined Lev's offer of evacuation. And so did Vova,
who still longed for Margo. She had rung him to make an
emotional confession. Nikolai, the giant of an NKVD officer,
had now started beating her up. Margo even admitted that she
had been excited at first when he had offered her rides in the
Voronok – the type of camouflaged vehicle in which the
NKVD secretly transported its prisoners.

Vova was not the only one to be unsettled by Lev. Mariya
Garikovna went with Lev to see off a close friend of hers at a
railway station. In tears, Mariya Garikovna murmured to her
evacuee friend, indicating Lev: 'I am afraid of him.' This may
well have been because Lev was even more ready to die in the

defence of Moscow than she was. Lev, after that time during
the Great Terror when he was trying to conquer any lingering
moral scruples with belief in the Soviet Motherland, was now
in a mood of exultant self-sacrifice.

The true reason for Lev's reappearance in Moscow with
Mariya Garikovna was indeed extraordinary. At the end of
that first week of October, Stalin had made it abundantly clear
to his close entourage, most notably Beria, that they faced
annihilation and must react with total ruthlessness. The
enemy's rear was to be harassed by partisan attacks. All houses
capable of offering shelter to German soldiers as winter
approached were to be destroyed, whatever the suffering this
entailed for Russian civilians trapped behind German lines.
Above all, the partisan war was to be extended to vengeance
operations with special stay-behind groups. Beria appointed
General Pavel Sudoplatov to be the chief of the Special Tasks
Group of the NKVD, in addition to his other responsibilities.

'In October of 1941,' wrote General Sudoplatov, 'when
Moscow was under serious threat, Beria ordered us to organize
an intelligence network in the city to be activated after its
capture by the Germans. We also created an autonomous
group which was to eliminate Hitler and his close associates if
they turned up in Moscow after its capture. This operation
was to be carried out by composer Lev Knipper, brother of
Olga Chekhova, and his wife Mariya Garikovna.' As well as
his immediate controller, Colonel of State Security Mikhail
Maklyarsky, Lev also reported to one of Beria's deputies,
Commissar of State Security Bogdan Kobulov. As a security
precaution, the NKVD chiefs had moved from the Lubyanka
to a training school for fire-fighters next to the Comintern
headquarters.

Lev and Mariya Garikovna were far from alone in this

underground resistance operation, even though their mission was the most ambitious. 'General Sudoplatov mobilized all his officers to take different posts,' recorded Zoya Zarubina, who was the NKVD liaison officer with Lev and Mariya Garikovna. 'I remember myself, I had two different passports, living in two or three different places at the same time, just to make sure. In one place I was registered with my baby, in the second I was just a student.' Lieutenant Colonel of State Security Shchors, who also liaised with Lev, was responsible for sabotaging the city's water supply if the Nazis came and his agent-wife was their radio operator. There were at least a dozen 'battle groups', each operating individually on a cell basis. They were provided with safe-houses, secret arms dumps and instructions on dead-letter drops. Sudoplatov's officers were to direct an unusual mixture of volunteers, including 'key figures among [the] Russian intelligentsia, who were important agents for [the NKVD]'.

Zarubina made contact with Lev and Mariya Garikovna as instructed. By a strange coincidence, she had known the exotic Mariya Garikovna from China, where she had been with her parents, both famous members of the OGPU and NKVD. She greatly admired Mariya Garikovna, not just for her elegance, beauty and intelligence, but also because she was such a brilliant agent, using her charm with devastating effect. Lev, on the other hand, she found introverted, but he was clearly very competent and energetic, even though he said little. Zoya Vasileevna Zarubina had been recruited in 1941, partly for her own foreign languages, but also because she could hardly have been better connected in NKVD circles. Her father, Vasily Mikhailovich Zarubin, had been the illegal *rezident* in Germany, Scandinavia and later Washington. Her stepmother, who worked with him, was Lisa Gorskaya, another famous OGPU and NKVD agent. Zarubina's stepfather was Nahum Eitingon (alias General Kotov), the organizer of Trotsky's assassination, director of partisan operations in Spain against Franco, and now Sudoplatov's deputy.

On 19 October, Lev wrote to his surrogate mother, Aunt Olya. This letter, churning with mixed feelings of sadness and fierce joy at his mission, is undoubtedly the most emotional and spontaneous of his life.

'The city has produced a very strange impression on me,' he wrote. 'It's a mixture of "Feast during a plague" [by Pushkin] and the well-known play by Hemingway [*The Fifth Column* (1937), set in Madrid during the Spanish Civil War]. I am feeling odd, too, like a bird sitting on a branch, knowing it might have to take off at any second . . . And it's not even so frightening to die. There are at last some powerful things in which I believe and which have helped to stiffen my spine . . . I am Russian, Russian to the marrow in my bones. I've realized that I love my ridiculous, idiotic, uncultured and dirty Motherland, love her with a tender Levitan love, and it's a pain to me to see her big, beautiful body violated. [Levitan, a great friend of Anton Chekhov, was the painter of wonderfully spiritual landscapes of Russia.] I know for sure what I will be fighting for and what, if needed, I will die for. And it's only now, grey-haired and balding, that I have begun to understand many things. But it's too late. I might die with the curtains of my soul still shut, with twilight in it, while there's so much sun around, so much joy, and so much of that most important thing that justifies life and which I have never had – love. Some people weep from happiness, and I weep for happiness. It will never come my way. And it's my own fault . . . Don't worry about me: I am not going to sell my life cheaply.'

The mission assigned to Lev and Mariya Garikovna was indeed special, and it went beyond Sudoplatov's terse description in his book. They had a second role beyond that of the other stay-behind groups. 'They were being prepared for a certain assignment to be sent to Germany to make contact with Olga,' Zarubina recounted with professional reticence, even more than sixty years after the event. 'The assignment was not very pleasant.'

This medium-term plan was for Lev and Mariya Garikovna to 'falsely defect' to the Germans if they found the opportunity. Otherwise, they would fight in the same way as the other 'battle groups'. Lev had eleven men, including a radio operator. They were equipped with 'remote control grenades, explosives, ammunition, everything that he needed for an active assault'. Their chief priority was to assassinate Hitler and any other Nazi leaders who came to Moscow to savour their triumph. Lev, with his Aryan looks, perfect German and mastery of its regional accents, could easily pass for a German officer. But assuming that he and Mariya Garikovna did manage to stage a defection, Lev was to claim that, as an artist and a German persecuted for his origins, he longed to work with the 'liberators' of the Soviet Union and rejoin his sister, Olga, in Berlin. The triumphant Germans would find it entirely natural that someone like Lev should hate Stalinism, so the security screening process was unlikely to be especially arduous. And his sister's well-known acquaintance with the Führer and some of the Nazi élite should help to confirm his good intentions.

Others sources, however, insist that Lev's task was to go no further than Turkey. His mission was to assassinate Franz von Papen, the German ambassador there. Papen was the politician who had allowed Hitler to come to power.

The panic of early and mid-October turned to mass courage in early November. Radio Moscow had broadcast Stalin's decision to stay in the city. On the eve of the anniversary of the revolution, Stalin made a powerful speech. 'If they want a war of extermination,' he declared, 'then they shall have one!'

The next day, 7 November, the annual parade on Red Square took place on Stalin's insistence. Beria and Molotov had been appalled at the threat of air attack, but Stalin ordered in all available anti-aircraft batteries and insisted on a fighter umbrella over the city. His idea, designed mainly for newsreels around the world, was that reinforcements for the Moscow front should march through Red Square, past the saluting base on Lenin's (now empty) mausoleum, and march on westwards towards the enemy.

The key elements in the battle for Moscow were the rapidly deteriorating weather, which was bound to favour the better-prepared Red Army, and Stalin's secret reinforcements from the Far East. Stalin, finally convinced by signal intercepts that the Japanese were indeed about to attack the Americans and not the Soviet Union (he had not trusted the reports of their brilliant spy in Tokyo, Richard Sorge), could now bring his Siberian armies westwards. Soon Soviet ski-troops were making surprise attacks on the German rear. Large cavalry formations mounted on shaggy Cossack ponies appeared out of forests to sabre the German supply personnel in their dumps. But the main battle was a frozen, bloody stalemate either side of the Minsk chaussé, the main road into the capital. The temperature had dropped to minus 20 centigrade and the ground was like iron.

Bock's army commanders, General Guderian and Field Marshal von Kluge, planned to withdraw without telling Hitler. Then General Zhukov sprang his surprise on 5 December, two days before the Japanese attacked Pearl Harbor. All the Siberian divisions and reserve tank units, of which the

Germans had no idea, were launched in a series of counter-attacks. The Germans were forced to fall back rapidly to avoid encirclement. Moscow was saved.

The great plan to kill Hitler in Moscow in fact proved a double miscalculation on the part of Stalin, Beria and General Sudoplatov. The city never fell and Hitler, they discovered after the end of the war, never had the slightest intention of visiting Moscow, even in the cursory manner of his early-morning tour of Paris in the summer of 1940. Both Lev and Mariya Garikovna nevertheless received medals from the NKVD for the defence of Moscow. Aunt Olya, hearing of the great battle for Moscow, was torn apart by worry. On 6 December, the day of the greatest Soviet counter-attack, she sent a telegram from Tbilisi to Lev at 23 Gogolevsky bulvar: 'Lyova my darling I am thinking of you please please write I am so worried kisses Olga.'

Lev Knipper, a Russian of pure German blood, had become passionately devoted to the cause of the Soviet Union in the Great Patriotic War. His sister, Olga Chekhova, on the other hand, appears to have become more and more Germanic, whatever she might have been prepared to do to help her relatives in the Soviet Union.

Her wartime passion for Jep, her lover in the Luftwaffe, and his for her, seems to have developed into a real telepathy, although they were usually several hundred miles apart. He claimed in his letters that he could hear her voice on the wind. He also recounted his dreams. In his favourite one, he had been forced to bale out by parachute over England. He found himself coming down in the small, overgrown park of a country house. And in this house, which had thick walls, he found her there all alone. The two of them knelt before the fire and she told him that he would find great peace in this place. He had wanted the dream to continue, but it had ended there.

Their separation was made unbearably poignant for him whenever he saw her picture in the newspapers or heard her on the radio. The local cinema near their air base in northern France sometimes showed movies which she had made. In March 1941, he had again been to see *Befreite Hände* – dubbed into French as *Les mains libres* – in a small local cinema. He simply wanted to feast on images of her even though it was very strange to watch her with a Frenchwoman's 'darker, veiled voice' issuing from her mouth on the synchronized soundtrack. The fact that Olga's co-star in the movie, Carl Raddatz, had been her lover at the time either does not appear to have bothered him or he did not know.

His greatest comfort when flying his Messerschmitt fighter was a small case she had given him with a photograph of her. It became a form of talisman for him. 'The case with the little photograph gives me such great happiness,' he wrote to her, 'because I can always take it with me. Whenever I feel like it, I can look at it thousands of metres over England, knowing that it will share the same fate as me – burnt with me or taken into a prisoner of war camp, or frozen with me in the icy sea.'

He seems to have known that he was going to die, and she must have expected it too, especially after the dream he had recounted. In December 1941, at the same time as Lev emerged unscathed from the battle for Moscow, Jep was shot down over England, no doubt still carrying her photograph in its little case.

18. A Family Divided by War

The battle for Moscow may have been the real turning point of the war, but few Muscovites experienced many immediate benefits, save one. Vova Knipper saw the carcasses of horses killed in the fighting on their way to the slaughterhouses in open trucks, with their legs in the air.

Vova still survived on the billycan of soup which his father brought back from lunch at the Central House of Workers in the Arts. His father usually poured some of his own soup into his son's plate. 'I looked down ashamed,' wrote Vova, 'because I did want more.' The main course consisted of some kasha, reheated on their little *burzhuika* stove, and a couple of *kotleta*, meatballs made from unidentifiable animals, but now probably from the Cossack mounts of the two cavalry corps which had been savaging the German rear. The freezing temperatures had kept the meat fit for human consumption.

After the successful defence of the city, Vova and his father were at least reassured that the restaurant for Workers in the Arts would not be closed, as they had feared during the panic in October. Yet Vova still found that he was so weak from lack of food that journeys on foot took almost twice as long as in peacetime. He often had to sit and rest. On one occasion he watched girls in steel helmets and Russian army boots launching barrage balloons into the evening sky.

Aunt Olya, meanwhile, fretted in Tbilisi, just as she had in 1920 during the civil war. On 27 December she wrote to her brother, Vladimir: 'Lyova has disappeared. I am so worried. My life now consists of waiting.' But before Vladimir could

reply to tell her that Lev had been in Moscow, she saw him
herself. 'Lyova suddenly turned up for the New Year with his
new wife,' she wrote again. 'Well, so what? If they love each
other, why shouldn't they live together? The news about
Lyova getting married has had a great effect on me. His letter
arrived at the end of December. I was very upset at first, but
then felt calmer when I met her. She's sweet, well-brought
up and unpretentious in her manner.'

When it became clear in the first week of December that the
Germans no longer stood any chance of taking Moscow, Lev
and Mariya Garikovna received new orders. They travelled
south-eastwards via the new government centre at Kuibyshev.
There Lev heard the first part of Shostakovich's Seventh
Symphony, which the composer had started writing in
Leningrad during the siege. Lev described the route as 'like
stations of the cross of evacuees – how can one forget the
lampposts with notes attached to them from which human
grief was crying at you – mothers looking for children, wives
for husbands and brothers for their sisters?'

In Tbilisi, Prokofiev showed him the new pieces which he
had so far composed during the war, but the most important
event there had been for Lev to introduce Mariya Garikovna
to Aunt Olya. The two of them moved on to Tashkent on
10 January 1942. Tashkent was where Lev's ex-wife and son
were stranded, without money and close to starvation, yet Lev
never visited them.

He must have avoided them out of what one can only
conclude was a callous moral cowardice. He consoled himself
with the idea that he had dedicated to his son 'some short
children's pieces for string and wind instruments'.

Lyuba and Andrei had been helped by Lev's friend Paul
Armand, the Lithuanian free-spirit. Although a Hero of the

Soviet Union from his bravery in the Spanish Civil War, Armand was consistently rejected when he tried to volunteer for the front. This may well have been the result of his arrest by the NKVD in 1938. He remained in a base unit in Tashkent, where he passed part of his rations to Lyuba and Andrei. Armand's requests for frontline service were finally permitted late that year after the Germans reached Stalingrad. He was killed there by a sniper's bullet.

Aunt Olya, meanwhile, went with the other members of the Moscow Art Theatre group down to Yerevan in Armenia. Her hands crippled with arthritis, the seventy-three-year-old actress found travelling over the rutted roads of the Caucasus both exhausting and excruciatingly painful. But her main concern at this time was the fate of her sister-in-law Masha in Yalta, which had been captured by the Germans in October 1941. 'I shudder to think about what has become of Mariya Pavlovna,' she wrote on 14 January 1942, just before she left for Yerevan.

Her other concern was for Lyuba and Andrei in Tashkent. She sent them money and tea and bacon lard when she replied to Lyuba's 'very agitated letter'. She told Vladimir that she had assured Lyuba that her feelings for her were not affected by Lev's new situation, 'but she had to find a new way of leading her life. It is all very hard.' The ever-generous Aunt Olya also sent Vladimir 1,000 roubles, even though she was starting to run short of money herself. Her main reassurance was that Lev seemed all right, mainly thanks to Mariya Garikovna. 'It seems as if he has finally found happiness,' she wrote. 'Mariya is very caring, she is fun, she is brave.'

Both Lev and Mariya Garikovna needed to be brave. The plan now was for the two of them to attempt a defection to the Germans via Iran, Turkey and then perhaps Bulgaria. They were not the only 'defectors' involved in this ambitious, if not desperate, operation. In Germany they were to make contact with an assassination group led by Igor Miklashevsky. Miklashevsky, a champion boxer and also the son of an actress at the Moscow Art Theatre, had defected soon after the battle for Moscow was over. He had an uncle by the name of Blumenthal who really had fled to the Germans at an early stage of the Moscow campaign. This uncle then became a radio announcer for the Nazi propaganda radio station destined to persuade the Soviet people that Hitler came as a liberator.

Miklashevsky was determined to kill his traitor uncle, but the NKVD had given him a higher priority. He was to pretend to defect to the Germans, saying that he wanted to join his uncle. Two other Soviet agents were instructed to join Miklashevsky in Berlin and await instructions. It appears that Lev and Mariya Garikovna were given the task by General Sudoplatov of 'defecting' via a new route, and then persuading Olga Chekhova to use her contacts and influence to get them into a position to assassinate Hitler in a suicidal attack. Although Olga must have expected some sort of approach at this critical period, she cannot have had any idea 'that her connections might be used for assassination plans'.

Lev's first visit to Iran was quite brief. He flew down, accompanied by Colonel of State Security Maklyarsky. It was presumably a reconnaissance. The Kremlin's interest in Iran at that time was considerable. With a young Shah precariously on the throne, the political situation had echoes of the late-nineteenth-century cloak-and-dagger 'Great Game' against British influence in the region. Lev apparently carried United States dollars for his mission hidden in the false bottom of a large tin of caviar.

Not long before, the Comintern chief, Georgi Dimitrov, wrote to Stalin on the situation in Iran. 'I don't think it expedient in the circumstances to restore the Communist Party there (as fascists would use it to scare the bourgeoisie). Communists must work within the People's Party and pursue their own line . . . I also think that it is not expedient to send a delegate from the Iranian Communists, as this would be used by our enemies in Iran. Instead we should probably send one of our own men there, a suitable one who could work under a legal cover and who could help our comrades in Iran.'

Lev, although highly suited for such a role, was not to be a 'legal', which meant working from within the Soviet embassy. He was to be an 'illegal', preparing his move with Mariya Garikovna from outside. The only cover was his work as a composer. He was there to research Iranian folk music and establish cultural contacts. It was thought that his defection to the Germans from within the embassy would have provoked far greater suspicion. But late that year, after Lev and Mariya Garikovna had returned to Iran for 'defection to Turkey and then via Bulgaria to Germany to join Olga there', the whole project, 'although endorsed by Beria and Merkulov, was cancelled by Stalin'.

Stalin had suddenly recognized the implications of the dramatically changed situation. The German Sixth Army had been encircled at Stalingrad with deep, tank-led thrusts far in its rear. Zhukov and Vasilevsky's restructuring of the Red Army had proved its worth. It was capable not just of heroic defence, but also of outwitting and outfighting the supposedly unbeatable Wehrmacht. The oil supplies of the Caucasus would soon be restored, and the United States was providing massive support in the form of Lend-Lease steel, vehicles and food.

Hitler could no longer defeat the Soviet Union in such circumstances and his own downfall was virtually inevitable. But Stalin now feared the consequences of an assassination.

With Hitler out of the way, the Western Allies might make peace with a new regime and leave the Soviet Union to fight on alone. For Stalin, who judged others by himself, the temptation seemed far too great for Roosevelt and Churchill to leave the Soviet Union and Germany to fight it out to the end. Hitler, who had sworn Stalin's defeat and destruction, now seemed to be his best guarantee of survival.

It was easy for the NKVD's First Directorate to warn Lev Knipper and Mariya Garikovna in Iran that the whole operation had been cancelled, but how Igor Miklashevsky was contacted is still not clear. Miklashevsky did, however, succeed in killing his traitor uncle in Berlin.

Aunt Olya, meanwhile, had fallen ill and recovered, but Nemirovich-Danchenko was now so unwell that he could not be moved. She and Kachalov, who still feared that his son, Vadim Shverubovich, had died, insisted on staying with Nemirovich-Danchenko, while the rest of the Moscow Art Theatre group left for Saratov. On 11 August, she had received a letter from Andrei asking where his papa was. Lev, however, on the way back to Iran, was himself passing through Saratov, where he saw the group's performance of *The Seagull*.

Aunt Olya was still very concerned for her sister-in-law, Aunt Masha, cut off in the Crimea several hundred miles behind German lines at Stalingrad. She had received some food supplies from friends just before the Germans captured most of the Crimea at the end of October the previous year. But the terrible siege of Sevastopol had continued until May 1942.

Masha, the staunch defender of her brother's memory and the Chekhov house-museum, did everything she could to prevent the Germans from occupying the house. 'On one occasion,' wrote a niece, 'a German officer turned up, a Major von Baake. He had a look at the house and demanded to be quartered in Anton Pavlovich's study and bedroom. Mariya Pavlovna would rather have died than give in. She had a long conversation and persuaded him that those rooms were relics. She was allowed to lock them up. The Herr Major lived in the dining room and his men on the ground floor. He only stayed for one week, and when leaving, he wrote on the door that the house was his, and this was why no Germans were quartered there afterwards.'

Masha survived only by selling her own clothes and possessions in order to buy food. Like most of the people in the occupied territories of the Soviet Union, she lived on the edge of famine. A little assistance of an unusual sort did, however, arrive at the Chekhov museum from an unexpected source. Aunt Masha received a picture postcard of Olga Chekhova from Berlin, with a message of greetings on the back from her sister, Ada. It was accompanied by two canvas bags filled with chocolates and biscuits.

There were unfounded rumours after the war that Olga Chekhova had exerted her great influence in Nazi circles to protect the museum. There was even one story that she had flown to Yalta to visit it in an aeroplane lent to her by Hitler.

One good reason why these stories of Olga Chekhova's extraordinary influence could never have been more than wishful thinking lay with Hitler himself. In an act of conspicuous self-denial, he had put all contact with movie stars and movies aside. 'I can't watch films while the war is on,' he told Eva Braun after she tried to coax him back to his favourite pastime, 'when the people have to make so many sacrifices and I must make such grave decisions. I must also save my sensitive eyes for reading maps and reports from the front.' Only Goebbels continued to take an interest in the UFA studios at Babelsberg. The minister for propaganda realized only too well, now that the war had turned against Germany, that escapism was needed as well as exhortation. This did not, of course, stop film stars from being roped into patriotic public messages. Newsreel footage showed some stars bicycling to work, the actor Heinz Rühmann arriving in a pony trap and Olga Chekhova on foot. She was furious to have been denied the use of her automobile.

The most revealing incident had come during Goebbels's notorious speech on 18 February 1943 at the Berlin Sportpalast, following the defeat at Stalingrad, when he had screamed at the audience, 'Do you want total war?' And they had bayed their reply. Newsreel cameras picked out various celebrities in the audience, who had been encouraged to attend by the propaganda ministry. Olga Chekhova was glimpsed briefly, hiding her head in her hands, as if in disbelief. This was not shown in the final *Deutsche Wochenschau* version.

In fact, Olga Chekhova was so much out of things that she would not have been of much use to Lev and Igor Miklashevsky if they had persisted in their assassination missions. She almost certainly had as little idea as the average Berliner of Hitler's whereabouts. He seldom left his gloomy *Wolfsschanze* headquarters in East Prussia and any movements were kept completely secret.

Olga Chekhova may have had little contact with the Nazi leadership at this time, but people still believed that she did. Vadim Shverubovich, acting as an interpreter in his prison camp, suddenly saw in a magazine a photograph of her in some movie role. Although slightly younger, Vadim had known her quite well in Moscow before the revolution because of his father's close friendship with Aunt Olya. 'Oh, that's Olenka Knipper,' he said without thinking to the German officer for whom he worked. 'I know her well.'

The officer was genuinely impressed. The photographs of Olga Chekhova with Hitler had created a strong impression of her influence in Germany too. He said to Vadim, one does not know how seriously: 'Let me tell that to the chiefs and you'll be in Berlin tomorrow.'

Vadim, suddenly alarmed, begged him to forget what he had just said. He knew instinctively that if he went to Berlin, he would never see Moscow again. Curiously, another Olga Chekhova myth arose after the war when it was claimed that she had arranged Vadim's escape. He did escape later, but it had nothing to do with her.

The war had completely cut the Berlin Knippers off from any news of the Moscow side of the family. Olga had no idea that her Uncle Vladimir, the one sent to fetch her back by Aunt Olya on the night of her elopement with Misha, had died on 12 November 1942. Nor did she know that Misha himself, now based in the United States, was making a movie in Hollywood called *The Song of Russia*. This Louis B. Mayer production might best be described as Hollywood's attempt at a second front in solidarity with the Soviet Union. The wonderfully implausible story has Robert Taylor as an American conductor visiting 'a collective farm where the peasants sing, smile and dance all day'. He then falls in love and marries 'a lovely Soviet peasant', the screen daughter of Misha. The Germans invade and the collective farmers resist heroically to the strains of Tchaikovsky. The script was indeed not up to much, but the two writers on it were treated very unfairly. When the movie was examined by the Committee on Un-American Activities after the war on the grounds that it was pro-Communist, Louis B. Mayer and Robert Taylor pointed the finger of political blame at the two scriptwriters and they were both blacklisted.

For his part, Lev was unaware of their mother's death in Berlin on 9 May 1943. The indomitable 'Baba' had succumbed to a combination of age and incessant smoking, not to mention the massive and relentless air raids of the US Air Force by day and the RAF by night.

To avoid the worst of the bombing, Olga decided to abandon her Kaiserdamm apartment in west Berlin and move out permanently to her dacha at Gross Glienecke, close to the UFA studios at Babelsberg. She brought with her the large stained-glass panel of the Knipper arms, that rather pretentious extravagance which she had commissioned some years before.

Lev returned to Moscow in 1943. He and Mariya Garikovna moved back into 23 Gogolevsky bulvar, despite the fact that his ex-wife Lyuba had returned from Tashkent and was living there once more with Andrei. Relations between them, however, were much easier, for Lyuba had now found a new man, a conductor, and the misery of 1941 was mostly forgotten.

According to Lev's liaison officer, Colonel Shchors, General Sudoplatov and General Kobulov visited the apartment, bringing supplies completely unobtainable in the shops, such as 'wine, different kinds of sausage, apples, oranges, canned milk'. This would indicate that even if Lev's immediate family had no more than suspicions about his work before the war, they must have known for certain that he was working for the NKVD by 1942 at the latest.

Lev returned to Iran from time to time, still under the cover of his musical activities. But in 1944 he was attached as a political officer – again with his Walther pistol – to either the 2nd or the 3rd Ukrainian Front, advancing into Romania. He still loved climbing, so he organized the ascent of a peak in the Carpathians.

The rapid advances of the Red Army also meant that the

Crimea had finally been liberated. Aunt Olya, to her great relief, received word that her sister-in-law was alive. Another example of Olga Chekhova myth-making in the Soviet Union also occurred after the Red Army liberated Yalta on 16 April 1944. A military interpreter told Vova Knipper following the war how he had entered liberated Yalta with the troops and on the first day went to see Mariya Pavlovna Chekhova at the Chekhov house-museum. He claims to have seen the photograph of a beautiful woman on her table and asked who she was. 'This is Olga Chekhova, the cinema actress,' Mariya Pavlovna had replied, according to him. 'I don't know whether the museum would have survived if it were not for her.'

This story is doubly dubious in the circumstances. The museum had survived almost unscathed, but Aunt Masha, who had been stricken with typhoid, was so weak when the Red Army arrived that she could not walk or even stand up. She simply sat there crying.

Vova himself, now just eighteen, had meanwhile been called up and was serving on the Kalinin Front. He had received letters from Aunt Olya, who was sorry for him, particularly after the death of his father, and she looked after him during a twenty-four-hour leave in Moscow. He had fallen asleep from exhaustion on Aunt Olya's bed soon after arriving. He woke briefly to see her ironing his uniform, which she had just washed for him.

The rapid advance of the Red Army in the south also meant that many prisoner of war camps had to be moved further westwards. Vadim Shverubovich found himself transferred to a camp in southern Austria, not that far from the Italian border. He managed to escape with an Italian prisoner and cross the border through the mountains. It was a terrible journey, for they had no boots, only scraps of cloth bound round their feet. On the Italian side, they sought shelter in the house of a village priest.

German troops, alerted of their escape, came to the priest's house, but they did not believe that the men could have made it over the mountains already. They just told the priest to keep his eyes open for them. 'They will be here tomorrow or the day after.' It was dangerous for the priest to shelter them any longer, so they were passed on down a chain to the Italian resistance.

When the Americans eventually arrived, Vadim was again able to make use of his great talent for languages. He worked for them as an interpreter, helping with the repatriation of displaced persons. In the meantime, his own family in Moscow had been informed officially that he must be dead. Kachalov, his father, refused to believe this and wrote begging for help to Stalin, who had always admired his theatrical genius.

In October 1944, with the Red Army on the border of East Prussia, the Western Allies close to the lower Rhine and German cities being bombed by day and by night, it was a welcome relief for actors to work away from the capital.

Olga Chekhova found herself filming in the ski resort of Kitzbühel in the Austrian Tyrol. There she encountered Julius Schaub, Hitler's personal adjutant, when he came over to join her at dinner in the hotel dining room. Schaub, she found, was almost totally deaf, having been with Hitler in the conference room at the *Wolfsschanze* when Stauffenberg's bomb went off. Schaub revealed a grim fascination in the experience, for he regaled Olga and her companions with all the grisly details of the explosion. He described how Hitler's arm and leg were burned and his clothes were literally hanging in tatters. She also heard that supplies of canned foods and weapons were being delivered to the Berghof above Berchtesgaden, but whether Schaub or somebody else told her this is not clear.

Olga Chekhova tried to pretend after the war that her outspoken comments to Goebbels on the invasion of the Soviet Union had led to her being blacklisted. Yet she made no fewer than eight films between 1942 and 1944 and she still received the odd invitation from Goebbels. In one of her movies, *Mit den Augen einer Frau*, she even managed to obtain another film role for her daughter, Ada, with whom she had acted in *Der Favorit der Kaiserin* in 1935. But with the relentless Allied bombing of the Berlin area, fewer films were made at Babelsberg. Prague, still virtually untouched by the war and with its shops full of luxuries unobtainable in Berlin, had become the new 'Mecca of the film-world'.

She also travelled to different cities within Germany for guest performances at theatres. In Cologne, however, her hotel was hit in a British bombing raid and burned down. She claimed that she had had to take the train back to Berlin still wearing her stage costume.

A major preoccupation of actors in Berlin appears to have been their cars and the impossibility of obtaining fuel. Olga Chekhova's former lover and close friend Carl Raddatz was reduced to a wood-burning contraption. She herself was furious with Goebbels for having refused her a supplementary ration for her Fiat Topolino. The maximum allowance was just fifteen litres a month, and buying fuel on the black market was very dangerous, since it was usually stolen from the Wehrmacht and therefore the offence could carry the death penalty. By the end of 1944, she was reduced to the S-Bahn suburban train and walking, sometimes up to six miles at a time.

Olga Chekhova had continued with one sort of war work, without any pressure from the propaganda ministry. She used to sing for the wounded soldiers in the Tübingen military

hospital. Goebbels still had his favourites, and 'the charming
Olga Chekhova', as he had so often described her in his diaries,
was no longer one of them, especially after the way her
mother, the formidable Baba, had snubbed him publicly in a
theatre. The propaganda minister's favourite actress during
the war was yet another foreigner, the Hungarian star Marika
Rökk. This time, however, Magda Goebbels approved of her
too. Marika Rökk was a brilliant all-rounder, famous for her
song and dance routines. Soviet intelligence sources, however,
claim that she was spying for them. 'When our troops reached
Germany,' wrote Beria's son, 'she moved to Austria, where
she set up her own movie company, not without support.'

   And yet the odd invitation from Goebbels still came from
time to time. To celebrate the five hundredth performance of
the play *Aimée*, Goebbels invited the cast to his country house
at Lanke, where they feasted on roast venison – a '*Wunder*' at
that stage of the war, with rations so drastically reduced. The
guests found that Goebbels was entertaining alone. His wife
and children were away on what Berliners called a 'bombing-
holiday' in Austria. Olga Chekhova asked Goebbels whether
he planned to extend the house, which by Nazi standards
was surprisingly small and unpretentious. 'The land does not
belong to me,' he replied, 'but to the local town, and in any
case for whom should I carry on building? If I am no longer
alive, should my children take on the burden of the hatred
directed at me?' The future of their children in the event of a
Nazi downfall was a subject which preoccupied him more
and more, yet he publicly berated as cowards and traitors
anybody who mentioned the possibility of defeat.

19. Berlin and Moscow 1945

On 1 February 1945, Olga Chekhova returned to Berlin by train from another acting engagement in Prague. It was the same day that forward units of Marshal Zhukov's 1st Belorussian Front crossed the frozen Oder to seize bridgeheads on the west bank. The Red Army was within sixty miles of Berlin. The news caused horror in the Nazi capital. As far as the propaganda ministry was concerned, the Mongol hordes were at the gates.

Olga's chief concern was for her family – her daughter, Ada, and her granddaughter, Vera. But she had also become extremely fond of another young officer called Albert Sumser. Bert Sumser, like a couple of her previous lovers, was a good deal younger than her: sixteen years in this case. A trainer of the Olympic athletics team, he had met her at a party in Wannsee, which was close to Potsdam, where he was serving as a signals officer. Sumser had no idea who she was, but he had been the only man to stand up when she entered the room, and they began to talk. She gave him her card and invited him to call. He 'did not even dare to think about making an advance towards this beautiful woman', and arrived at the dacha bringing, 'instead of red roses', a brace of wild duck he had shot. With food in such short supply, the very practical Olga Chekhova had greatly appreciated the gesture, as well as his good manners. Then, in the early spring of 1945, when he fell ill, she walked all the way to his barracks in Potsdam with some food for him. It was a round trip of nearly twelve miles on foot through the Königswald pine forest, because by then there was no fuel for the car. Their relationship, 'all based on her initiative', was no doubt made more intense by the dangers and difficulties of the moment.

Olga apparently refused several offers of evacuation. She had decided to stay with her daughter and granddaughter out at the dacha in Gross Glienecke. Ada's husband, a gynaecologist called Wilhelm Rust, had been called up as a Luftwaffe doctor. He was away in the north, attached to the headquarters of General Stumpff, who later signed the final surrender to Marshal Zhukov with Field Marshal Keitel. Their daughter, Vera (who had also, with remorseless predictability, been christened Olga), was only four years old. When Zhukov finally launched the great offensive against Berlin in April, all that Olga and Ada knew of Wilhelm Rust's whereabouts was that his field hospital had been withdrawn northwards towards Lübeck, on the Baltic coast.

Within the family, they had discussed whether Wilhelm should desert and whether they could hide him successfully out at Gross Glienecke, but the pitiless execution of deserters by the SS and Feldgendarmerie made them decide against the idea. To make matters worse, the Luftwaffe airfield at Gatow was only a mile away. Olga later told her SMERSh interviewers in Moscow, 'We agreed that he would surrender at the first opportunity and refer to me, and I could give all the guarantees for him.' Lübeck was expected to fall to the Red Army and Olga Chekhova's 'guarantees' on his behalf could have come only from her intercession with the Soviet authorities. It was a highly significant indication of the influence she knew she wielded in Moscow.

The potential problem there, which she probably did not realize at the time, lay with the barriers of secrecy between the different departments and organizations of Soviet intelligence. Beria was her principal protector as a result of

Mariya Garikovna and Lev, yet he and his deputy, Merkulov, whom she had seen in November 1940, did not even inform their own First Department of the NKVD about the identity of certain agents. And they certainly did not tell SMERSh, the Soviet counter-intelligence force attached to the Red Army.

SMERSh was headed by Beria's former deputy, Viktor Semyonovich Abakumov, who had been promoted by Stalin to provide a counterbalance to Beria's power. On 14 February, exactly two weeks after Olga Chekhova's return to Berlin, Abakumov became the first Soviet officer to enter the *Wolfsschanze*, Hitler's secret headquarters in East Prussia. His very detailed report was addressed to Stalin, but a copy was also sent to Beria, a man far too dangerous to alienate.

While the population of Berlin, especially the women, felt they were now living on the edge of a volcano, Muscovites longed for the peace which finally seemed within their grasp.

'We are already dreaming of the Crimea,' Aunt Olya's friend Sofya wrote to Vova Knipper on 2 April. 'Lyova is going there very soon for about two weeks. He needs rest. He has been working a lot. Yesterday his last piece for the Symphony Orchestra was performed. He conducted it himself.' Lev had returned to Moscow from his role as a commissar in the Balkans, where no doubt his excellent German had been used once again in the hunt for Fascist spies.

His sister at Gross Glienecke, meanwhile, was preparing for the storm to come. Like many Berliners, they began to bury their silver and any other valuables in the garden, and prepared for a siege with food and drinking water in jars in their cellar. Because Olga spoke Russian, neighbours, including the Afghan ambassador and Carl Raddatz and his wife, began to inquire whether they could join her and her companions when the Red Army arrived, as she would be the only person able to communicate with the conquerors.

The great onslaught began on the Oder front before dawn on 16 April. Out at Gross Glienecke, beyond the western edge of Berlin, the three generations of Chekhovas could not hear the massive bombardment, but throughout the eastern suburbs of the city the vibration was so great that walls shook, pictures fell from their hooks and telephones rang on their own.

Goebbels and his wife, Magda, made a last visit to their lakeside villa at Schwanenwerder. While Magda carried out an inventory of the house to which she knew she would never return, Goebbels destroyed his correspondence and personal memorabilia. That was when he showed a colleague who had come to say goodbye the signed photograph of Lida Baarova, which he had kept hidden in his desk since 1938. 'Look,' he said, 'that's a woman of perfect beauty.' He then threw her picture into the flames.

On Friday 20 April, Goebbels attended Hitler's birthday in the bomb-damaged Reichschancellery, the last reception of the Nazi regime. It was a beautiful day, Führer weather, according to Nazi superstition. But the anniversary was also well known to the US Air Force, whose Flying Fortresses appeared over the city in a penultimate raid. Along with all the other dignitaries of the Wehrmacht and the Nazi Party, Göring appeared, having just dynamited his characteristically vulgar country house, Karinhall. Ribbentrop was also there, arrogant and ill at ease. The occasion was a little like the final gathering of a corrupt stock-company going into liquidation. The directors were longing to slip away. The only question in their minds was whether the founder, to whom they owed everything, would fly out of the city or stay to shoot himself.

These were the men with whom Olga Chekhova had been associated in their heyday. This again begs the question whether she had been an 'adventuress', as Aunt Olya believed, or a dedicated agent of the Soviet Union. As is so often the case, neither alternative tells the whole truth. Olga Chekhova had accepted the invitations to Nazi receptions, partly to safeguard her career and partly out of curiosity. She was neither a Nazi nor a Communist. As one White Russian acquaintance testified, when interrogated by SMERSh later, her politics belonged to the pre-Nazi era. Like her mother, she despised Hitler and his entourage, but she knew that she had to work with them. She genuinely loathed their anti-Semitism and had helped a Jewish actor called Kaufmann and his family. The simple answer is that Olga Chekhova, ever since the collapse of her marriage to Misha Chekhov, had been a determined survivor, prepared to make whatever compromises were necessary. She had a number of failings, particularly her relationship with the truth, yet she remained a brave and resourceful woman whose main priority was to protect her family and close friends.

Also on 20 April, Olga Chekhova walked all the way to Potsdam again to Bert Sumser's barracks. 'I have to talk to you,' she said to him. 'What do you want to do after the war? Or do you want to die? I want to save you. Come and stay with me. I will hide you.' Sumser decided to follow her. He escaped from the barracks on an army motorcycle, just as his unit was marched off to defend Potsdam from the Soviet armies about to encircle Berlin. Hitler gave the very weak division, under General Helmuth Reymann, the preposterously inflated title of Army Group Spree. It did little to help them as the Soviet 3rd and 4th Guards Tank Armies advanced from the south-east.

Olga was also concerned at that stage about her sister, Ada,

202 The Mystery of Olga Chekhova

and her daughter, Marina Ried, who were living further out from the city. Yet they were the first to be liberated by the Red Army. 'My darling, darling Auntie Olya!' Ada wrote on 26 April, presumably just after the Red Army arrived. 'I am writing to you at this first opportunity. We are alive and in good health – miracles do happen. I still know nothing about Olga and Olechka – they are in Glienecke. I am living with Marina and her husband near Berlin – all that we had in the city has been destroyed by bombs. Mama died two years ago.' This breathless letter continued and then finished: 'I'm so excited, I can hardly write.' How Ada managed to send the letter is unknown. Perhaps she persuaded an impressionable young Soviet officer that it must be all right to send a letter to the widow of the great Anton Pavlovich Chekhov.

Stalin had ordered Marshal Zhukov and Marshal Konev to encircle the city. This was to prevent both the Nazi leaders from escaping and the Americans from slipping into the city from the south-west. Packed into her little air-raid shelter, the first that Olga Chekhova and her companions would have heard was the battle on 26 April for Gatow airfield, just the other side of a thin barrier of pine trees. There, a mixture of Luftwaffe cadets and elderly Volkssturm militia depressed the barrels of the 88mm anti-aircraft guns to minimum elevation and took on the Soviet tanks advancing through the chaos of wrecked and burned-out aircraft. Their resistance lasted most of the day.

The Soviet troops were from the 47th Army, which had advanced north of Berlin via Oranienburg and then swept south to meet up with the 3rd Guards Tank Army near Potsdam. On that evening and the following day, Soviet soldiers fanned out, searching the area for German stragglers. Their faces were masked by the dirt of the last ten days of fighting.

Olga Chekhova's version of their arrival is characteristically melodramatic. The Katyusha rocket launchers have fallen silent. Only isolated shots can be heard. A Red Army soldier suddenly appears in the doorway to their cellar. There is blood on his forehead. He staggers, and they realize that he is mortally wounded. He points his sub-machine-gun at them, but just as he looks as if he is about to fire, he falls dead at their feet. Her cinematic instincts clearly got the better of her. The dead soldier's comrades burst in. One of them says accusingly: 'You killed Kolya!' Then they march Olga and her family off to the Soviet kommandatura. 'The sentence was execution,' she wrote. 'Just like a film.' But to judge by the general state of affairs at this time, if the soldiers had for a moment believed that their comrade had been killed, they would have immediately gunned down every occupant of the house. And a local kommandatura would not have been set up and operational before the neighbourhood had been secured.

Albert Sumser's version is more convincing. They were sitting in the house, waiting for the first Russians. He was next to Olga and had her little dog, Kuki, on his lap. The first soldiers, surprised to find that Olga spoke Russian, appear to have called a woman commissar. He remembered her black, greasy hair and enormous breasts, and above all her fury. She screamed at Olga that she was a traitor to the Motherland, then grabbed her by the throat, shouting threats. She was fortunately interrupted by the arrival of a colonel, who demanded to know what was happening. Olga immediately told him who she was. The colonel promptly turned on the woman commissar and began yelling at her, telling her she was stupid and ignorant if she had never heard of Chekhov. He ordered her out and told two of the soldiers to stay there and guard the house. No doubt he reported his discovery to higher command, and word was passed to SMERSh counter-intelligence.

The next evening, a staff car containing two Soviet officers pulled up under the tall pine trees outside the house. Olga Chekhova was told to pack a few things and to accompany them. She said goodbye to her daughter, granddaughter and Bert Sumser, who, although of military age, had not been taken away as a prisoner. The two officers were escorting her to the headquarters of Marshal Zhukov's 1st Belorussian Front. This was in the former military engineers school at Karlshorst, on the other side of Berlin, and a wide detour was necessary to avoid the fighting which still continued in and around the centre of the city.

At Karlshorst, she was interrogated on the following day, 29 April, by Colonel Shkurin of SMERSh. It was a strangely restrained and truncated interrogation, almost as if the interrogator had received instructions to do little more than go through the motions. This, it must be remembered, was at a time when White Russians found in Berlin were either executed on the spot or rounded up, ready to be turned into 'camp dust' in the Gulag. The next morning, 30 April, Colonel Shkurin's protocol was sealed in an envelope with a covering letter from Lieutenant-General Aleksandr Anatolievich Vadis, the head of SMERSh attached to the 1st Belorussian Front. Two days later, Vadis, harried by telephone calls and signals from Moscow, was in charge of the hunt for Hitler's corpse in the Reichschancellery.

The package containing the documents on Olga Chekhova was handed to her chief escort officer. It was addressed to Viktor Semyonovich Abakumov, the chief of SMERSh, who had received the Order of Kutuzov 1st Class on 21 April and would soon be promoted to Colonel General, even though the only shots he had ever heard fired had been those of execution squads. Olga Chekhova and her escort were then taken by staff car, probably an American Willys, and driven eastwards to Poznan, captured after a brutal siege in late February. There, an aircraft sent from Moscow awaited her.

Twenty-five years after leaving the Belorussky station, Olga Chekhova found herself back in Moscow. According to Soviet intelligence sources, she was taken 'for a 72-hour rendezvous' to an NKVD safe-house in central Moscow. Abakumov's habit of taking 'actresses, cheating wives, secretaries and foreign visitors' to safe-houses for his illicit affairs compromised these secret locations and was well known within the NKVD. This weakness later featured on the list of charges against him under the category of ignoring 'Communist moral principles'.

General Ivan Serov, the NKVD chief in Berlin, when attacked by Abakumov later – almost certainly on Stalin's orders – wrote a letter of denunciation to Stalin on 2 February 1948, describing Abakumov's behaviour during the battle for Moscow in late 1941: 'Let Abakumov tell the Central Committee about his cowardly behaviour during the hardest period of the war when the Germans were near to Moscow. He went round like a wet hen, moaned and sighed about what would happen to him and did not do anything. His cowardly behaviour influenced the subordinates of the department. His obsequious servant Ivanov, who was responsible for his household, was sent to us to measure up for boots to be made for running away from Moscow. The generals who stayed in Moscow witnessed Abakumov's behaviour. Let Abakumov refute the evidence that during the desperate days of the war, he went to Moscow and chose girls of easy virtue and brought them to the Hotel Moskva.'

In May 1945, Abakumov was thirty-seven years old. 'The very ideal of a Chekist', he was tall and quite good-looking, with sensual lips and 'a shock of black hair'. Like Beria, he was a sex addict, although he resorted less to rape. And also like Beria, he was a sadist who thoroughly enjoyed torturing his victims. Solzhenitsyn recorded that in order not to spoil the Persian carpet in his office, 'a dirty runner bespattered with blood was rolled out' before the unfortunate prisoner was brought in.

Abakumov was also obsessed with stage and film stars, which was perhaps part of the reason for his interest in Olga Chekhova, even though, at forty-seven, she was ten years older than him. He later arrested General V. V. Kryukov, a dashing cavalry commander and close friend of Marshal Zhukov, tortured him personally, and then had his wife, Russia's most famous singer, Lydia Ruslanova, dragged in. She spurned him and Abakumov sent her straight to a Gulag labour camp.

There is no clear indication whether Olga Chekhova slept with Abakumov, either under duress or because she considered it a necessary insurance. Perhaps nothing happened between them at all. But if Abakumov did sleep with Olga Chekhova and he had known of Beria's patronage, he would very probably have sought his agreement first. Abakumov would not have risked antagonizing Beria at this stage. Olga Chekhova's two subsequent letters to him, released by the KGB along with the other papers, are far from conclusive on the issue, despite the fact that she asks in one of them, 'When are we going to meet?' and they were both addressed to 'Dearest Vladimir Semyonovich'. Even the 'Dearest' is inconclusive, since it may have been an actress's professional effusiveness, and the fact that she called him Vladimir instead of Viktor apparently reflects Abakumov's habit of using a *nom de guerre* even in unmilitary situations.

Olga Chekhova's account of her time in Moscow is significantly evasive and flat, though she could have made a wonderfully melodramatic story, as she had of her adventures in Nazi Germany. She claims that she was lodged with the wife of a Red Army officer still listed as missing in Germany. In her version, charming officers who spoke several languages visited her constantly, played chess with her, chatted and then took her off for interrogation sessions in the Kremlin, the only purpose of which was to fill in details about Hitler's circle.

It is certainly true that, for Stalin, the interrogation of all those close to Hitler was a very high priority. Stalin was still obsessed with his enemy and the source of his power over the German people. The copy of Olga Chekhova's handwritten deposition, which the KGB released to Vova Knipper just as the Soviet regime was collapsing, tends to support this. Yet this deposition is far from complete and in any case it was written for SMERSh military counter-intelligence, not for the Foreign Intelligence Department of the NKVD, or Beria's innermost circle. The KGB, not for the first or last time, was shamelessly playing games with a highly selective release of material.

Yet even the limited selection of material made available is enough to demonstrate that Olga Chekhova was taken extraordinarily seriously by the chiefs of Soviet intelligence – one suspects far too seriously. This is amply confirmed by the VIP treatment accorded to her on her return to Berlin some eight weeks later.

During her time in the Moscow apartment after the first safe-house, Olga Chekhova pretended to keep a diary and hide it. She must have known that her SMERSh guardians would find it and read it secretly. 'All that Olga Chekhova wrote,' Sergo Beria surmised years later, 'was clearly written for Abakumov's men to read. Apparently, Abakumov's men really believed that the woman could be naïve enough to keep a diary while living in a safe-house of military intelligence.'

Olga Chekhova, a 'talented actress', he concluded, 'was not and could not have been a naïve person'. An excerpt from her supposedly secret diary was quoted in another document by Major General Utekhin, the head of SMERSh's foreign counter-intelligence. 'Rumours circulating about me are worthy of a novel,' Olga Chekhova scribbled. 'Apparently, there's information about me being intimate with Hitler. My God, I laughed a lot about it. How come and what are all these intrigues about? Incredible and mean slander! When one's conscience is clear, nothing can affect one. And how wonderful it is to speak the truth. Time will show whether they will believe me or not.'

An even more bizarre event took place in Moscow while Olga Chekhova was there under SMERSh protection. Aunt Olya received a telephone call from a Red Army officer whom she did not know, to say that he had brought a parcel for her from Berlin. She asked a friend of the family called Sofya Stanislavovna Pilyavskaya to go and fetch it. Aunt Olya must have been uneasy at anything coming from Berlin after sighting her niece at the end of the victory performance of *The Cherry Orchard*.

The parcel which she fetched was addressed to 'Olga Knipper-Chekhova'. Aunt Olya opened it, read the accompanying letter and suddenly exclaimed in alarm: 'It isn't for me!' The parcel contained evening dresses and the letter was from Olga Chekhova's daughter, Ada, who had sent on these extra clothes, assuming that her mother had been taken back to the Soviet Union to perform in some guest performances at the Moscow Art Theatre.

Aunt Olya rang Kachalov to tell him what had happened and ask him if he knew anything about an invitation to her niece to perform in the Soviet Union. Kachalov was a friend of the military governor of Berlin, the very popular General Berzarin, and managed to put a call through to him. To his consternation, Berzarin was most unwelcoming and abrupt. 'I know nothing about Olga Chekhova, and don't call me any more, forget about it.'

A very confused and alarmed Aunt Olya felt that she had even more reason to hasten down to the Crimea. She wanted, with Aunt Masha, to burn all the letters and postcards from their nieces in Germany.

Aunt Olya, despite the holiday in her beloved Crimea, soon fell seriously ill. Whether or not it was hastened by nervous exhaustion and the strain of recent times, it is impossible to tell. Lev was with her, and when Vova Knipper wrote to Aunt Olya from Moscow about his engagement to Margo, it was Lev who replied.

'Dear Vova,' he wrote. 'I read your letter out to Aunt Olya. She's been in bed since the 6th. Her seventy-fifth birthday on the 22nd was a sad day. And she had an operation on the 23rd. For two weeks her temperature ranged between 38 and 39 degrees. Now she's feeling better after the operation. We think that she'll be out of the hospital by the 30th. We are very happy for you. We are glad that Margo's family has received you so warmly. This means that you won't be so lonely in Moscow at the start of your stay there. It's good that you have completed your studies. Nowadays one does need an education, especially if one wants to be an actor. By the way, I did not know that you were interested in this profession. It is hard work. You have to work hard on yourself. Masses of reading, thinking, and most important for any artistic profession are inner discipline, self-control, and an ability to withstand failures, which are usually much more numerous than successes, even for talented actors. But you saw how your father could work. And Aunt Olya is still working. Knippers are hard-working and they persevere in achieving their goals. Well, that's enough moralizing. I will be in Moscow around 10 October and Aunt Olya later, when she's feeling better. She sends her kisses. I shake your hand. Say hello to Margo for me because I do not know their telephone number in Moscow. Yours Lev Knipper.'

Aunt Olya may have had an additional reason for not wanting to reply in person. She had apparently heard unsettling rumours that Vova had not acquitted himself well during the war and an air of disgrace hung over him within the family. But there was at least one major reassurance for her at this time. On the occasion of her seventy-fifth birthday on 22 September, the veteran actress received the Order of Lenin on the instructions of the Central Committee. Apart from the prestige attached to the award, it was a clear signal that the Knipper family was not under threat from the NKVD.

20. Return to Berlin

On Beria's orders, Olga Chekhova was flown back to Berlin in the last week of June. Her lover, Albert Sumser, described her as looking exhausted and shaken. Those weeks in the snakepit of Soviet intelligence had clearly been a considerable nervous strain, especially since SMERSh was not to know about her relationship with Beria and Merkulov. It would also have been a very unpleasant shock for her if she had heard from Beria or Merkulov about Lev and the plan to use her in the assassination attempt. Her family and everything that she had ever worked for would have been destroyed in such a desperate attempt. One wonders how much this affected her relationship with Lev. They never saw each other again, and it appears, despite some remarks she made at the end of her life, that they did not communicate.

The proof of the importance which Soviet intelligence accorded to Olga Chekhova comes in a letter from General Vadis, by then the chief of all SMERSh groups in Germany, to Abakumov, just after her return to Berlin. Vadis reported on everything that they had done for her. 'According to your instructions, on 30 June 1945, Chekhova, Olga Konstantinovna, together with her family and her belongings, was moved from the place Gross Glienecke to the eastern part of Berlin, the town of Friedrichshagen, where she was given a house in Spree Strasse No. 2. The move was carried out using the resources of the counter-intelligence department SMERSh of the Group of Soviet Occupation Troops in Germany.'

The large house into which Olga Chekhova was moved had been carefully chosen, and one suspects that she had a decisive voice in the matter. Built between the wars, with heavy tiles and a rough stucco finish, it was in many ways a far more spacious version of her dacha at Gross Glienecke. It too had a private, peaceful setting, looking out across water, with its own wooden jetty and heavy willows. The only sound was of ducks quacking gently. The previous occupant had been moved out by a detachment from the 11th NKVD Rifle Brigade.

'After the move,' Vadis continued, 'we satisfied the following of Chekhova's requests, either directly or through the military commandant. 1. Cleaning and partial repairs of the house have been performed. 2. Two cars belonging to Chekhova have been repaired. 3. Chekhova has been supplied with food (two months' rations). 4. Food ration cards provided for the whole family. 5. A supply of milk has been organized. 6. Coal has been purchased for heating. 7. She has been given money, 5,000 Marks. 8. Guards have been placed on the house: three soldiers from the 17th (NKVD) Independent Rifle Battalion.'

The only one of Olga's demands which they refused was that she should be provided with an escort of soldiers whenever she went visiting friends or her dressmaker, to make sure that Soviet soldiers did not steal her car. Although she seemed unconcerned about such a conspicuous indication of her relationship with the Soviet authorities, they wanted to be more discreet. 'We don't give her an escort, using well-founded pretexts,' Vadis explained.

There was absolutely no restriction on her movements. She was visiting the western sectors of the city just as much as the Soviet zone, where she paid courtesy calls on the Red Army commandant and other officials. (In her memoirs she even tries to pretend that she was not living in the Soviet sector.) The report ended: 'Chekhova has expressed great satisfaction with our care and attention. Signed Vadis.'

Olga Chekhova was careful not to make any comment to SMERSh officers on her future plans. Her daughter, however, made polite noises about wanting to go and live and work in the Soviet Union, but their main preoccupation at the time was trying to find out what had happened to Ada's gynaecologist husband, Wilhelm Rust, who was thought to be a prisoner of war with the British. On 24 July, Willi Rust suddenly turned up at the house at Spree Strasse. General Vadis was instinctively suspicious, presumably because Rust had been released fairly rapidly by the British. 'He was being kept in a prisoner of war camp in Denmark,' Vadis reported to Abakumov, 'where he continued to work as a doctor. Apparently, at his own request, he was transferred to another camp in the town of Braunschweig. He was provided with necessary documents, an ambulance with medical supplies and a medical assistant who was also a prisoner of war. Under the pretext of moving to the new place of work in the zone of Berlin occupied by English troops, Rust arrived at Chekhova's house in the ambulance. While travelling in occupied German territory, he was stopped several times by English and Soviet patrols, which let him proceed after checking his documents and the vehicle . . . The circumstances of Rust's return to Berlin arouse suspicion and demand thorough investigation. I need your instructions. Vadis.'

The Soviet military authorities must also have offered Olga Chekhova their postal facilities. Ada had been able to send the parcel of dresses to Moscow and now Olga Chekhova, who had presumably seen a photograph of Aunt Masha in some Soviet publication, sent her another postcard of herself: 'Dear Aunt Masha, Judging by your photographs, you have remained the same, and this is why I have also decided to become a vegetarian. Kisses your [Olga].' Whether or not the two aunts had recovered from their fright by this stage is unknown, but they must have remained uneasy until the award of the Order of Lenin was announced.

Olga Chekhova still managed to surprise her protectors, even though it would appear from several reports that the Spree Strasse house must have been bugged by SMERSh or the NKVD before she was moved there; and one also wonders to whom her Russian maid, Nadia, reported. Despite such surveillance, SMERSh suddenly woke up to the fact that there was another person living in the Spree Strasse house for whom they had not accounted. This, according to the report to Abakumov in Moscow, was 'someone called Sumser, Albert, born 1913, German teacher at the academy of physical education in Berlin, champion in field and track athletics, who lives with Chekhova and has intimate relations with her'. The fact that Bert Sumser had been with the household all along appears to have escaped their attention.

Very soon after Willi Rust returned late in July, Olga Chekhova made a quick trip to Vienna. Travel was not easy at the time, but no doubt General Vadis arranged her journey down there. On her return, she wrote Aunt Olya a letter which was intercepted by the NKVD and ended up in the KGB archive. 'My dear and dearest Aunt Olya, finally I can write to you. I was stuck in Vienna. Now I'm back here organizing my new home. [Ada] and her husband and Ver-ochka are living with me. Dr Rust has started to work here in the hospital. Today I visited Ada [her sister] and Marina and laughed until I cried when I saw how Ada milked her cow. They've got quite a household now.' It is hard to imagine Ada also acquiring the very rare luxury of a cow without Olga's help, since almost all livestock had been seized by the

Red Army. The idea of them each having their own household cow was perhaps prompted by Olga's memory of Chaliapin's cow, which had kept her daughter alive in Moscow during the first winter of the revolution.

'You're so mobile,' she continued in her letter to Aunt Olya, 'that it won't be a problem for you to come and visit. We are all so looking forward to seeing you. You know all the events of the last years from Ada and [Olga's daughter Ada] and Marina. Poor Mama did not survive to see the victory of Russians, to which she had been looking forward so much. I can't tell you much about myself, because the move has exhausted me completely. Simonov has visited us and told us a lot about Lev.'

Konstantin Simonov, the novelist and poet, who later became a great friend of Marshal Zhukov, reached Berlin as a war correspondent at the very end of the fighting. One longs to know what he told them about Lev, and this reference may have been the reason why this particular letter was intercepted.

Olga Chekhova had other visitors, including Western journalists. SMERSh operatives carefully noted their comings and goings. General Zelenin, who took over from General Vadis as head of SMERSh in Germany, reported to Abakumov that she had been visited by an American, a Dr Gun. Dr Nerin E. Gun was a journalist who had recently been liberated from Dachau by US Forces. He later produced a biography of Eva Braun and on these visits was no doubt getting Olga Chekhova's reminiscences of the Nazi leadership. Other visitors, including a French general, were congratulating her on her aunt receiving the Order of Lenin. The British commandant, on the other hand, was given a conspicuously cold reception when he invited her to dinner.

Olga Chekhova cannot have felt any better disposed to the

British when, on 14 October, a London Sunday newspaper, the *People*, published a sensational article about her entitled 'The Spy Who Vamped Hitler'. The author of this piece, Willi Frischauer, poured forth every rumour about her. 'Olga Tschechova [*sic*],' it began, 'famous German stage and screen actress, now lives in a castle on the eastern outskirts of Berlin, fêted by the Russians . . .' It claimed that during the war she had a room reserved for her at Hitler's field headquarters 'wherever he went'. Hitler was 'casting his covetous eyes upon her' and her allure was so effective, the article claimed, that Nazi leaders almost queued up to ask her to persuade the Führer to do this or that. She was portrayed as a 'Polish' Mata Hari and Madame de Pompadour rolled into one. According to Frischauer, her chauffeur was her courier. He rushed off after each meeting with her little notebook, and the details written with her diamond-studded pencil were on their way to Moscow. The inventions and inaccuracies were flagrant, but the article set off a media storm.

Olga Chekhova heard of the article the following day and marched into General Zelenin's office. He reported the whole scandal to Abakumov and included a letter which she wrote to Abakumov on 18 October. This made no mention of the row and was clearly intended to win his support: 'Dearest Vladimir Semyonovich, I take this opportunity to send you my heartfelt greetings and my gratitude for everything. I am giving a lot of performances both for our people [*sic*] and for Germans glorifying Russian literature. I so wanted to see you in my house and if you do come over again, please do visit me. I had a letter from the Crimea from Olga Leonardovna . . .'

'Chekhova is extremely worried by the publication of this article,' Zelenin reported to Abakumov in a covering letter. He also included a copy of the interrogation of a childhood acquaintance of hers, a White Russian called Boris Fyodorovich Glazunov, accused of being part of 'the intelligence organ Zeppelin'. SMERSh, in true Stalinist fashion, suspected everyone and often beat confessions of anti-Soviet conspiracies from any of the usual suspects, of whom the first were Russian émigrés.

Less than a month later, on 14 November, *Kurier*, a German-language newspaper in the French zone of Berlin, recycled stories from the *People* article, and claimed that Olga Chekhova, the movie star, 'the Queen of Nazi society', had received a major decoration from Stalin for her intelligence services during the war.

Olga was furious. A young German woman had spat in her face in the street and called her a traitor. She went straight to Red Army headquarters at Karlshorst and demanded that the Soviet authorities act at once. *Kurier* was forced to print the following statement on 19 November. 'The information bureau of the Soviet Military Administration has informed us that it has been authorized to announce the following:

The article reprinted in *Kurier* from *Mainzer Anzeiger* about the German actress Olga Chekhova does not reflect the true facts. The truth is that the Praesidium of the Supreme Council of the USSR on 22 September 1945 decorated not the German actress Olga Chekhova but the Russian actress Olga Leonardovna Knipper-Chekhova on her seventy-fifth birthday. Olga Chekhova in turn wrote us a letter from which we would like to quote the following:

1. I never received such a high Russian decoration, particularly from Generalissimo Stalin himself. So far I have not had the honour of meeting Generalissimo Stalin. Olga Chekhova, Anton Chekhov's widow, who is my aunt, received the medal on her seventy-fifth birthday.

2. Ex-foreign affairs minister Ribbentrop met me only at official

receptions. I never met foreign affairs minister Count Ciano. I never entered the Führer's headquarters and I did not even know where it was.

3. I know nothing of my influence on Hitler because, like my colleagues, I saw him only at official receptions and I hardly spoke to him. This is why there is confusion about my influence on Hitler in various military and business circles.

4. It is also incorrect that a general whom I knew asked me to intervene with Hitler to ask for the production of special guns.

5. It is also incorrect that the Gestapo arrested my driver in the last few days of the war. I have not had a driver for six years. I could not have a driver because Dr Goebbels, for propaganda purposes, took away my car four years ago so that the people would see that even celebrities had to walk. So now you see what great influence I had on Hitler.'

Kurier finished its grovelling apology with a tribute to 'Frau Chekhova, whom we respect very much'.

This time General Serov, the NKVD chief in Germany, reported the whole matter to Beria, sending copies for Abakumov and Beria's deputy, Merkulov. 'With regard to Olga Chekhova's visit to Moscow in May this year, English newspapers were also publishing different rumours about her connections with Russian intelligence. I put this to you and it is for you to come to a decision and give orders. Signed Serov.' Beria scrawled across his copy: 'Comrade Abakumov, what do you suggest should be done about Olga Chekhova?' It was a Delphic remark, yet when he signed it and wrote the date – 22.11.45 – a stamp appeared immediately underneath: 'Taken under control. Secretariat of the NKVD of the USSR'.

When this copy of the report reached Abakumov, he added his own instruction: 'Comrade Utekhin. Provide a reference on all materials concerning Chekhova. 22.11.45'. General

Utekhin of the 4th Department was SMERSh's most feared
mole-hunter. Did Abakumov suddenly wonder whether he
had been taken in by a double agent? Her friendship with
Glazunov of the so-called Zeppelin Group clearly rang alarm
bells. But it would appear that Beria intended to keep Olga
Chekhova in place and unharmed, ready for use at a later date,
this time against the Western Allies.

The procession of Western journalists to Olga Chekhova's
house in Spree Strasse did not stop, as General Zelenin told
Abakumov on 24 November. She took these opportunities to
deny the stories of her spying, but it did not seem to do much
good. An American journalist called Sam Wagner apparently
told her that she should not deny them. They could make her
a fortune if she came to act in the States. He brought cigarettes
and Cognac as a goodwill offering. SMERSh assumed that
all these journalists were really intelligence officers in disguise,
just because they wore the uniform of war correspondents.

Olga Chekhova finally managed to win peace a few years
later when a Stuttgart newspaper repeated the story of the
medal from Stalin, illustrating their claim with a ridiculous
forgery of photo-montage. They took a still from *Befreite
Hände*, her movie with Carl Raddatz, in which she is holding
up a small statuette, then replaced the object with a Soviet
decoration. Olga sued on the grounds that this was damaging
her career and she won. But her relationship with the Soviet
intelligence services had still not ended.

21. After the War

By the time Olga Chekhova returned from Moscow, the endless work parties of German women had cleared most of the streets and sidewalks. Many of these exhausted *Trümmer-frauen*, or 'rubble-women', tried to live without thinking. Their only hope was to rebuild some normality into their children's lives.

It was easier for most not to reflect on the war which had just ended. They had reached '*Stunde Null*' – the hour zero of their country's lowest moment. For the majority, exhaustion and the shock of defeat, combined with the demands of the Allies to accept partial guilt for the concentration camps, made thinking seem too hard. All they could do was to keep putting one foot in front of the other.

Their husbands were still in Soviet camps and these women, in all too many cases, had faced rape on their own, just as they had had to face the relentless Allied bombing of the city and the Soviet onslaught. Many were deeply scarred by their experiences, some were shattered, but it seems that most were immeasurably toughened by the need to survive the downfall of Nazi Germany.

Signs of the determination to move forward arose rapidly from the ruins. The black market flourished, with a standing souk around the Brandenburg Gate and in the Tiergarten. Prostitution was the shortest route to food and other necessities, but the ubiquity of venereal infection was terrifying. The newly arrived British troops said that in Berlin VD stood for 'Veronika danke-schön'. Flyposters on burned-out tanks advertised dance classes in a strange city of foreign soldiers and German women whose husbands and boyfriends were their prisoners.

Olga Chekhova, whose strength had come from surviving the Russian Revolution, had been spared the suffering of other German women in 1945. Yet the nervous strain of her time in Moscow should not be underestimated. Considering the dangerous game in which she was involved, her nerve was remarkable. At a time when the discovery of a firearm in a house would trigger the instant execution of every inhabitant, Olga Chekhova fired off her pistol at drunken Soviet soldiers who tried to steal her car one night. The fact that she had been provided with a gun is significant enough. And she promptly wrote to Abakumov, asking for more sentries to guard her waterside mansion in Friedrichshagen.

For Olga Chekhova, *Stunde Null* did not exist. She was in any case determined to keep working as an actress. Since few films were likely to be made in Berlin at that time, she gave guest performances and 'chanson evenings' in improvised or patched-up theatres, mainly in west Berlin. Even the deepening division of Berlin between the Soviet and Western sectors did not hamper her freedom of movement.

Perhaps the most extraordinary story of survival in the younger Chekhovian circle was that of Kachalov's son, Vadim Shverubovich. Having escaped into Italy from the Wehrmacht prison camp in Austria, an outrageous fate awaited him entirely in character with the brutal indifference of the Soviet system.

His father's letters to Stalin about him finally had an effect. Vadim was located in the American camp in north Italy, where he was helping to translate in refugee camps. His return to the Soviet Union was organized, but almost as soon as he was back in the country, the NKVD arrested him simply because he was a former prisoner of war. Any Red Army soldier who had surrendered to the Germans was being screened for treason. Most were sent to labour camps. Nobody believed his story that he had been ordered back to report in the capital. 'What, in Moscow?' the NKVD officer asked contemptuously. 'Well, you need to work a bit more – felling trees.' Vadim was sent to a Gulag camp which was just as bad as the German ones he had experienced. He was there in the summer and autumn of 1945. Then, after another inquiry from the Kremlin, he was again traced by the authorities. The NKVD camp administration shipped him back to the Lubyanka. He was by then in a terrible state, ill, emaciated and not very far from death. To cover up the blunder, he was kept there for a month and fattened up on a 'double officer's ration'. At the end of the month, he was suddenly told he was free to go home. His prison clothes had rotted, so he was issued with a smart suit that was almost new. Shverubovich, when putting it on, found that it had two small holes high in the back of the jacket. It had evidently come from the NKVD warehouse of good-quality clothes saved from the corpses of their most distinguished victims. He received nothing else, and he had to make his own way on foot to his parents' apartment on Bryusov pereulok.

Aunt Olya often went out to the Kachalov dacha after the war. She and her fellow actor had been friends as well as colleagues for fifty years, and they sat together on the veranda surrounded by tall trees. The strain of the war years had taken its toll on both of them, with Aunt Olya worrying about Lev and Kachalov about Vadim. 'I've distanced myself from life,' she wrote to Olga's sister, Ada, in Berlin. 'I no longer have the strength to live at a modern pace.' Her only journey away from Moscow was to the Crimea to stay at her beloved Gurzuf. Lev and Mariya Garikovna came to visit her there, bringing their large black poodle, Judy. But by 1947 she was becoming more and more house-bound, often finding it hard to breathe.

Yet even if she had distanced herself from life, life continued to come to her in the form of friends and admirers. 'In the evenings, there is always somebody dropping by, and Sofya [Baklanova] always cooks something delicious.' The immediate post-war New Year's Eve parties at her apartment, especially that of 1947, were memorable. Candles were lit on a Christmas tree, food laid out and the grand piano prepared for Lev and other musician friends, such as Svyatoslav Richter. Lev's former wife, Lyuba, came, with her new husband, the conductor Nikolai Pavlovich Anosov, and the Kachalovs came with their family.

The following year, 1948, marked the fiftieth anniversary of the Moscow Art Theatre. Kachalov, the only other survivor from the early days, was not at all well by then, so Aunt Olya went out to his dacha as often as she could. 'We sit together – he and I – the last two of the Old Guard.' The forty-fourth anniversary of Anton Chekhov's death was also approaching, she observed to Ada in a letter, 'and I am still alive'.

There was also a big party each year for Aunt Olya's birthday on 22 September. Kachalov's granddaughter, Mariya Shverubovich, remembers Lev with his hair turning white and his 'very charming face' which 'always looked tanned'. Lev at this time was starting to lose the hard, haunted look of earlier photographs.

It was impossible to forget the war, even in the most unlikely places. When Lev had the chance in 1947, he organized another mountaineering expedition in the Caucasus. With a small group, he tackled the ascent of Mount Elbrus, the highest mountain in Europe. During the climb, they found bunkers, food depots and the corpses of German Alpine troops frozen into the snow. Preserved by the cold, their skin had gone a dark brown. These were members of General Konrad's 49th Mountain Corps, who had fought on the flanks of the mountain in 1942, just at the start of the battle for Stalingrad. One group had managed to reach the top, a feat trumpeted by Goebbels in the Nazi press.

During his immediate post-war travels, Lev frequently encountered German prisoners of war repairing roads or working on construction projects. He evidently enjoyed their surprise and curiosity when he chatted to them with his perfect command of the language. Lev was to remain under General Sudoplatov's command until 1949 – there was still the task of identifying anti-Communist Russians abroad – but he was never called upon once the war was over. It may well have been this gradual sense of retirement from the NKVD which allowed him to relax at last.

Perhaps it was no coincidence that his relationship with Mariya Garikovna, in a way the most intense point of his involvement with the NKVD, should have begun to disintegrate. In the summer of 1947, she had to stay in Moscow with her mother, who was dying from stomach cancer, while Lev took his son, Andrei, climbing in the Caucasus. While friendship with his first wife, Lyuba, had been restored, Lev's current marriage was giving way to his next.

It is hard to know whether Mariya Garikovna was still afraid of Lev, but she certainly remained in awe of his music. Whenever anybody came to visit and Lev was composing, she would tiptoe up to them and whisper: 'Lyova is working!' Judy, the dog, was locked in the other room so that the maestro would not be disturbed. Even after Lev left her, Mariya Garikovna was very upset when Lev failed to receive some important prize. 'How is it,' she would way, 'that they didn't include Lyova?'

Mariya Garikovna, a brilliant linguist, continued to work for Soviet intelligence. It was on the very morning of her state exam at the Institute of Foreign Languages that Lev told her he was leaving her. She replied with bitter humour that he might have waited until she had finished the exam. When he left Mariya Garikovna that morning, Lev took only his brief-case with him: a point of honour among Russian males when leaving a wife. His first wife's new husband, the conductor, had rushed round soon afterwards with a heavy overcoat. 'Lyova,' he said, 'don't be a fool, it's winter!'

Lev's suffering was, however, minimal in comparison to that of Mariya Garikovna. She was so upset when the truth sank in that she virtually lost her sight for a week. Some time later Lev dropped by to visit her and suggested that they could remain friends and lovers. She slapped his face.

Even though Mariya Garikovna continued to admire Lev the composer, his musical career was not enjoying the same success as before the war. He had been one of the composers invited to create a new national anthem, but his version was not chosen. Then, in 1948, at a time when Stalinism was entering another manic period, the Soviet authorities con-demned Prokofiev and Shostakovich for 'Formalism'. Stalin's enforcer in cultural matters, Andrei Zhdanov, is said to have picked out tunes on the piano to show the sort of music the party wanted. Apparently Lev was out of favour too for speaking imprudently on Prokofiev and Shostakovich's behalf. But he was also frustrated with his own work. Aunt Olya often had to remind him that there had to be failures as well as successes in life. Failure seems to have come partly from his concession to the political pressures of the late 1930s. A few years later Lev admitted that many people thought that his symphonies were in some ways like 'propaganda posters'.

★

Lev's sister remained even more of a mystery. Olga Chekhova and the whole family suddenly moved in 1949 from their SMERSh-sponsored house in Friedrichshagen to a new apartment in Charlottenburg in the western sector. That she managed to do this at the height of tension during the Berlin Airlift and the tight Soviet cordon on the western sectors of the city is striking to say the least.

Olga Chekhova had been in contact since 1947 with the NKVD's star agent, Aleksandr Demyanov, working with Lev's old paymaster, Colonel Shchors. She apparently also maintained her contacts with Abakumov and General Utekhin, until shortly before both were purged in August 1951. In his inimitably devious way, Stalin had used Abakumov against Beria, then he allowed Beria to destroy him, slowly and cruelly. Abakumov was held in appalling conditions, not knowing from one day to the next whether he was to be released or killed. Photographs showed a dramatic ageing in five years. Olga Chekhova, because of her known contact with Abakumov, was regarded as dangerous, but it appears that Beria still wanted to keep her as a card up his sleeve.

In 1952, the Berlin-Karlshorst KGB *rezident* was ordered to find out everything he could on Olga Chekhova. Somebody at Moscow Centre had heard 'a rumour' that she had been flown to the Soviet capital at the end of the war. They wanted to ascertain why, thus demonstrating the confusion caused by watertight compartments within the intelligence world.

Stalin's death in March 1953 produced an outpouring of grief in the Soviet Union, even among families who had suffered during the Terror. Ordinary people wept openly in the street. Hundreds of thousands queued for days and nights to walk past Stalin's coffin. They cried as much in fear as from a sense of loss. What would happen to them now that the great leader was gone? Would there be another war?

The inter-regnum which followed was uneasy, mainly because the inner circle of the Politburo was nervous, and with good reason. Lavrenty Beria seized back control of Soviet intelligence and security. They knew that he was not just powerful because of his position, he was also the most energetic and intelligent of them all. And Beria, they soon discovered, had a master plan. He wanted to end the Cold War through the reunification of Germany in return for massive aid to the Soviet Union from the United States. It may seem ironic that the most feared name of the Soviet system should have wanted to do this. Yet Beria, although never one of nature's democrats, was at least a pragmatist. He knew that the Soviet Union could not catch up and beat the West economically through heavy-handed autarchy.

Beria first needed to sound out the West's likely reaction through unofficial channels. He called on Prince Janusz Radziwill again and warned him to prepare to visit the United States, acting as his personal emissary. He also decided to find out what leading West Germans would feel by using Olga Chekhova. But Soviet intelligence still 'over-estimated the importance of Olga Chekhova in both the cultural and political life in Germany'. In June, Beria summoned the head of the KGB German Department, Colonel of State Security Zoya Ivanovna Rybkina, who had been Zarah Leander's controller during the war. She was instructed to fly to Berlin to meet Olga Chekhova and brief her on her task. On 17 June, East German workers rioted. Red Army tanks were ordered in to suppress the revolt. Beria, despite the alarm sown among his colleagues by events in Germany, decided to press ahead with his plan.

On 26 June, Rybkina met Olga Chekhova in East Berlin.

We have no idea whether any of the Western intelligence services had their eye on Olga Chekhova and became aware of this meeting. In any case, the whole project was doomed for a very different reason. That very morning in the Kremlin, on Nikita Khrushchev's instructions, several senior officers, armed with pistols and led by Marshal Zhukov, burst into a meeting and arrested Beria. The plan to reunify Germany had been denounced by his rivals as 'a direct capitulation to imperialism'.

Olga Chekhova must have slipped back into West Berlin unnoticed. Rybkina, meanwhile, was the one in greatest danger. Khrushchev, who had some idea of what was afoot, wasted no time. He ordered General Grechko, who was in Berlin with a 'special commission', to investigate KGB activities there. Officers at the headquarters at Karlshorst were interrogated to find out if anybody from Moscow Centre had turned up in the city.

Rybkina was saved by one of Grechko's GRU military intelligence officers whom she had known during the war. He helped her on to a plane back to Moscow while other KGB personnel loyal to Beria were rounded up. The purge was even more thorough in Moscow. General Sudoplatov, who had worked closely with Beria during the war, was sentenced to fifteen years' imprisonment on one of the usual trumped-up charges. Many others of more junior rank suffered too. Lev's former liaison officer during the battle for Moscow, Zoya Zarubina, was thrown out of the KGB simply for having been one of Sudoplatov's group. Rybkina also had to leave the KGB. She was sent as part of the Gulag labour camp administration to Kolyma in the far north-east of Siberia.

To the astonishment of her chief in the KGB, she made no protest. 'Do you realize where you are going?' he asked. 'Yes, I do,' she replied. She went to Kolyma and spent two years there. She tried to help those prisoners whom she knew. She even met a German there, a prisoner whom she had met before the war, when he came to Moscow with a German opera group.

Mariya Garikovna also suffered, as another member of Soviet intelligence closely associated with Beria. She was thrown out of the KGB and could not get another job. It was, of course, a small hardship in comparison to what would have happened to her a dozen years before, but she found herself reduced to poverty for the first time in her life. According to her nephew, she was down to a single set of underwear, which she washed each night and dried on the radiator. This penury continued for several years until suddenly a new intelligence regime realized that her linguistic gifts were wasted. She was recalled for foreign service, mainly in Western Europe. It seems as if she was now acting as an 'archangel' to delegations sent on cultural and economic missions abroad. This was a sad waste of her talents, but that was a common fate. Even sadder was the manner of her death. Before a trip to Paris, she underwent plastic surgery on her face. In the Soviet Union such rarely practised techniques were crude to say the least. Mariya Garikovna died the following day from unforeseen complications.

Of the younger Chekhovian circle of cousins from Moscow in 1914, one of the first to die was Misha Chekhov. Aunt Olya showed Sergei Chekhov, who had almost worshipped him, a copy of an American newspaper dated 30 September 1955. It announced that the actor Mikhail Chekhov had died in Beverly Hills. Misha, the anointed of Stanislavsky, had been the 'Method' guru to many actors, including Gregory Peck and Marilyn Monroe. Aged just sixty-four, he had looked much older than his years. Sergei felt, as perhaps Misha did himself, that he had never sustained the brilliant promise of his days with the Moscow Art Theatre as Hamlet, Erik XIV, Malvolio and Gogol's Government Inspector. Did the genius simply wither, once separated from his Motherland, or did he burn himself out with alcohol?

Misha's former wife, Olga, on the other hand, never seemed to burn out, partly because she was a strong pragmatist. Unlike Misha, she never allowed herself to suffer the disillusionment of dashed ideals. Misha himself had been her only ideal, and she was probably grateful in retrospect for the harsh lesson of their failed marriage.

She knew that her profession had increasingly little to offer a woman of her age, but she was determined not to give in. Her slightly raffish and voluptuous elegance had served her well in so many movie roles, but she knew those days were past. She would try other roles more suited to her fifties. To take advantage of the great appetite for the cinema in West Germany during those hard years before the economic miracle, she even set up her own film production company, 'Venus–Film München/Berlin'. Olga made contact with the new Communist regime at the old UFA studios at Babelsberg to attempt co–productions and to sell her films to East Germany. Her big mistake, however, was to make herself the star in three consecutively unsuccessful movies, and 'Venus–Film' collapsed. Yet she still made the most of that boom period. Between 1949 and 1974 she had parts in twenty–two films, nearly half of them in 1950 and 1951.

With Babelsberg in the Soviet sector, the German movie industry was reborn in Munich, with American support. Olga Chekhova moved there herself in 1950. So did her granddaughter, Vera, who also wanted to become an actress. Olga realized at this time that she needed a new parallel career as her movie-making days came to an end. In 1952 she published her first volume of colourful and misleading memoirs under the shameless title *Ich verschweige nichts!* (*I Conceal Nothing!*). She also made her first move into the world of cosmetics, with the publication of a 'beauty and fashion guide' entitled *Frau ohne Alter* (*Ageless Woman*). Although full of Olga Chekhova's rather trite philosophy of beauty, it adopted a surprisingly sexy approach for that repressive decade in Germany. Encouraged by the response, she decided to form her own cosmetics company.

'Olga Tschechowa Kosmetik' was set up in Munich in 1955, and 'expanded very rapidly'. Considering that 'the millions which she had earned during her career were lost' at the end of the war, and that 'Venus-Film' had so recently failed, it poses the question of where she managed to obtain financing. This is of interest because Soviet intelligence sources are absolutely convinced that Olga Tschechowa Kosmetik was set up almost entirely with money from Moscow. One even considers that it offered a very useful opportunity for making contact with the wives of NATO officers.

One must, however, treat such assertions with caution, since Russians still take great pride in the Soviet Union's intelligence coups. This has encouraged exaggeration and myth-making. Stalin is even quoted as having said in 1943 that 'the actress Olga Chekhova will be very useful in the post-war years'. On the basis of the evidence currently available, this seems an unlikely remark, yet perhaps there was more to her career than we know. SMERSh certainly treated her with an extraordinary degree of care and respect on her return to Germany in the summer of 1945. The KGB officers who passed Vova Knipper the batch of papers about his cousin referred to the case as 'a complicated and somewhat unusual story'. There remain a considerable quantity of documents on the subject which have not seen, and probably never will see, the light of day.

Olga Chekhova, although not one of nature's businesswomen considering her failures in the past, was nevertheless immensely disciplined and hard-working. Her extraordinary vitality, which had attracted men so much younger than herself, did not desert her even in her sixties. She still found time to appear in another six films while running Olga Tschechowa Kosmetik. She also encouraged her granddaughter, Vera, in her acting career.

Vera had caught the eye of the most famous member of the United States Army. On 2 March 1959, Private First Class Elvis Presley drove with his two companions, Lamar Fike and Red West, to Munich to visit Vera Chekhova at her grandmother's house in Fresenius Strasse in Obermenzing. Presley had fallen for Vera, by then a beautiful nineteen-year-old, soon after he joined the US Seventh Army near Frankfurt am Main. During his visit to Munich, Vera was acting each evening in a play called *Der Verführer* (*The Seducer*), but the young couple saw a good deal of each other during the day. Presley even sat through a special screening of all her films, and he returned again in June.

In 1962, Olga Chekhova received the *Deutscher Filmpreis*, in her case a life-time achievement award 'For many years of outstanding contribution to German Film'. More intriguing, after the row over her supposed Order of Lenin, was her award from the West German government in 1972. The President decorated her with the *Bundesverdienstkreuz*, the Cross of the Order of Merit of the Federal Republic. She received it along with Konrad Lorenz.

In 1964, five years after Aunt Olya's death, Olga Chekhova wrote to her companion, Sofya Baklanova. She announced that she intended to visit Moscow, accompanied by a small retinue including her masseur, her secretary and her doctor. She wanted a suite in the Hotel National and proposed to visit the graves of Uncle Anton and Aunt Olya in the Novodeviche cemetery. Among the forms she filled in, she claimed once again that she had acted at the Moscow Art Theatre under Stanislavsky's direction. In the end, she never went. It was her last chance of seeing Lev.

Lev did, however, reply to a letter from Ada ten years later. He was still travelling, mostly in Siberia and Central Asia, and planning more musical projects. He was off to East Germany to produce a Symphony-Oratorium on Germany between 1933 and 1945. He was also working on an opera, *Count Cagliostro*, based on the novel by Aleksei Tolstoy, whom he had persuaded to return to the Soviet Union fifty years before. Lev continued to compose obsessively right up to his very last hours in July 1974. A final consolation for this morally tormented patriot was to receive the title of 'People's Artist of the USSR' a few days before his death.

His sister clearly never suffered from political angst in any form. She continued to live in Obermenzing, where she refused to watch a single documentary on television about the war. She complained in a letter to her sister, Ada, that her cosmetics company was getting too large, with 140 employees. This authoritarian matriarch was clearly fed up with all the social aspects and personnel relationships involved. 'A proletarian will always be a proletarian,' she wrote. 'The demands get bigger and bigger but the faculty of reason does not keep up!'

At the very end of her life, Olga Chekhova demonstrated both courage and an urge to follow family tradition. At the age of eighty-three, she was dying painfully from leukaemia, but never complained. On 9 March 1980, knowing that the end was near, she whispered her last request to her granddaughter, Vera.

When Anton Chekhov was on his deathbed in Baden-weiler, he had told Aunt Olya that he would like a glass of champagne. He had drunk his champagne and then died. Olga Chekhova decided to follow his example. She was even able to direct Vera to the correct shelf in the wine cellar. When Vera returned, Olga Chekhova drank down the glass. Her last words were, 'Life is beautiful.'

Although of German blood, Lutheran by baptism and German by nationality for over half a century, Olga Chekhova left instructions that she was to be buried according to Russian Orthodox rites.

Rumours about her mysterious life continued to grow. A German newspaper wrote that Himmler had wanted to arrest her in 1945, because by then he was convinced of her treachery. In Russia it was claimed that on Stalin's personal order Olga Chekhova, with the help of the SS General Walter Schellenberg, went to the concentration camp where Stalin's son, Jakov Djugashvili, was held, but she did not manage to save him. Some time later, the President of Russia, Boris Yeltsin, made a dramatic announcement about the Amber Room – that magnificent present from a Prussian King to a Russian Tsar, seized back by the Wehrmacht during the war and lost. Yeltsin claimed that he knew where this treasure was hidden in Thuringia and that the codename of this bunker was Olga. It would have been so suitable if it had proved true. Olga Chekhova was part of that ancient fascination between Russia and Germany, a dangerous borderland of shifting frontiers and loyalties.

OLGA CHEKHOVA'S FILMS

1917 *Anya Kraeva*
1918 *Kaliostro*
      Poslednie priklucheniya Arsena
          Lupena
1921 *Schloß Vogelöd*   Friedrich W. Murnau
      Hochstapler
      Violet
1922 *Der Todesreigen*   William Karfiol
      Tatyana
1923 *Puppenhaus*
      Nora   Berthold Viertel
      Die Pagode   Olga Tschechowa
      Der Kampf ums ich
      Der verlorene Schuh
      Die Fahrt ins Glück
1924 *Soll und Haben*
      Die Venus vom Montmartre
      Die Bacchantin
      Das Meer
1925 *Mädels von heute*
      Die Millionenkompagnie
      Das alte Ballhaus
      Soll man heiraten?
      Der Mann aus dem Jenseits /
          Feldgrau
      Die Stadt der Versuchung

1926	*Trude, die Sechzehnjährige*	
	Der Feldherrnhügel	
	Der Mann im Feuer	
	Sein großer Fall	
	Kreuz in Moore	
	Familie Schimeck	
	Die Gesunkenen	Rudolf Walther-Fein
	Brennende Grenze	
	Die Mühle von Sanssouci	
1927	*Der Florentiner Hut / Le Chapeau de Paille d'Italie*	René Clair
	Diane – Die Geschichte einer Pariserin	
	Feuer	
	Die selige Exzellenz	
	Der Meister der Welt	
1928	*Moulin Rouge*	Ewald André Dupont
	Marter der Liebe	
	Weib in Flammen	Olga Chekhova
	1812	
	After the Verdict / Die Siegerin	
1929	*Stud. chem. Helene Willführ*	
	Blutschande	
	Irrlichter	
	Auf Befehl der Republik	
	Die Liebe der Brüder Rott	
1930	*Die Drei von der Tankstelle*	
	Der Narr seiner Liebe	Olga Tschechowa
	Liebling der Götter	
	Liebe im Ring	
	Troika	
	Der Detektiv des Kaisers	
	Die grosse Sehnsucht	

	Zwei Krawatten	
	Ein Mädel von der Reeperbahn	
	Love on Command / Liebe auf Befehl	
	Mary / Sir John greift ein	Alfred Hitchcock
1931	*Liebelei*	Max Ophüls
	Panik in Chicago	
	Die Nacht der Entscheidung	Dmitri Buchowetzki
	Das Konzert	Leo Mittler
	Nachtkolonne	
1932	*Der Choral von Leuthen*	Carl Froelich
	Trenck	
	Die Galavorstellung der Fratellini / Spione im Savoy-Hotel	
1933	*Ein gewisser Herr Gran*	Gerhard Lamprecht
	Wege zur guten Ehe	Adolf Trotz
	Der Polizeibericht meldet	Georg Jacoby
	Um ein bißchen Glück	
	Heideschulmeister Uwe Karsten	Carl Heinz Wolff
1934	*Maskerade*	Willi Forst
	Peer Gynt	Fritz Wendhausen
	Maria Walewska	
	Zwischen zwei Herzen	Herbert Selpin
	Die Welt ohne Maske	Harry Piel
	Was bin ich ohne dich!	Arthur Maria Rabenalt
	Abenteuer eines jungen Herrn in Polen	Gustav Fröhlich
	Regine	Erich Waschneck
	Der General	
1935	*Lockspitzel Asew*	Piel Jutzi
	Liebesträume	Heinz Hille
	Künstlerliebe	Fritz Wendhausen

	Ein Walzer um den Stefansturm	J. A. Hübler-Kahla
	Chemin de Paradis	
	Die ewige Maske	Werner Hochbaum
	Sylvia und ihr Chauffeur	
1936	*Der Favorit der Kaiserin*	Werner Hochbaum
	Burgtheater	Willi Forst
	L'argent	
	Hannerl und ihre Liebhaber	Werner Hochbaum
	Seine Tochter ist der Peter	Heinz Helbig
1937	*Liebe geht seltsame Wege*	Hans Heinz Zerlett
	Unter Ausschluß der Öffentlichkeit	Paul Wegener
	Die Gelbe Flagge	Gerhard Lamprecht
	L'amour	
	Gewitterflug zu Claudia	Erich Waschneck
1938	*Zwei Frauen*	Hans Heinz Zerlett
	Das Mädchen mit dem guten Ruf	Hans Schweikart
	Rote Orchideen	Nunzio Malasomma
	Es leuchten die Sterne	
	Verliebtes Abenteuer	Hans Heinz Zerlett
1939	*Befreite Hände*	Hans Schweikart
	Bel Ami	Willi Forst
	Ich verweigere die Aussage	Otto Linnekogel
	Parkstraße 13	Jürgen von Alten
	Die unheimlichen Wünsche	Heinz Hilpert
1940	*Angelika*	Jürgen von Alten
	Leidenschaft	Walter Jansen
	Der Fuchs von Glenarvon	Max W. Kimmich
1941	*Kameraden*	
	Menschen im Sturm	Fritz Peter Buch
1942	*Mit den Augen einer Frau*	Karl Georg Külb
	Das große Spiel	
1943	*Reise in die Vergangenheit*	Hans Heinz Zerlett

	Andreas Schlüter	Herbert Maisch
	Gefährlicher Frühling	Hans Deppe
1944	*Der ewige Klang*	Günther Rittau
	Melusine	Hans Steinhoff
	Shiva und die Galgenblume	
1945	*Mit meinen Augen/Im Tempel der Venus*	Hans Heinz Zerlett
1949	*Eine Nacht im Séparée*	
1950	*Kein Engel ist so rein*	
	Aufruhr im Paradies	
	Maharadscha wider Willen	
	Zwei in einem Anzug	
	Der Mann, der zweimal leben wollte	
1951	*Eine Frau mit Herz*	
	Begierde/Die Perlenkette	
	Talent zum Glück/Das Geheimnis einer Ehe	
	Mein Freund, der Dieb	
	Alles für Papa	
1952	*Hinter Klostermauern*	
1953	*Heute Nacht passiert's*	
1954	*Rittmeister Wronski*	
	Rosen-Resli	
1955	*Die Barrings*	
	Ich war ein hässliches Mädchen	
1958	*U-47 Kapitänleutnant Prien*	Harald Reini
1970	*Gestrickte Spuren*	
1971	*Duell zu Dritt*	
1973	*Die Zwillinge vom Immenhof*	
1974	*Frühling auf Immenhof*	

REFERENCES

Abbreviations

AD-MCM   Arkhiv doma-muzeya Chekhova Melikhovo
(Archive of the Chekhov house-museum at
Melikhovo)

AD-MCY   Arkhiv doma-muzeya Chekhova Yalta (Archive of
the Chekhov house-museum at Yalta)

BA-FA   Bundesarchiv – Filmarchiv, Berlin

GARF   Gosudarstvenny Arkhiv Rossiiskoy Federatsii (State
Archive of the Russian Federation), Moscow

MMKhAT   Muzei Moskovskogo Khudozhestvennogo
Akademicheskogo Teatra (Archive of the Moscow
Art Academic Theatre Museum)

OR   Russian State Library manuscript section

PAK/T   Privatarchiv Knipper/Tschechowa, Berlin

RGALI   Rossiisky Gosudarstvenny Arkhiv Literatury i
Iskusstva (Russian State Archive for Literature and
the Arts), Moscow

RGASPI   Rossiisky Gosudarstvenny Arkhiv Sotsialno-
Politikeskoi Istorii (Russian State Archive for
Social-Political History), Moscow

TB-JG   Die Tagebücher von Joseph Goebbels – Im Auftrag
des Instituts für Zeitgeschichte. Edited Elke
Fröhlich, Munich, 2001

VAR   *Voennye arkhivy Rossii*, No. 1, 1993

Interviews

Lev Aleksandrovich Bezymenski (formerly Major GRU); Professor Tatyana Alekseevna Gaidamovich (widow of Lev Knipper); Vadim Glowna (Olga Chekhova's grandson-in-law); Academician Andrei Lvovich Knipper (son of Lev Knipper); Aleksandr Aleksandrovich Melikov (Mariya Garikovna Melikova's nephew); Eduard Prokofievich Sharapov (former Colonel KGB); Igor Aleksandrovich Shchors (former Colonel KGB); Mariya Vadimovna Shverubovich (granddaughter of Vasily Kachalov); Professor Anatoly Pavlovich Sudoplatov (son of General Pavel Sudoplatov); Albert Sumser (Olympic trainer and lover of Olga Chekhova in 1945); Vera Tschechowa (Olga Chekhova's granddaughter); Zoya Vasileevna Zarubina (former Captain First Directorate NKVD, liaison officer for Lev Knipper and Mariya Garikovna).

SOURCE NOTES

1. The Cherry Orchard of Victory

p. 1 'Attention, this is Moscow . . .', quoted Porter and Jones, p. 210.

p. 1 'Gorky Street was thronged', Ehrenburg, p. 187.

p. 2 'kissed, hugged and generally fêted', *Manchester Guardian*, quoted Porter and Jones, p. 210.

p. 2 'What immense joy . . .', ibid.

p. 2 Muscovites and clothes, Berezhkov, 1994, p. 322.

p. 4 *The Cherry Orchard* special performance, AD-MCM, V. V. Knipper Fond.

p. 4 Maxim Gorky (1868–1936) was a pen name. His real name was Aleksei Maximovich Peshkov.

p. 4 'deathly pale', 'smelled of a funeral', Stanislavsky, 1924, p. 422.

p. 5 Stanislavsky's real name was Konstantin Sergeievich Alekseiev, but to hide his youthful passion for acting from his father, Moscow's most distinguished merchant, he adopted the stage name of Stanislavsky.

p. 5 'a huge chapter', Olga Leonardovna Knipper-Chekhova to Stanislavsky, Tiflis, 19 September 1920, Vilenkin (ed.), Vol. II, p. 122.

p. 5 'Just as he could wear . . .', quoted Benedetti, 1988, p. 140.

p. 5 Stalin's order for the execution of Meyerhold, Isaac Babel, Koltsov (the original of Karpov in Hemingway's *For Whom the Bell Tolls*) and 343 others was signed on 16 January 1940. Meyerhold was shot on 2 February 1940, Shentalinsky, p. 70; Montefiore, p. 287.

p. 6 Beria's former mistress, V. Matardze, and Meyerhold apartment, Parrish, p. 37.

p. 6 Tiflis is now Tbilisi.

p. 6 Moscow Art Theatre request in 1943 for honour for Olga Leonardovna Knipper-Chekhova refused, AD-MCM, V. V. Knipper Fond.

p. 7 Thousandth performance, letter to Olga Leonardovna Knipper-Chekhova, 12 November 1943, Vilenkin (ed.), Vol. II, p. 206.

p. 7 Chekhov and Ranyevskaya. On 14 October 1903, he wrote to Olga Leonardovna Knipper-Chekhova that the part 'will be played by you, there's no one else', Chekhov, *Pisma*, XI, pp. 273–4, quoted Benedetti, 1988, p. 128.

p. 8 'One pair of hands is enough . . .', Vilenkin (ed.), Vol. I, p. 226, quoted Pitcher, p. 183.

p. 8 Stanislavsky's sound effects. His admitted 'enthusiasm for sounds on the stage' during *The Cherry Orchard* provoked a sharp joke from Chekhov. '"What fine quiet," the chief person of my play will say,' he remarked to somebody nearby so that Stanislavsky could hear. '"How wonderful! We hear no birds, no dogs, no cuckoos, no owls, no clocks, no sleigh bells, no crickets"', quoted Stanislavsky, 1924, p. 420.

p. 8 Olga Leonardovna Knipper-Chekhova sights Olga Konstantinovna Chekhova, AD-MCM, V. V. Knipper Fond. The exact date of this special performance has been impossible to find in the files of the Moscow Art Theatre, which are clearly incomplete since there is no record of her appearing in any production of *The Cherry Orchard* between 1938 and 1948, though she completed her thousandth performance in 1943.

2. Knippers and Chekhovs

p. 9 August Knipper, the actress's grandfather, however, was a metalworker. His son, Leonhardt Knipper, left Germany to seek his fortune as an engineer at the age of twenty-five. Leonard Knipper (he had soon dropped the Germanic spelling of his first name) moved to Glazov in the Urals to run a paper factory. His wife, Anna Salza, a talented pianist, came from Baltic German stock. She was ten years younger than him. Leonard and Anna spoke German at home and remained Lutherans, even though they took on Russian nationality. Konstantin, their eldest child, had been born before their move to Glazov, and Olga was born there, but in 1872 the family moved to Moscow, where a second son, Vladimir, or Volodya, was born later. They spent their winters there in a villa on the Novinsky bulvar. Knipper ancestry, V. V. Knipper, pp. 26–30; Helker and Lenssen, p. 22; and Andrei Lvovich Knipper, interview, 22 September 2002. In her memoirs Olga Chekhova claims that the Knippers were of noble descent. This is not really true. The Knipper ancestor who had been the court architect of Wenceslas III, the Elector of Westphalia, had been ennobled, but the title was stripped from him later. Olga Chekhova's father, Konstantin Leonardovich Knipper, was automatically ennobled according to Peter the Great's 'Table of Ranks', purely because of his post as an official in the Ministry of Transport, but then so was Lenin's father as an inspector of schools. Another branch of the Knipper family had gone to Russia in the eighteenth century. Karl Knipper, a ship-owner, had set up and sponsored a group of German actors in St Petersburg in 1787. V. V. Knipper, p. 22.

p. 10 'my vaulting-horse', quoted Rayfield, n. 37, p. 622.

p. 11 'cows who fancy . . .', 'Machiavellis in skirts', quoted Rayfield, 1997, p. 183.

p. 11 'Have you been carried away by his moiré silk lapels?', quoted ibid., p. 505.

p. 12 Just before Chekhov's death in 1904, Gorky was so provoked by a jealous attack from Olga Leonardovna Knipper-Chekhova's former lover Nemirovich-Danchenko that he severed his ties with the Moscow Art Theatre. For the row between Nemirovich-Danchenko and Gorky in April 1904, see Benedetti, 1988, pp. 139–48.

p. 13 'little skeleton', OR 331/62/27, quoted Rayfield, 1997, p. 118.

p. 13 'Natalya is living in my apartment . . .', 24 October 1888, quoted ibid., p. 179. These two children, Nikolai (Kolya) and Anton, were the children of Aleksandr and his common-law wife, the divorcée Anna Ivanovna Khrushchiova-Sokolnikova.

p. 14 'thunderous voice', Čechov, 1992, p. 12.

p. 15 'Am in the Crimea', ibid., p. 20.

p. 15 'Misha is an amazingly intelligent boy', Sergei Mikhailovich Chekhov, MS, AD-MCM/Sakharova/File 81.

p. 16 Konstantin Knipper's wife's name in her passport had been Yelena Yulievna Ried, but within the family she was Luise or Lulu, and later, when a grandmother, Baba.

p. 16 Her school records give her date of birth as 13 April 1897, but that was according to the old Orthodox calendar, RGALI 677/1/4087.

p. 16 Olga Konstantinovna Chekhova's birthplace according to official documents, AD-MCM, V. V. Knipper Fond.

p. 17 'a hunting lodge', Tschechowa, 1952a, p. 53.

p. 18 'I hellishly wanted . . .', quoted Rayfield, 1997, p. 573.

p. 18 'which looked like a see-saw', Andrei Lvovich Knipper, interview, 22 September 2002.

p. 18 'first music shock', L. K. Knipper, p. 11.

p. 20 'unruly character', ibid.

p. 20 Olga Chekhova's school record, Stroganov Art School, personal file of Olga Konstantinovna Knipper, 1913, RGALI 677/1/4087.

p. 20 'such a beauty . . .', Tatyana Alekseevna Gaidamovich, interview, 4 January 2003.

p. 20 'You will definitely . . .', Tschechowa, 1973, p. 37. Needless to say, her conversation with Duse is different in the two versions of her memoirs. In the 1952 version Duse also gives her a tiny pair of silver ice-skates for a doll and says: 'You are so beautiful that you should be kept away from the theatre!', Tschechowa, 1952a, p. 69.

3. Mikhail Chekhov

p. 21 Mikhail Chekhov at Maly Theatre School, Sergei Mikhailovich Chekhov, MS, AD-MCM/Sakharova/File 81.

p. 21 October 1911, Čechov, 1992, p. 44.

p. 21 'He was short, thin and moved restlessly . . .', Sergei Mikhailovich Chekhov, MS, AD-MCM/Sakharova/File 81.

p. 22 'as if I had to . . .', Čechov, 1992, p. 57.

p. 22 'Thank you, Aunt Masha . . .', quoted Sergei Mikhailovich Chekhov, MS, AD-MCM/Sakharova/File 81.

p. 22 Aleksandr Chekhov's death, Čechov, 1992, pp. 28–9.

p. 23 'I visited Mishka several times . . .', Valdimir Ivanovich Chekhov, 19 August 1913, quoted Sergei Mikhailovich Chekhov, MS, AD-MCM/Sakharova/File 81.

p. 23 'second-rate people', Sergei Mikhailovich Chekhov, MS, AD-MCM/Sakharova/File 81.

p. 24 'Volodya wrapped in this carpet . . .', ibid.

p. 24 'My darling Mashechka, calm down . . .', ibid.

p. 25 'Agitation is expressed . . .', Stanislavsky, *Sobranie sochineny*, Vol. VI, p. 48, quoted Benedetti, 1988, p. 191.

p. 25 Breakfasts with Stanislavsky, Čechov, 1992, p. 58.

p. 26 Prechistensky bulvar was renamed Gogolevsky bulvar in the early 1920s, after the revolution.

p. 26 *The Rose and the Cross*, L. K. Knipper, p. 13.

4. *Misha and Olga*

p. 27 'From my earliest youth . . .', Čechov, 1992, p. 33.

p. 28 Misha's only comment on their engagement was: 'Olga Leonardovna Knipper-Chekhova had two nieces staying with her and I decided to marry one of them', ibid., p. 71. He was, however, more generous about the failure of their marriage later.

p. 29 If such a man kissed me', Tschechowa, 1973, p. 53. See also Tschechowa, 1952a, pp. 83–4 for other variations.

p. 30 To this day, a passport in Russia is also the state internal identity card.

p. 30 'Oh, but your nephew . . .', Sergei Mikhailovich Chekhov, MS, AD-MCM/Sakharova/File 81. According to Olga Chekhova, Olga Leonardovna Knipper-Chekhova rang the apartment to find out why Misha had failed to appear at the theatre, Tschechowa, 1973, pp. 86–7.

p. 31 'I said that [Olga] herself . . .', Sergei Mikhailovich Chekhov, MS, AD-MCM/Sakharova/File 81.

p. 31 'Come at once', Tschechowa, 1973, p. 56.

p. 32 'Thank God . . .', ibid.

p. 32 If Olga's father, Konstantin Knipper, was there at that time, then it was probably on a brief visit. Between 1912 and 1915 he was based mostly in Ekaterinburg, where Olga's imagined friends the Grand Duchesses were to be murdered four years later.

p. 32 'crying her eyes out', Tschechowa, 1973, p. 57.

p. 32 Olga's threatened suicide, Tschechowa, 1952a, p. 87.

p. 32 'We're already in Petrograd for a week . . .', Sergei Mikhailovich Chekhov, Sakharova (ed.), p. 264.

p. 33 'Beautiful Mashechka . . .', quoted Sergei Mikhailovich Chekhov, MS, AD-MCM/Sakharova/File 81.

p. 33 'I was at the family dinner . . .', ibid.

p. 33 'two left hands', Tschechowa, 1973, p. 58.

p. 33 'waiting for one's call-up . . .', Čechov, 1992, p. 148.

p. 34 'surge of false patriotism', L. K. Knipper, p. 14.

5. *The Beginning of a Revolution*

p. 35 'patriotic plays', 'art showed that it had . . .', Stanislavsky, 1924, p. 548.

p. 36 'the miraculous liberation of Russia', Stanislavsky to Kotliarevsky, 3 March 1917, quoted Benedetti, 1988, p. 225.

p. 37 'I hope you aren't angry . . .', quoted Sergei Mikhailovich Chekhov, MS, AD-MCM/Sakharova/File 81.

p. 37 'Deep effect', 'a true Russian', 'Paper! Pen! . . .', Tschechowa, 1952a, pp. 88–9.

p. 37 'My dear Masha . . .', AD-MCM/Sakharova/File 81.

p. 38 'small, utterly primitive . . .', Tschechowa, 1973, p. 65.

p. 38 Olga Chekhova and meningitis, Silvia Honold, 'Gespräch mit Olga Tschechowa', Munich, 1962, unpublished MS, p. 136, quoted Helker and Lenssen, p. 60.

p. 40 'hysterical hedonism', Figes, p. 283.

p. 40 'The ethical side of the theatre . . .', Stanislavsky to Nemirovich-Danchenko, 11 August 1916, quoted Benedetti (ed.), p. 303.

6. *The End of a Marriage*

p. 41 'She had been brought up . . .', Sergei Mikhailovich Chekhov, MS, AD-MCM/Sakharova/File 81.

p. 41 'In the drawer . . .', Čechov, 1992, p. 72.

p. 42 Bread queues, Figes, pp. 299–300.

p. 42 Lev Knipper and military career, Andrei Lvovich Knipper, interview, 23 September 2002.

p. 42 'would probably collapse . . .', quoted Figes, pp. 321, 276.

p. 44 Olga Chekhova on Kerensky, Tschechowa, 1952a, p. 92.

p. 44 'done over', Stanislavsky, quoted Benedetti, 1988, p. 225.

p. 45 'gray-clad mobs', etc., Stanislavsky, 1924, pp. 553–4. For *The Cherry Orchard* at the Theatre of the Soviet of Workers' Deputies, see Benedetti, 1988, p. 226.

p. 46 'The Bolsheviks are ruining . . .', V. V. Knipper, p. 83.

p. 47 'like a carved . . .', Čechov, 1992, p. 80.

p. 48 'He was an adventurer . . .', 'already in her overcoat', ibid., pp. 78–9.

7. *Frost and Famine*

p. 52 *Anya Kraeva*, etc. Olga Chekhova's movies made in Russia were never mentioned on her curriculum vitae in later years. As far as her version of history is concerned, *Schloß Vogelöd*, the first film she made in Germany, was her first film.

p. 52 'Proletkult', Figes, pp. 736–7, 742, 745.

p. 53 'always served beauty . . .', 'we have become . . .', Stanislavsky, 1924, pp. 556, 563.

p. 53 'Masha my dearest . . .', Olga Leonardovna Knipper-Chekhova to Mariya Pavlovna Chekhova, Moscow, 28 February 1918, Vilenkin (ed.), Vol II, p. 118.

p. 54 'the devastation and neglect . . .', 'It's not revolution . . .', ibid., pp. 119, 74, quoted Pitcher, p. 217.

p. 56 42 per cent of Moscow's prostitutes, 'ruined by the revolution', Figes, p. 605.

p. 56 'I was playing . . .', Olga Leonardovna Knipper-Chekhova to Mariya Pavlovna Chekhova, Moscow, 10 April 1918, Vilenkin (ed.), Vol. II, p. 119.

p. 57 'Every day, my sister Ada and I . . .', Silvia Honold, 'Gespräch mit Olga Tschechowa', Munich, 1962, unpublished MS, p. 51, quoted Helker and Lenssen, p. 62.

p. 57 'Sugar is seventy-five roubles . . .', Olga Leonardovna Knipper-Chekhova to Mariya Pavlovna Chekhova, Moscow, 22–26 January 1919, Vilenkin (ed.), Vol. II, p. 120.

p. 59 Death of Natalya Aleksandrovna, Čechov, 1992, p. 121; and Sergei Mikhailovich Chekhov, MS, AD-MCM/Sakharova/File 81.

8. Surviving the Civil War

p. 61 'You've got red devils . . .', Andrei Lvovich Knipper, interview, 22 September 2002.

p. 61 Lev Knipper's version of his role in the Russian civil war, L. K. Knipper, p. 15.

p. 62 Cheka atrocities, Figes, pp. 646–7 for examples.

p. 63 'catastrophe', Stanislavsky, 1924, p. 557.

p. 63 Shverubovich was Kachalov's real family name; Kachalov was just a stage name.

p. 63 This account of the Moscow Art Theatre group in Kharkov is based mainly on that of the stage manager, S. Bertensson, *Vokrug iskusstva*, Los Angeles, 1957, quoted Pitcher, pp. 219–25.

p. 65 'took away all chance . . .', Stanislavsky, 1924, p. 557.

p. 66 'Stanislavsky is a real artist . . .', quoted N. I. Komarovskaya, *Videnoe i perezhitoe*, Moscow, 1965, p. 139, quoted Benedetti, 1988, p. 230.

p. 67 'Auntie Manya, Uncle Vanya . . .', Mayakovsky, SS, Vol. IX, pp. 107–8, quoted Benedetti, 1988, p. 248.

p. 67 'We interpreted Mayakovsky's suicide', quoted Shentalinsky, p. 48. Mayakovsky killed himself in 1930. Stalin later insisted, with unparalleled cynicism, that Mayakovsky was 'the most talented poet of our Soviet epoch' and that 'indifference to his memory is a crime'.

p. 67 Anton Chekhov's day. Less than five years later, Stanislavsky wrote: 'The life that Chekhov painted is gone, but his art is still with us. Many young people know nothing of that life, for they appeared on the scene long after it passed. Revolutions and wars created cruel but interesting moments in the life of man, who in one day, sometimes in one hour, passed through what it took a man of the generation before tens of years to experience', Stanislavsky, 1924, p. 565.

9. *The Dangers of Exile*

p. 70 Lev Knipper in civil war, Andrei Lvovich Knipper, interview, 23 September 2002.

p. 70 Kachalov group in the Caucasus. This account comes mainly from Pitcher, pp. 221–6, which in turn comes partly from S. Bertensson, *Vokrug iskusstva*, Los Angeles, 1957.

p. 71 Vadim Shverubovich, Mariya Vadimovna Shverubovich, interview, 16 September 2003.

p. 72 Novorossiisk, Figes, p. 679.

p. 73 Likani Palace, Montefiore, p. 546.

p. 73 'I have been suffering . . .', Olga Leonardovna Knipper-Chekhova to Mariya Pavlovna Chekhova, Tiflis, 11 September 1920, Vilenkin (ed.), Vol. II, p. 121.

p. 74 ' "Our life in this house is over" . . .', Olga Leonardovna Knipper-Chekhova to Stanislavsky, Tiflis, 19 September 1920, ibid., p. 122.

p. 74 'You don't understand . . .', Olga Leonardovna Knipper-Chekhova to Mariya Pavlovna Chekhova, Tiflis, 11 September 1920, ibid., p. 121.

p. 75 Wrangel army at Gallipoli. 'One fifth of the corps left Gallipoli prior to its exodus to the Balkan countries [principally Bulgaria]. One soldier in four and one officer in six became refugees and left the peninsula before the rest of the army. Only 3.67 per cent returned to Soviet Russia, of which a little over 0.5 per cent were officers', N. D. Karpov, 'Krym – Gallipoli – Balkany', *Voenno-istorichesky arkhiv*, No. 1 (16), 2001, pp. 4–16.

p. 77 'real mother', Tschechowa, 1973, p. 85.

p. 77 Krupskaya signing Olga Chekhova's exit pass, Silvia Honold, 'Gespräch mit Olga Tschechowa', Munich, 1962, unpublished MS, quoted Helker and Lenssen, p. 63; Lunacharsky, Tschechowa, 1973, pp. 85–6.

p. 78 'They have written to me . . .', Olga Leonardovna Knipper-Chekhova to Mariya Pavlovna Chekhova, Tiflis, 11 September 1920, Vilenkin (ed.), Vol. II, p. 121.

10. The Far-Flung Family

p. 79 Hamsun novel, *In the Claws of Life*, Pitcher, p. 227.

p. 79 'rushed towards the orchestra pit . . .', Vilenkin (ed.), Vol. II, p. 344, quoted Pitcher, p. 227.

p. 80 'We lit candles. . . .', Olga Leonardovna Knipper-Chekhova to Stanislavsky, Zagreb, January–February 1921, Vilenkin (ed.), Vol. II, p. 123.

p. 80 'the aunt who gave birth . . .', Andrei Lvovich Knipper, interview, 23 September 2002.

p. 80 The complications in the return to Moscow, Mariya Vadimovna Shverubovich, interview, 25 September 2003.

p. 81 'Are you staying . . .', Tschechowa, 1973, p. 87.

p. 81 Pension in Gross-Beeren-Strasse, ibid., p. 89. This version is rather more convincing than Olga Chekhova's earlier account, in which she claimed that she rang Gräfin von Trittleben, whose daughter had stayed with the Knipper family in Moscow, and was received in luxury, Tschechowa, 1952a, p. 101. Perhaps the schoolfriend was the Trittleben daughter, but it is sometimes very hard to unravel the different versions.

p. 81 The ring smuggled under her tongue. This was according to Tschechowa, 1973, p. 86. But Tschechowa, 1952a, p. 101, states that it was 'sewn into my overcoat'.

p. 82 'that she had the quintessential face . . .', ibid., p. 103.

p. 83 'I could not imagine . . .', Olga Chekhova to Olga Leonardovna Knipper-Chekhova, 16 March 1924, MMKhAT, K-Ch No. 2761.

p. 83 The première of *Schloß Vogelöd*, Helker and Lenssen, p. 82.

p. 84 'We will be playing . . .', Olga Leonardovna Knipper-Chekhova to E. N. Konshina, Prague, 12–18 September 1921, Vilenkin (ed.), Vol. II, pp. 124–5.

p. 84 'Kachalov was looking beautiful', Olga Leonardovna Knipper-Chekhova to Stanislavsky, Prague, 18–19 September 1921, ibid., pp. 126–7.

p. 84 'with a family name . . .', Vilenkin, p. 184.

p. 84 'I have been ill recently', Olga Leonardovna Knipper-Chekhova to E. N. Konshina, Prague, 12–18 September 1921, Vilenkin (ed.), Vol. II, pp. 124–5.

p. 85 'You mustn't think . . .', quoted ibid., p. 127.

p. 85 'I have just come back . . .', Olga Leonardovna Knipper-Chekhova to Nemirovich-Danchenko, Berlin, 14 February 1922, ibid., p. 130.

11. The Early 1920s in Moscow and Berlin

p. 87 'standard-bearer of the bourgeoisie', quoted Benedetti (ed.), 1991, p. 316.

p. 87 'When we play the farewell . . .', Stanislavsky to Nemirovich-Danchenko, Berlin, 1922, Stanislavsky, *Sobranie sochineny*, Vol. VII, p. 29, quoted Benedetti, 1988, p. 249.

p. 87 'the same old snub-nosed little idiot Petrushka', ibid., p. 247.

p. 88 'the vivid, external . . .', Stanislavsky, *Sobranie sochineny*, Vol. VI, p. 256, quoted Benedetti, 1988, p. 246.

p. 88 'unforgettable', 'As the play finished . . .', Sergei Mikhailovich Chekhov, MS, AD-MCM/Sakharova/File 81.

p. 88 'I am staying with Misha . . .', ibid.

p. 90 UFA development in 1920s, see Beyer, 1992, pp. 10–11.

p. 91 'At last!', 'It will be very interesting . . .', quoted Vladimir Bonch-Bruevich, 'Zritel i slushatel', *Sovetskoe iskusstvo*, 29 January 1934, quoted Turovskaya, pp. 206–7.

p. 91 'Here I am in Moscow . . .', Olga Leonardovna Knipper-Chekhova to Mariya Pavlovna Chekhova, Moscow, 6 June 1922, Vilenkin (ed.), Vol. II, p. 131.

p. 92 'There was a small . . .', V. V. Knipper, p. 56.

p. 92 'For you, Olga Leonardovna . . .', ibid.

p. 93 Ada did not marry the father of her daughter, Marina Ried. Ried was Ada's mother's maiden name. Olga Leonardovna Knipper-Chekhova also writes in the same letter of 6 June 1922 that she is sad that her sister-in-law is to take Olga's little daughter to Berlin, a city 'which I hate'. This indicates that the plan for Olga's mother to take little Ada to Berlin had been established well before Konstantin Knipper's death in January 1924. Olga's sister, Ada, was again living with their aunt at 23 Prechistensky bulvar. 'I am living here with my niece Ada . . .', Olga Leonardovna Knipper-Chekhova to P. F. Sharov, Moscow, 3 August 1922, Vilenkin (ed.), Vol. II, p. 132.

p. 93 'On my return to Moscow . . .', L. K. Knipper, p. 23.

p. 93 'after he returned . . .', Lev Bezymenski, *Die Zeit*, 15 October 1993, and interview, 17 September 2003. See also Sudoplatov, 1995, p. 159. According to Anatoly Pavlovich Sudoplatov, interview, 24 September 2003, there is a file in the Lubyanka of secret correspondence between Lev and Olga. In December 1921, the Cheka had become the OGPU (Obeyedinyonnoy Gosudarstvennoy Politischeskoy Upravlenie), or Unified State Political Directorate. It became part of the NKVD in 1934.

p. 95 'Lev has just turned up . . .', Olga Leonardovna Knipper-Chekhova to P. F. Sharov, Moscow, 3 August 1922, Vilenkin (ed.), Vol. II, p. 132.

p. 95 'a committee of professors . . .', 'to join the theatre on paper', L. K. Knipper, pp. 47–8. Lev's only son, Academician Andrei Lvovich Knipper, says himself that the only possible explanation for his father being allowed abroad so soon after his return was that he was working for the OGPU, interview, 23 September 2002.

p. 95 'From time to time . . .', quoted Lev Bezymenski, *Die Zeit*, 15 October 1993.

p. 95 For Cheka and OGPU operations against émigré groups, see Andrew and Gordievsky, pp. 67–78. INO was founded in 1920 and headed by Mikhail Abramovich Trilisser. In 1941 INO became INU, Inostrannoye Upravlenie, or the Foreign Intelligence Directorate of the NKGB.

p. 96 'main foreign target', ibid., p. 115.

p. 96 Lev Knipper and Aleksei Tolstoy, Anatoly Pavlovich Sudoplatov, interview, 24 September 2003.

p. 97 For the Russian émigré community in Berlin, see the catalogue of the exhibition 'Das russische Berlin 1918–1941', May 2002.

p. 98 'And when are we going to hear the real chimes?' The *Tsar Fyodor* production in Berlin is described in Benedetti, 1988, pp. 252–3.

12. Home Thoughts from Abroad

p. 100 'My fate has torn me away . . .', Olga Leonardovna Knipper-Chekhova to E. N. Konshina, Paris, 12–14 December 1922, Vilenkin (ed.), Vol. II, pp. 134–5.

p. 100 'It's so noisy . . .', Olga Leonardovna Knipper-Chekhova to F. N. Mikhailsky, New York, 19 January 1923, ibid., p. 136.

p. 101 'He's thin and angular', 'There's suffering in his face . . .', 'It is so touching . . .', Olga Leonardovna Knipper-Chekhova to E. N. Konshina, New York, 18 November 1923, ibid., p. 143.

p. 102 'I'm plunged into expressionism', Freiburg, 14 June 1923, MMKhAT, K-Ch No. 2733.

p. 102 'I spent only three days . . .', Olga Leonardovna Knipper-Chekhova to V. L. Knipper, Freiburg, 27 June 1923, V. V. Knipper, p. 102.

p. 103 'more slave labour in America . . .', Olga Leonardovna

Knipper-Chekhova to V. V. Knipper, Freiburg, 31 August 1923, ibid., p. 103.

p. 103 'What was our horror . . .', *Krokodil*, 28 October 1923, quoted Benedetti, 1988, p. 263.

p. 104 'Moscow accuses us of disloyalty . . .', Stanislavsky to Nemirovich-Danchenko, 28 December 1923, ibid.

p. 104 *Prozhektor* photograph, V. V. Knipper, p. 106.

p. 104 'a trustful relationship . . .', Sudoplatov, 1996, p. 146.

p. 105 Olga Chekhova as 'sleeper', Anatoly Pavlovich Sudoplatov, interview, 25 September 2003.

p. 105 'Here at last, Comrades . . .', quoted Andrew and Gordievsky, p. 58.

p. 106 'Down with anti-Bolshevism!', Helker and Lenssen, p. 89.

p. 106 'fellow-traveller', Anatoly Pavlovich Sudoplatov, interview, 24 September 2003.

p. 107 'Papa gestorben . . .', 8 January 1924, MMKhAT, K-Ch No. 2735.

p. 107 'sobbed like a child', etc., L. K. Knipper to Olga Leonardovna Knipper-Chekhova, 7 January 1924, MMKhAT, K-Ch No. 2734.

p. 108 'Everyone was such a formalist . . .', E. A. Akulov, 25 October 1990, clipping in AD-MCM, V. V. Knipper Fond, File 22.

13. The End of Political Innocence

p. 111 'be happy to play the mayor's wife', Olga Leonardovna Knipper-Chekhova to Nemirovich-Danchenko, Freiburg, 5 July 1924, Vilenkin (ed.), Vol. II, p. 147.

p. 111 'I have left the Gnesina . . .', L. K. Knipper to Olga Leonardovna Knipper-Chekhova, Moscow, 8 February 1924, MMKhAT, K-Ch No. 2738.

p. 112 'Darling and dearest Aunt Olya . . .', 10 March 1924, MMKhAT, K-Ch No. 2761.

p. 112 'The Most Important Theatrical . . .', Tschechowa, 1973, p. 270.

p. 112 'The theatre is full all the time . . .', 16 March 1924, ibid.

p. 113 Olga's daughter, Ada (Olga Mikhailovna Chekhova), saying goodbye to Mikhail Chekhov, Sergei Mikhailovich Chekhov, MS, AD-MCM/Sakharova/File 81.

p. 113 'with a slightly guilty smile', V. V. Knipper, p. 21.

p. 114 'I am working for the Soviet state . . .', Mariya Pavlovna Chekhova to Olga Leonardovna Knipper-Chekhova, Yalta, 10 October 1924, Vilenkin (ed.), Vol. II, p. 147.

p. 114 'The commemoration . . .', Olga Leonardovna Knipper-Chekhova to Maria Pavlovna Chekhova, Moscow, 24 October 1924, ibid., p. 148.

p. 115 For the arrival of Lulu Knipper and the children in Berlin and Olga's life at this time, see Helker and Lenssen, pp. 94–100.

p. 116 'Dear Aunt Olya!' Olga Konstantinovna Chekhova to Olga Leonardovna Knipper-Chekhova, Paris, 23 April 1926, MMKhAT, K-Ch No. 2762.

p. 116 'I am stuck here again . . .', Olga Konstantinovna Chekhova to Olga Leonardovna Knipper-Chekhova, 15 July 1926, MMKhAT, K-Ch No. 2763.

p. 117 'I will be here . . .', Olga Konstantinovna Chekhova to Olga Leonardovna Knipper-Chekhova, Berlin, 25 September 1927, MMKhAT, K-Ch No. 2764.

p. 118 Invitation to stay, Olga Konstantinovna Chekhova to Olga Leonardovna Knipper-Chekhova, 19 May 1929, MMKhAT, K-Ch No. 2765. The name Prechistensky was regarded as too religious by the Bolsheviks and changed to honour the dramatist Gogol.

p. 118 'I am studying singing . . .', Olga Konstantinova Chekhova to Olga Leonardovna Knipper-Chekhova, Hochgebirge, Bavaria, 23 September 1929, MMKhAT, K-Ch No. 2766.

p. 118 *Love on Command (Liebe auf Befehl)*, Olga Chekhova in the United States, see Helker and Lenssen, pp. 120–23.

p. 119 'It was shameful . . .', L. K. Knipper, *Sovietskaya muzyka*, No. 12, 1978, p. 89.

p. 119 'My dream was to perform . . .', ibid.

p. 119 'They are making such . . .', L. K. Knipper to Olga Leonardovna Knipper-Chekhova, Leningrad, 13 February 1927, MMKhAT, K-Ch No. 2739.

p. 120 'My life is still . . .', L. K. Knipper to Olga Leonardovna Knipper-Chekhova, 18 July 1927, MMKhAT, K-Ch No. 2741.

p. 120 *North Wind*, L. K. Knipper, *Sovietskaya muzyka*, No. 12, 1978, p. 89.

p. 120 'politically unreliable' and Major Viktor Ilin, Anatoly Pavlovich Sudoplatov, interview, 25 September 2003.

p. 120 Olga Knipper-Chekhova as an informer at the Moscow Art Theatre. Professor Donald Rayfield, the biographer of Anton Chekhov, kindly drew my attention to 'plausible Moscow Arts Theatre folklore emanating from the late actor Mark Prudkin, for instance her remark to one of her scandalously many and young lovers: "If you make love to me especially tenderly, I shall save you [from the NKVD]."' While Olga Leonardovna Knipper-Chekhova was certainly a lot more manipulative and unscrupulous in the theatrical world than is shown in the heavily expurgated versions of her letters – the vicious gossip has been entirely suppressed – there can be no doubt that she was gossiped against in her turn. Her German origins and her marriage to Anton Chekhov provoked many hostile comments, most of which were probably unfounded.

p. 121 'his enemies spread. . . .', Sergei Mikhailovich Chekhov, MS, AD-MCM/Sakharova/File 81.

p. 122 'I both accept the West . . .', Ada Konstantinovna Knipper to Olga Leonardovna Knipper-Chekhova, Paris, 10 December 1931, MMKhAT K-Ch, No. 2574.

p. 123 Lyubov Sergeevna Zalesskaya and Gogolevsky bulvar, Andrei Lvovich Knipper, interviews, 22 and 23 September 2002.

p. 123 'I was addicted for ever', L. K. Knipper, *Sovietskaya muzyka*, No. 12, 1978, p. 89.

14. The Totalitarian Years

p. 125 'hot air factory', Haffner, p. 97.

p. 126 'pass through the brown shit', quoted Burleigh, p. 286.

p. 126 *Die Nacht der Entscheidung.* This work fascinates movie buffs because it has a single scene which runs for 175 feet.

p. 126 'Adele had some fluffy garment . . .', recounted by Vera Tschechowa, quoted V. V. Knipper, p. 10.

p. 127 Viktor Semyonovich Abakumov was born in 1908. His father was a stoker, his mother a laundress. He joined the NKVD in 1932 and in 1939 he became its head in Rostov. Helped by the purges, and the number of dead men's shoes to be filled, he became Deputy Commissar of NKVD on 26 February 1941.

p. 127 'Did you happen to meet . . .', protocol of interrogation, 29 April 1945, by Colonel Shkurin, AD-MCM, V. V. Knipper Fond, File 22.

p. 127 Goebbels is estimated to have seen more than 1,100 films, Beyer, 1991, p. 7.

p. 128 'Sing lower, Blondi . . .', Junge, p. 92. Zarah Leander (1907–81) and Soviet intelligence, *The Times*, 11 July 2003; and Anatoly Pavlovich Sudoplatov, interview, 24 September 2003. Rybkina was operating under the codename 'Yartseva'.

p. 129 'What sort of good manners . . .', Tschechowa, 1973, p. 126.

p. 130 'So late, Frau Chekhova', V. V. Knipper, p. 47.

p. 130 'Oh, if you . . .', Junge, p. 95.

p. 131 'Oh, him with his little worm!', Beyer, 1991, p. 13.

p. 132 Lida Baarova finally returned to Germany in 1975 to play in Rainer Werner Fassbinder's *Die bitteren Tränen der Petra von Kant* (*The Bitter Tears of Petra von Kant*).

p. 133 'If you won't go . . .', Lenin, quoted Shentalinsky, p. 234.

p. 133 'That doesn't matter', reply to Ivan Gronsky, quoted ibid., p. 257.

p. 134 'Revolution violates art . . .', Stanislavsky, 1924, p. 566.

p. 135 'unexpectedly asked to join . . .', L. K. Knipper, *Sovietskaya muzyka*, No. 12, 1978, p. 89.

p. 135 'Nonsense instead of Music', Shentalinsky, pp. 303–4.

p. 135 'I am thinking about you . . .', 16 February 1932, MMKhAT, K-Ch No. 2744.

p. 136 'Songs don't live long . . .', quoted V. V. Knipper, p. 112.

p. 136 Life at 23 Gogolevsky bulvar, Andrei Lvovich Knipper, interviews, 22 and 23 September 2002.

p. 138 'Our Olga has . . .', Berlin, 9 October 1936, MMKhAT, K-Ch No. 2575.

p. 138 Invitation to the Reichschancellery, Helker and Lenssen, p. 162.

p. 138 'I will do it gladly . . .', TB-JG, Teil 1, Aufzeichnungen 1924–1941, Band 3/II, p. 250.

p. 139 'own little corner . . .', Ada Konstaninovna Knipper to Olga Leonardovna Knipper-Chekhova, Brussels, 23 January 1937 (on Olga Chekhova-Robyns personal blank), MMKhAT, K-Ch No. 2577.

p. 139 'We have had guests . . .', Ada Konstantinovna Chekhova to Olga Leonardovna Knipper-Chekhova, Berlin, 17 November 1937, MMKhAT, K-Ch No. 2578.

15. The Great Terror

p. 141 'Papa flew into a fury . . .', V. V. Knipper, pp. 58–9.

p. 142 *The Kremlin Crag-dweller*, Shentalinsky, p. 173. In the final version of this poem, the 'cockroach whiskers' or 'cockroach moustaches' (depending on the translation) was replaced by 'cockroach eyes' when Mandelstam wrote out the poem himself for Shivarov, his OGPU interrogator.

p. 143 19 million people arrested, over 7 million died, Andrew and Gordievsky, p. 106.

p. 143 'The execution squads . . .', Shentalinsky, p. 222.

p. 143 Ada sent two postcards asking for the document, AD-MCY.

p. 144 'There were not any persons . . .', Mariya Pavlovna Chekhova and Mikhail Pavlovich Chekhov, RGALI 2316/3/146.

p. 145 '*Gospoda!*' V. V. Knipper, p. 107.

p. 145 'My life has become a lot more complicated . . .', L. K. Knipper to Olga Leonardovna Knipper-Chekhova, Yalta, 4 April 1937, MMKhAT, K-Ch No. 2745.

p. 146 'You see, my dearest Aunt Olya . . .', L. K. Knipper to Olga Leonardovna Knipper-Chekhova, Yalta, 25 April 1937, MMKhAT, K-Ch No. 2746.

p. 148 Barber's shop in the proezd Serova, V. V. Knipper, p. 140.

p. 149 'She was sitting . . .', Leo Rabeneck, 'Posledniye minuty Chekhova', *Vozrozhdeniye*, Vol. 84, Paris, December 1958, quoted Malcolm, p. 62.

p. 149 'worries and joys', 9 October 1937, TB-JG, Teil 1, Aufzeichnungen 1924–1941, Band 3, p. 294, and 'professional concerns', 5 May 1939, TB-JG, Teil 1, Aufzeichnungen 1924–1941, Band 6, p. 338. See also 4 February 1938.

p. 149 'prima donna of the Nazi film . . .', Berezhkhov, 1972, p. 109.

p. 150 'Well, that's life!', 16 September 1938, TB-JG, Teil 1, Aufzeichnungen 1924–1931, Band 6, p. 93.

p. 150 'The piece was not up to much', TB-JG, Teil 1, Aufzeichnungen 1924–1941, Band 6, p. 337.

p. 150 'a beautiful, sunny May Sunday', TB-JG, Teil 1, Aufzeichnungen 1924–1931, Band 6, p. 348.

p. 151 'poking their noses . . .', Tschechowa, 1973, p. 190.

p. 152 'our people in Scandinavia', Lev Bezymenski, *Die Zeit*, 15 October 1993.

p. 152 'Prince, people like you . . .', Anatoly Pavlovich Sudoplatov, interview, 24 September 2003.

p. 153 General Nikolai Baldanov, Aleksandr Aleksandrovich Melikov, interview, 18 October 2003.

p. 153 General Baldanov's imprisonment and execution. According to Lieutenant Colonel of State Security Igor Aleksandrovich Shchors, after Baldanov visited military plants in France and Germany he was denounced, probably by another member of the delegation, and accused of being a French agent. He was sentenced to ten years with no right of correspondence.

Shchors saw his file and three petitions from his work colleagues, asking for him to be released. The reply to all three petitions was the same: 'His crimes are too grave for the case to be reconsidered.' Shchors became involved in this when, in 1943 or 1944, Mariya Garikovna asked him to tea. She was a very clever woman and he was sure she had her reasons for doing this. She asked some questions, in her charming, nonchalant manner, and then showed him a letter she wrote to the KGB leadership asking them to reconsider Baldanov's case once again.

She wrote that perhaps now that she had proved her devotion to her country and her eagerness to die for it, they would trust her more and believe her that her former husband was innocent. She asked Shchors to pass the letter on to his bosses. Shchors told her that the best way was for her to put the letter into the box for petitions in the building in the Dzerzhinskogo Square (now Lubyanka Square). Her letter reached its addressees. Some time later

Sudoplatov asked Shchors to trace Baldanov in the camp and, if he had not received an additional term, to release him. He found out that Baldanov was a prisoner at a certain camp. The reply from there was that he had died from typhus in 1939 (long before the petitions were submitted). Just to be thorough, Shchors checked whether there had been any cases of typhus in that period. The answer was negative. Baldanov had probably been executed. Igor Aleksandrovich Shchors, interview, 7 December 2003.

p. 153 Mariya Garikovna and Beria, Anatoly Pavlovich Sudoplatov, interview, 24 September 2003, and Zoya Vasileevna Zarubina, interview, 25 September 2003. An ancestor, Prince Kochubei, featured in Pushkin's epic *Poltava*.

p. 154 'Lyovka, you son of a bitch! . . .', Andrei Lvovich Knipper, interviews, 22 and 23 September 2002.

p. 154 Lev's mission in Poland, Anatoly Pavlovich Sudoplatov, interview, 24 September 2003.

16. Enemy Aliens

p. 156 'Edification and Cheerfulness in Hard Times', Tschechowa, 1973, p. 179.

p. 156 'tall and sure of himself, but without a trace of arrogance', Tschechowa, 1973, p. 180.

p. 158 'For singing that song . . .', Berezhkov, 1982, p. 20.

p. 159 'to assess personally . . .', Anatoly Pavlovich Sudoplatov, interview, 25 September 2003. On Merkulov in Berlin, see also Andrew and Gordievsky, pp. 203–4.

p. 160 'Occasionally, he would put . . .', Berezhkov, 1982, p. 27.

p. 162 Message from Lev, Anatoly Pavlovich Sudoplatov, interview, 24 September 2003.

p. 162 'Frau Olga Tschechowa in sincere . . .', Tschechowa, 1973, p. 165.

p. 162 'We've got to look after ourselves', V. V. Knipper, p. 96.

p. 163 Lev's relationship with Mariya Garikovna, Igor Aleksandrovich Shchors, interview, 7 December 2003.

p. 163 'Who's that?' V. V. Knipper, p. 47.

17. Moscow 1941

p. 165 'One has to take . . .', quoted Turovskaya, p. 8.

p. 165 'This was when . . .', Lev Knipper, *Sovietskaya muzyka*, No. 12, 1978, p. 89.

p. 166 'Don't be surprised . . .', L. K. Knipper to Olga Leonardovna Knipper-Chekhova, 23 June 1941, MMKhAT, K-Ch No. 2748.

p. 168 'They have been asked . . .', Olga Leonardovna Knipper-Chekhova to V. L. Knipper, 7 September 1941, V. V. Knipper, p. 61.

p. 168 'We are at a complete loss . . .', Sofya Ivanovna Baklanova to V. L. Knipper, 11 September 1941, ibid.

p. 170 'they were left to die . . .', Mariya Vadimovna Shverubovich, interview, 25 September 2003, and *Moskovsky Khudozhestvenny Teatr: 100 Let*, Vol. II, Izd. 1998, MMKhAT.

p. 171 'We were walking . . .', V. V. Knipper, p. 70.

p. 173 Volga German, ibid., p. 15.

p. 174 'from Leningrad to the Far East', Parrish, p. 99.

p. 174 'People sitting round . . .', V. V. Knipper, pp. 19–20.

p. 175 'Well, you should remember . . .', ibid., p. 49.

p. 175 'I am afraid of him', Aleksandr Aleksandrovich Melikov, interview, 18 October 2003.

p. 176 Sudoplatov's role, Andrew and Gordievsky, p. 252. Lieutenant General Pavel Anatolyevich Sudoplatov was the head of the NKVD Partisan Administration and later head of the post-war Spetsburo, which carried out foreign assassinations. His deputy, Major General Eitingon, had organized Trotsky's assassination.

p. 176 'In October of 1941 . . .', Sudoplatov, 1996, p. 159.

p. 177 'General Sudoplatov mobilized . . .', Zoya Vasileevna Zarubina, interview, 26 September 2003.

p. 177 'key figures . . .', Anatoly Pavlovich Sudoplatov, interview, 24 September 2003.

p. 177 Zarubina, after finishing as case officer for Lev Knipper and Mariya Garikovna, worked on the translation of all the papers brought to Moscow from the Soviet spies within the Manhattan project. Zoya Vasileevna Zarubina, interview, 26 September 2003.

p. 178 'The city has produced . . .', Moscow, 19 October 1941, MMKhAT, K-Ch No. 2748. This letter was sent by a friend of Lev's called Sidorenko and so there was much less chance of it being censored by the NKVD.

p. 179 'They were being prepared . . .', Zoya Vasileevna Zarubina, interview, 26 September 2003.

p. 179 'falsely defect', Anatoly Pavlovich Sudoplatov, interview, 24 September 2003.

p. 179 Sudoplatov and Zarubina are convinced that Lev and Mariya Garikovna were to be sent to Germany to make contact with Olga Chekhova. Colonel Shchors, on the other hand, believes that Lev's target was Franz von Papen in Turkey.

p. 180 'If they want a war . . .', Werth, p. 246.

p. 181 'Lyova my darling . . .', Olga Leonardovna Knipper-Chekhova to L. K. Knipper, Tbilisi, 6 December 1941, collection of S. M. Chekhov, RGALI 2540/1/36.

p. 182 'The case with the little photograph . . .', Tschechowa, 1973, p. 181.

18. A Family Divided by War

p. 184 'Lyova suddenly turned up . . .', Olga Leonardovna Knipper-Chekhova to V. L. Knipper, Tbilisi, 3 January 1942, V. V. Knipper, pp. 122–3.

p. 184 'like stations of the cross . . .', L. K. Knipper, p. 94.

p. 184 Prokofiev, *Sovietskaya muzyka*, No. 12, 1978, p. 89.

p. 184 'some short children's pieces . . .', V. V. Knipper, p. 114.

p. 184 Paul Armand in Tashkent, Andrei Lvovich Knipper, interviews, 22 and 23 September 2002.

p. 185 'I shudder to think...', Olga Leonardovna Knipper-Chekhova to V. L. Knipper, 14 January 1942, V. V. Knipper, p. 123.

p. 185 'very agitated letter', Olga Leonardovna Knipper-Chekhova to V. L. Knipper, Tbilisi, 26 March 1942, ibid., pp. 134–5.

p. 186 Sudoplatov believes that Lev Knipper was due to meet up with Miklashevsky, but other Soviet intelligence experts, such as Boris Volodarsky, consider that most unlikely. He thinks that the NKVD would have preferred two separate operations against Hitler. Meanwhile, Colonel Shchors, as mentioned earlier, thinks that Lev was part of the Papen assassination attempt in Turkey. Anatoly Pavlovich Sudoplatov, interview, 24 September 2003; Boris Voladarsky, e-mail to the author, 13 November 2003; Igor Aleksandrovich Shchors, interview, 7 December 2003.

p. 186 'that her connections...', Anatoly Pavlovich Sudoplatov, interview, 24 September 2003. The NKVD, perhaps out of eagerness to please Stalin, who longed to get rid of Trotsky, was extremely interested in assassination plots. Kim Philby's original task in Spain had been to organize the assassination of General Franco.

p. 186 Lev accompanied by Colonel Maklyarsky and caviar tin with false bottom, Igor Aleksandrovich Shchors, interview, 7 December 2003. Colonel Shchors continued as Lev's paymaster and confirmed that he was a fully paid agent of the NKVD.

p. 186 'I don't think it expedient in the circumstances...', RGASPI 558/11/66.

p. 187 'defection to Turkey...', Anatoly Pavlovich Sudoplatov, interview, 25 September 2003.

p. 188 'On one occasion', Yevgenia Mikhailovna Chekhova, Sakharova (ed.), p. 210.

p. 189 Olga Chekhova and Mariya Pavlovna Chekhova, information provided by the director of the Chekhov house-museum, Yalta.

Source Notes 267

p. 189 'I can't watch films . . .', quoted Junge, p. 70.

p. 190 Film stars on newsreel, *Deutsche Wochenschau Zwölf Minuten Magazine*, UFA BA-FA 3246/1944.

p. 190 Olga Chekhova during the Goebbels speech on 18 February 1943. I am most grateful to Vadim Glowna for bringing this to my attention. The footage was cut from the newsreel shown: *Deutsche Wochenschau*, BA-FA DW 651/1943/Roll 1.

p. 190 Vadim Shverubovich in prison camp, Mariya Vadimovna Shverubovich, interview, 25 September 2003.

p. 191 'a collective farm where . . .', Hal Erickson, *All Movie Guide*, MSN Entertainment. *The Song of Russia* was based on the novel *Scorched Earth* by Leo Mittler.

p. 193 'This is Olga Chekhova, the cinema actress', Vladimir Ivanovich Stezhensky, quoted V. V. Knipper, p. 176.

p. 193 Aunt Masha's state on the liberation of Yalta, Sergei Mikhailovich Chekhov, MS, AD-MCM/Sakharova/File 81.

p. 194 Schaub conversation. The film she was making was presumably *Mit meinen Augen*, released early in 1945. It was one of the very last movies made under the Third Reich. Deliveries of supplies and weapons to Berghof, V. V. Knipper, p. 190.

p. 195 'Mecca of the film-world', Tschechowa, 1973, p. 195.

p. 196 'When our troops reached Germany', Beria, p. 127.

p. 196 'bombing-holiday', 'The land does not belong . . .', Tschechowa, 1973, pp. 211–12.

19. Berlin and Moscow 1945

p. 197 'did not even dare . . .', 'all based on her initiative', Albert Sumser, interview, 26 September 2003.

p. 198 'We agreed that he would surrender . . .', Olga Chekhova's handwritten deposition in Moscow to SMERSh, unsigned and undated, but almost certainly May 1945, AD-MCM, V. V. Knipper Fond, File 22.

p. 199 Abakumov report on *Wolfsschanze*, 15 February 1945, GARF, 9401/2/93, pp. 6–15.

p. 199 'We are already dreaming of the Crimea...', Sofya Ivanovna Baklanova to V. V. Knipper, 2 April 1945, AD-MCM, V. V. Knipper Fond, File 22.

p. 200 Olga Chekhova's household, as the Red Army approached, consisted of Ada, Vera, a maid and a Russian dressmaker.

p. 200 'Look, that's a woman of perfect beauty', Beyer, 1991, p. 15.

p. 201 Olga Chekhova's political beliefs. 'As to her political views, she is in favour of the pre-Hitler system in Germany', from interrogation of Boris Fyodorovich Glazunov, b. 1895 in Leningrad, by Captain Tereshchenko, senior investigator of 1st Division, 4th Department Counter-Intelligence SMERSh, of the Group of Soviet Occupation Troops in Germany, 10 October 1945, AD-MCM, V. V. Knipper Fond, File 22.

p. 202 'My darling, darling Auntie Olya!' Ada Konstantinovna Knipper to Olga Leonardovna Knipper-Chekhova, Berlin, 26 April 1945, MMKhAT, K-Ch No. 2580.

p. 203 'You killed Kolya!', quoted V. V. Knipper, p. 180.

p. 203 Albert Sumser's version, interview, 15 October 2003.

p. 204 Interrogation by Colonel Shkurin, AD-MCM, V. V. Knipper Fond, File 22.

p. 205 'for a 72-hour rendezvous', Deriabin, p. 59. Deriabin was at the time an officer of the NKVD Guards Directorate in charge of protecting Soviet leaders, and was thus in a position to know.

p. 205 'Let Abakumov tell...', *VAR*, pp. 208–13.

p. 205 'The very ideal of a Chekist', 'a shock of black hair', Kuznetsov, pp. 149–50.

p. 206 'a dirty runner bespattered...', Solzhenitsyn, *The Gulag Archipelago*, Vol. I, 1974, p. 126.

p. 206 Abakumov and Beria, Anatoly Pavlovich Sudoplatov, interview, 25 September 2003.

p. 206 KGB papers. According to Professor Sudoplatov, the papers released represent only a tiny proportion of those on the whole case. In fact the KGB revealed only the papers which concern SMERSh, when SMERSh had no idea of Olga's true relationship with the NKVD. The key document – if the proceedings were ever trusted to paper – would be her NKVD debriefing for Beria and Merkulov, but that is unlikely to be released, especially since the KGB officially denied that there were any more papers.

p. 206 'When are we going to meet?' AD–MCM, V. V. Knipper Fond, File 22.

p. 207 Olga Chekhova and Soviet intelligence, see also Beria, pp. 123–30; Parrish, pp.126, 317; Deriabin, pp. 59–60; Sudoplatov, 1996, pp. 146, 159; Anatoly Pavlovich Sudoplatov, interview, 25 September 2003.

p. 207 'All that Olga Chekhova wrote . . .', Beria, pp.123–30.

p. 208 'Rumours circulating about me . . .', AD–MCM, V. V. Knipper Fond, File 22.

p. 208 'It isn't for me!', Mariya Vadimovna Shverubovich, interview, 25 September 2003.

p. 209 'Dear Vova', L. K. Knipper to V. V. Knipper, 25 September 1945, AD–MCM, V. V. Knipper Fond, File 22. It would appear that either Olga Knipper-Chekhova herself or the Soviet authorities had decided to reduce her age by two years, considering that her date of birth was 22 September 1868 and her seventy-fifth birthday had already taken place in 1943.

20. Return to Berlin

p. 211 Olga and Lev after the war. Lev's son is certain that he never went abroad again after the war, except to East Germany, and he is virtually certain that his father never heard from Olga. Andrei Lvovich Knipper, interview, 22 September 2002.

p. 211 'According to your instructions . . . ,' AD–MCM, V. V. Knipper Fond, File 22.

p. 213 'He was being kept in a prisoner of war camp in Denmark . . .', AD-MCM, V. V. Knipper Fond, File 22.

p. 213 'Dear Aunt Masha . . .', Olga Konstantinovna Chekhova to Mariya Pavlovna Chekhova, 2 August 1945, AD-MCY.

p. 214 'My dear and dearest . . .', Olga Konstantinovna Chekhova to Olga Leonardovna Knipper-Chekhova, Berlin, 2 August 1945, AD-MCM, V. V. Knipper Fond, File 22.

p. 216 'Dearest Vladimir Semyonovich . . .', Olga Konstantinovna Chekhova to Viktor Semyonovich Abakumov, 18 October 1945, AD-MCM, V. V. Knipper Fond, File 22.

p. 216 'Chekhova is extremely worried . . .', Lieutenant General Zelenin to Viktor Semyonovich Abakumov, Berlin, 22 October 1945, AC-MCM, V. V. Knipper Fond, File 22.

p. 217 *Kurier* and correspondence, AD-MCM, V. V. Knipper Fond, File 22.

p. 218 'With regard to Olga Chekhova's visit . . .', document headed: 'To Beria from Serov, 21 November 1945. Copy to Abakumov. Copy to Merkulov. Top Secret. NKVD of the USSR', AD-MCM, V. V. Knipper Fond, File 22.

p. 218 'Taken under control . . .', Anatoly Pavlovich Sudoplatov, interview, 24 September 2003.

21. After the War

p. 222 'What, in Moscow? . . .' Mariya Vadimovna Shverubovich, interview, 25 September 2003.

p. 222 'I've distanced myself . . .', 'In the evenings . . .', Olga Leonardovna Knipper-Chekhova to Ada Knipper, 17 January 1947, PAK/T.

p. 223 'We sit together . . .', 'and I am still alive', Olga Leonardovna Knipper-Chekhova to Ada Knipper, 18 July 1948, PAK/T.

p. 223 Lev's 1947 expedition to Caucasus and Elbrus, Andrei Lvovich Knipper, interview, 22 September 2002.

p. 224 Lev under General Sudoplatov until 1949, Anatoly Pavlovich Sudoplatov, interview, 24 September 2003.

p. 224 'Lyova is working!', Aleksandr Aleksandrovich Melikov, interview, 18 October 2003.

p. 225 'Lyova, don't be a fool, it's winter!', Tatyana Alekseevna Gaidamovich, interview, 4 January 2003.

p. 225 Lev and Mariya Garikovna split up, Aleksandr Aleksandrovich Melikov, interview, 18 October 2003.

p. 225 Dmitry Dmitrievich Shostakovich condemend for 'Formalism', Shentalinsky, pp. 303–4. Shostakovich was awarded the Lenin Prize in 1957.

p. 225 'propaganda posters', *Sovietskaya muzyka*, No. 12, 1978, p. 89.

p. 226 Olga Chekhova and Aleksandr Demyanov, Igor Aleksandrovich Shchors, interview, 7 December 2003.

p. 226 Olga Chekhova's contacts with Abakumov and General Utekhin, Anatoly Pavlovich Sudoplatov, interview, 24 September 2003. Abakumov's misery dragged on. His greatest mistake had been to conceal from Stalin the suspicion that Zhdanov's doctors had somehow been responsible for his death. He was finally charged with a failure to take 'active measures' against Zionists, at a time when Stalin saw 'Cosmopolitanism' as treachery. Stalin's xenophobia was now taking a more anti-Semitic form. Abakumov was also accused of the misappropriation of government funds and, as mentioned earlier, 'ignoring Communist moral principles'. In December 1954, he was tried and sentenced to 'suffer the highest degree of punishment: death by shooting'. Deriabin, p. 176.

p. 226 'a rumour', Deriabin, pp. 59–60.

p. 227 'over-estimated the importance of Olga Chekhova', Anatoly Pavlovish Sudoplatov, interview, 24 September 2003.

p. 227 Zoya Rybkina's mission to Berlin, June 1953, Eduard Prokofievich Sharapov, interview, 22 September 2003; see also Sudoplatov, 1994, p. 336.

p. 228 'a direct capitulation to imperialism', quoted Lev Bezymenski, *Die Zeit*, 15 October 1993.

p. 228 'Do you realize where you are going?', Eduard Prokofievich Sharapov, interview, 22 September 2003.

p. 229 Mariya Garikovna and end of her life, Zoya Vasileevna Zarubina, interview, 26 September 2003, and Aleksandr Aleksandrovich Melikov, interview, 18 October 2003.

p. 229 Death of Misha Chekhov, Sergei Mikhailovich Chekhov, MS, AD-MCM/Sakharova/File 81. Misha left his small ranch in California to Ada (his daughter with Olga Chekhova), but Ada died as a result of a plane crash in 1966.

p. 230 'Venus-Film . . .', Helker and Lenssen, pp. 210–11.

p. 231 'expanded very rapidly', Renata Helker, interview, 13 October 2003.

p. 231 'the millions which she had earned . . .', Helker and Lenssen, p. 214.

p. 231 Soviet intelligence sources and Olga Tschechowa Kosmetik, Anatony Pavlovich Sudoplatov, interview, 24 September 2003; Eduard Prokofievich Sharapov, interview, 22 September 2003; Beria's son, Sergo, also wrote: 'Olga Chekhova was rewarded for her intelligence work. Her financial well-being was secured by the Soviet Union. But she never received any medals. And no one in the West was ever able to prove that she had been a Soviet spy', Beria, pp. 123–30.

p. 231 'the actress Olga Chekhova . . .', Lev Bezymenski, *Die Zeit*, 15 October 1993.

p. 231 'a complicated and somewhat unusual story', V. V. Knipper, p. 179.

p. 233 Symphony-Oratorium and *Count Cagliostro*, L. K. Knipper to Ada Knipper, 9 May 1974, PAK/T. He also wrote a ballet, *The Source of Happiness*, which was based on Tadjik music. *Sovietskaya muzyka*, No. 12, 1978, p. 89. Also Tatyana Alekseevna Gaidamovich, interview, 26 September 2003.

p. 233 'A proletarian will always be a proletarian . . .', Olga Chekhova to Ada Knipper, 28 November [?], PAK/T.
p. 234 Death of Olga Chekhova, Vera Tschechowa, interview, 16 October 2003.

SELECT BIBLIOGRAPHY

Andrew, Christopher, and Gordievsky, Oleg, *KGB: The Inside Story of Its Foreign Operations from Lenin to Gorbachev*, London, 1990

Applebaum, Anne, *Gulag*, London, 2003

Beevor, Antony, *Berlin: The Downfall 1945*, London, 2002

Benedetti, Jean, *Stanislavski*, London, 1988

Benedetti, Jean (ed.), *The Moscow Art Theatre Letters*, New York, 1991

Berezhkov, Valentin, *On Diplomatic Mission*, Moscow, 1972

—— *History in the Making*, Moscow, 1982

—— *At Stalin's Side*, New York, 1994

Beria, Sergo, *Moi otets: Lavrenty Beria*, Moscow, 1994

Beyer, Friedemann, *Die Ufa-Stars im Dritten Reich: Frauen für Deutschland*, Munich, 1991

– *Die Gesichter der UFA*, Munich, 1992

Boner, Georgette, *Hommage an Michael Tschechow*, Zurich, 1994

Burleigh, Michael, *The Third Reich*, London, 2000

Čechov, Michail A., *Leben und Begegnungen, Autobiographische Schriften*, Stuttgart, 1992

—— *Die Kunst des Schauspielers: Moskauer Ausgabe*, Stuttgart, 1998

Chekhov, Mikhail Aleksandrovich, *see* Čechov, Michail A.

Chekhova, Olga Konstantinovna, *see* Tschechowa, Olga

Deriabin, Peter, *Inside Stalin's Kremlin*, Washington, DC, 1998

Ehrenburg, Ilya, *Men, Years – Life*, Vol. V, New York, 1964

Figes, Orlando, *A People's Tragedy*, London, 2002

Haffner, Sebastian, *Defying Hitler*, London, 2002

Helker, Renata, and Lenssen, Claudia, *Der Tschechow-Clan*, Berlin, 2001

Junge, Traudl, *Until the Final Hour: Hitler's Last Secretary*, London, 2003

Kachalov, V. I., *Sbornik Statei, Vospominany, Pisem*, Moscow, 1954

Karpov, N. D., 'Krim – Gallipoli – Balkany', *Voenno-istorichesky arkhiv*, No. 1 (16), 2001

Knipper, Lev Konstantinovich, *Vospominaniya, dnevniki, zametki*, Moscow, 1980

Knipper, Vladimir Vladimirovich, *Pora galliutsinatsy*, Moscow, 1995

Komissarzhevsky, V., *Teatry Moskvy*, Moscow, 1959

Kuznetsov, I. I., 'Stalin's Minister V. S. Abakumov 1908–1954', *Journal of Slavic Military Studies*, Vol. 12, No. 1, March 1999

Malcolm, Janet, *Reading Chekhov*, New York, 2001

Marshall, Herbert, *The Russian Theatre*, New York, 1977

Montefiore, Simon Sebag, *Stalin: The Court of the Red Tsar*, London, 2003

Parrish, Michael, *The Lesser Terror: Soviet State Security, 1939–1953*, Westport, Conn., 1996

Peschersky, Vladimir, *Krasnaya kapella*, Moscow, 2000

Pitcher, Harvey, *Chekhov's Leading Lady*, London, 1979

Porter, Cathy, and Jones, Mark, *Moscow in World War II*, London, 1987

Rabeneck, Lev L., 'Serdtse Chekhova', *Vozrozhdeniye*, Vol. 92, Paris, August 1959

Rayfield, Donald, *The Cherry Orchard: Catastrophe and Comedy*, London, 1994

—— *Anton Chekhov*, New York, 1997

Sakharova, E. M. (ed.), *Vokrug Chekhova: Memuary*, Moscow, 1990

Shentalinsky, Vitaly, *The KGB's Literary Archive*, London, 1997

Sitsky, Larry, *Music of the Repressed Russian Avant-Garde*, Westport, Conn., 1994

Stanislavsky, *My Life in Art*, Boston, 1924

—— *Sobranie sochineny*, 8 vols., Moscow, 1951–64

Sudoplatov, Pavel, *Special Tasks: The Memoirs of an Unwanted Witness*, New York, 1994

—— *Spets operatsii*, Moscow, 1995

—— *Razvedka i Kreml*, Moscow, 1996

Tschechowa, Olga, *Ich verschweige nichts!*, Berchtesgaden, 1952a

—— *Frau ohne Alter*, Munich, 1952b

—— *Meine Uhren gehen anders: Erinnerungen*, Munich, 1973

Turovskaya, M., *Olga Leonardovna Knipper-Chekhova 1868–1959*, Moscow, 1959

Vilenkin, V. Ya, *Kachalov*, Moscow, 1976

Vilenkin, V. Ya (ed.), *Olga Leonardovna Knipper-Chekhova*, Vol II, *Perepiska O. L. Knipper-Chekhovoi (1896–1959), Vospomininaniya ob O. L. Knipper-Chekhovoi*, Moscow, 1972

Werth, Alexander, *Russia at War*, London, 1964

Wolf, Vitali, *Teatralnyi dozhd*, Moscow, 1998

Zolotnitsky, David, *Meyerhold: Roman s sovetski vlastyu*, Moscow, 1999

ACKNOWLEDGEMENTS

The original spark which led to this book came in 2000 from Dr Galya Vinogradova, with whom I stayed in Moscow while researching *Berlin: The Downfall 1945*. Her daughter Dr Lyuba Vinogradova, to whom I owe so much for all her help over the last ten years, then suggested that she should drop by the Chekhov museum at Melikhovo, which is not that far from their dacha. This is where the Chekhova story started in earnest.

From then on many people have helped in many different ways, both large and small. I am extremely grateful to Judith Baum, Professor Anatoly Aleksandrovich Chernobayev, Professor Tatyana Alekseevna Gaidamovich, Wolf Gebhardt, Angelica von Hase, the film historian Renata Helker, who generously gave me access to her Privatarchiv Knipper/Chekhova, Academician Andrei Lvovich Knipper, Lesley Levene, Douglas Matthews, Igor Aleksandrovich Shchors, Mariya Vadimovna Shverubovich, Professor Anatoly Pavlovich Sudoplatov, Boris Voladarsky and Zoya Vasileevna Zarubina.

Once again it has been a great pleasure and an enormous help working with the BBC. I am extremely grateful to Laurence Rees, Jonathan Stamp and Thecla Schreuders, the director, whose constant well-aimed questions produced an enjoyable and very useful debate.

Andrew Nurnberg is mercifully still my agent and Eleo Gordon my editor at Penguin. I owe them both, as always, a very great deal. But naturally my deepest thanks go to my wife, Artemis Cooper, who along with everything else vastly improved the manuscript with her editing.

INDEX

The numbers in italics refer to illustrations.

Beria, Lavrenty – *cont.*
  interviews Janusz Radziwill, 152
  establishes spy network, 153
  and Mariya Melikova, 153–4
  disbelieves war reports on
    German advance, 169
  restores order in wartime
    Moscow, 173
  reaction to German invasion,
    176
  and risk of air attack on
    Moscow parade, 180
  and assassination plot against
    Hitler, 181
  and Lev and Mariya's bogus
    defection to Germans, 187
  as Olga Chekhova's protector,
    198
  sadism, 206
  on Olga Chekhova's diary, 207
  orders Olga Chekhova's return
    to Berlin, 211
  considers Olga Chekhova's
    future, 218–19
  and newspaper attacks on Olga
    Chekhova, 218
  destroys Abakumov, 226
  seizes control after Stalin's
    death, 227
  arrested, 228
Berlin
  Olga Chekhova first arrives in,
    81–2, 84
  Kachalov group visits, 85
  Russian émigré community in,
    96–7, 115
  Moscow Art Theatre touring
    company plays in, 97–8
  Olga Chekhova's life and homes
    in, 102–3, 115

  Nazi unpopularity in, 125
  bombed, 192, 195, 220
  Olga Chekhova moves from
    during war, 192
  and Red Army advance, 197,
    199–203
  Olga Chekhova returned to
    (1945), 211–13
  women in, 220–21
  airlift (1949), 226
  Olga Chekhova and family
    move house to
    Charlottenburg, 226
Berliner Renaissance-Theater,
  110, 112
Bertensson, Sergei, 91, 103
Berzarin, General Nikolai, 209
Blaufuchs, Der, 139
Blok, Aleksandr
  The Rose and the Cross, 26
Blum, Vladimir, 87
Bock, Field Marshal Fedor von,
  167, 169, 180
Bolsheviks
  and February revolution, 45
  takeover in Moscow (1917),
    45–6
  low vote in 1917 election, 50
  dominance, 55
  White Army's detestation of,
    61–2
Boner, Georgette, 122
Borzhomi, Georgia, 73
bourgeoisie
  repressed, 55–6
Braun, Eva, 189, 215
*Brennende Grenze (Burning
  Frontiers),* 116, 130, *18*
Brest-Litovsk, Treaty of (1918), 50
Brussels, 138–9

Knipper, Vladimir – *cont.*
  threatened in Bolshevik
    revolution, 46
  discourages Lev from musical
    career, 93
  letters to Olga Knipper-
    Chekhova in USA, 101
  letter from Olga Knipper-
    Chekhova in Berlin, 102
  at Konstantin's death, 107
  and Olga Chekhova's
    association with Hitler, 162
  in Second World War, 167–8,
    173–5, 183
  Olga Knipper-Chekhova sends
    money to, 185
  death, 191
Knipper, Vova (Vladimir's son)
  on Olga Knipper-Chekhova's
    room in Moscow, 92
  and Lev's composing, 136
  Olga Chekhova sends
    childhood gifts to, 141
  and NKVD interrogators, 148
  on Olga Chekhova and Olga
    Knipper-Chekhova in Berlin,
    149
  admires Lev, 163–4
  innocence, 164
  wartime rations, 167
  and Olga Knipper-Chekhova's
    departure for Caucasus, 168
  in wartime Moscow, 171,
    173–5, 183, 199
  romance and engagement with
    Margo, 173, 175, 209–10
  army service, 193
  given Olga Chekhova's post-
    war deposition and papers,
    207, 231

and Olga Knipper-Chekhova's
    illness in Crimea, 209
  behaviour in war, 210
Knipper, Yelena Luise (Olga
    Chekhova's mother), *see*
    Ried-Knipper, Yelena Luise
Knipper-Chekhova, Olga
    (Anton's wife; 'Aunt Olya'),
    3, 5, 9, 10
  plays in 1945 production of *The
    Cherry Orchard*, 4, 7–8
  in civil war (1919), 6, 65
  as émigrée, 6, 77, 79–80
  under Soviet disfavour, 6–7
  acting style, 7–8
  background, 9
  love affair and marriage with
    Chekhov, 10–12
  as Nemirovich-Danchenko's
    mistress, 10, 85
  birth and parentage, 16
  childhood, 16–17
  fondness for Lev Knipper, 17,
    19
  musical interests, 19
  in Aleksei Tolstoy's *Tsar Feodor*,
    21, 96
  Olga Chekhova stays with in
    Moscow, 26
  reaction to Misha's marriage to
    Olga Chekhova, 30–31
  First World War theatrical
    tours, 37
  letters to Masha after revolution,
    53, 57
  dyes hair, 54
  and food shortages in early
    revolution days, 54
  on pointlessness of revolution,
    54–5

Vadis, Lieutenant-General
Aleksandr, 204, 211–14
Vasilevsky, Marshal Aleksandr,
187
Veidt, Conrad, 126, *23*
Venus-Film München/Berlin
(company), 230–31
Verführer, Der, 232
Verlorene Schuh, Der, 106
Vienna
Olga Chekhova visits (1945),
214
Voltaire, François Marie Arouet
Candide, 119
Volunteer Army (anti-Bolshevik),
51, 60

Wagner, Sam, 219
West, Red, 232
White Army
in civil war, 6, 60–62, 64–5,
67–8, 75
evacuated, 72, 74–6
White Guard movement
activities abroad, 96
White Russians
émigrés, 96–7, 100, 115
Wolf, Friedrich, 174
Wolf, Koni, 174
Wolf, Markus, 174
World War, First (1914–18)
outbreak, 24–5

Russian army defeats in, 35, 39
popular attitude to, 36
food shortages, 42
World War, Second (1939–45)
Russia enters, 165
see also Red Army
Wrangel, Baron Pyotr, 62, 64,
74–5

Yagoda, Genrikh, 121, 133
Yalta, 67, 113–14, 116, 193; *see
also* Crimea
Yeltsin, Boris, 234
Yerevan, Armenia, 185
Yezhov, Nikolai, 143, 154
Yorck, 129
Yousoupov, Prince Feliks, 104
Yudenich, General Nikolai, 63, 67
Yugoslavia, 80, 157

Zarubin, Vasily (Zoya's father),
177
Zarubina, Zoya, 177, 179, 228
Zelenin, General, 215–16, 219
Zeppelin (intelligence group), 217,
219
Zhdanov, Andrei, 225
Zhukov, Marshal Georgi, 1, 180,
187, 197–8, 202, 215, 228
Ziller, Xenia Karlovna, *see*
Chekhova, Xenia
Zinoviev, Grigori, 105

Stalingrad: The Fateful Siege, 1942–1943

The International #1 Bestseller

"A fantastic and sobering story . . . fully and authoritatively told."
—Richard Bernstein, *The New York Times*

Historians and reviewers worldwide have hailed Antony Beevor's magisterial *Stalingrad* as the definitive account of World War II's most harrowing battle. In August 1942, Hitler's huge Sixth Army reached the city that bore Stalin's name. In the five-month siege that followed, the Russians fought to hold Stalingrad at any cost, then caught their Nazi enemy in an astonishing reversal. As never before, *Stalingrad* conveys the experience of soldiers on both sides as they fought in inhuman conditions, and of civilians trapped on an urban battlefield. Antony Beevor has interviewed survivors and discovered completely new material in a wide range of German and Soviet archives, including reports of prisoner interrogations, desertions, and executions. The battle of Stalingrad was the psychological turning point of World War II; as Beevor makes clear, it also changed the face of modern warfare. As a story of cruelty, courage, and human suffering, *Stalingrad* is unprecedented and unforgettable.

WINNER OF THE WOLFSON HISTORY PRIZE
WINNER OF THE SAMUEL JOHNSON PRIZE FOR NONFICTION
WINNER OF THE HAWTHORNDEN PRIZE
ISBN 0-14-028458-3

The Fall of Berlin 1945

"The best account yet written on the death knell of Hitler's vaunted Thousand Year Reich."
—Carlo D'Este, *The New York Times Book Review*

The Fall of Berlin 1945 is a gripping, street-level portrait of the harrowing days of January 1945 in Berlin when the vengeful Red Army and beleaguered Nazi forces clashed for a final time. The result was the most gruesome display of brutality in the war, with tanks crushing refugee columns, mass rapes, pillage, and destruction. Making full use of newly disclosed material from former Soviet files as well as other archives, Beevor has reconstructed the different experiences of those millions caught up in the death throes of the Third Reich, depicting not only the brutality and desperation of a city under siege but also rare moments of extreme humanity and heroism.

ISBN 0-14-200280-1

The Spanish Civil War

"A rare book which cannot be supplemented."
—John Keegan, *The Sunday Times* (London)

The Spanish Civil War is a compelling account of one of the most hard-fought and bitter wars of the twentieth century: a war of atrocities and political genocide that was a military testing ground before the Second World War for the Russians, Italians, and Germans. With his thorough and contemporary examination of the Spanish civil war, historian Antony Beevor unravels the complex events from the coup d'etat which started the war in July of 1936 to the final defeat of the Republicans in 1939. This highly readable account leaves out none of the familiar aspects, exploring them with a clear eye and providing important new insights into the war—its causes, course, and consequences.

ISBN 0-14-100148-8

Paris after the Liberation 1944–1949
Revised Edition
With Artemis Cooper

"A wondrous account that thoroughly matches the brilliance of its subject." —*The Boston Globe*

"Enormously enjoyable . . . It is hard to see how it could have been done better." —*The Sunday Telegraph* (London)

In this brilliant synthesis of social, political, and cultural history, Antony Beevor and Artemis Cooper present a vivid and compelling portrayal of the City of Lights after its liberation. Paris became the diplomatic battleground in the opening stages of the Cold War. Against this volatile political backdrop, every aspect of life is portrayed: scores were settled in a rough and uneven justice, black marketers grew rich on the misery of the population, and a growing number of intellectual luminaries and artists—including Hemingway, Beckett, Camus, Sartre, de Beauvoir, Cocteau, and Picasso—contributed new ideas and a renewed vitality to this extraordinary moment in time.

ISBN 0-14-243792-1